VARIETIES OF UNIONISM

Varieties of Unionism:
Strategies for Union
Revitalization in a
Globalizing Economy

Edited by
CAROLA FREGE AND JOHN KELLY

OXFORD

UNIVERSITY PRESS

OXFORD

UNIVERSITY PRESS

Great Clarendon Street, Oxford OX2 6DP

Oxford University Press is a department of the University of Oxford.
It furthers the University's objective of excellence in research, scholarship,
and education by publishing worldwide in

Oxford New York

Auckland Bangkok Buenos Aires Cape Town Chennai
Dar es Salaam Delhi Hong Kong Istanbul Karachi Kolkata
Kuala Lumpur Madrid Melbourne Mexico City Mumbai Nairobi
São Paulo Shanghai Taipei Tokyo Toronto

Oxford is a registered trade mark of Oxford University Press
in the UK and in certain other countries

Published in the United States
by Oxford University Press Inc., New York

© Oxford University Press 2004

The moral rights of the author have been asserted
Database right Oxford University Press (maker)

First published 2004

British Library Cataloguing in Publication Data

Data available

Library of Congress Cataloging in Publication Data

Data available

ISBN 0-19-927014-7 (hbk.)

Typeset by Newgen Imaging Systems (P) Ltd., Chennai, India
Printed in Great Britain
on acid-free paper by
Biddles Ltd., King's Lynn, Norfolk

Dedication

CF: To Karolus and June, the oldest and the currently youngest of the Frege clan
JK: To my mother

Contents

List of Illustrations

Tables

Figures

Notes on Contributors

Carola Frege is Reader in the Industrial Relations Department at the London School of Economics and Political Science and Associate Professor at the School for Management and Employment Relations at Rutgers University, USA.

John Kelly is Professor of Industrial Relations at the London School of Economics and at the Department of Management, Birkbeck College, London.

Lee Adler is Professor in the School of Industrial and Labor Relations at Cornell University.

Martin Behrens is Programme Director for European Employment Relations at the Wirtschafts-und-Sozialwissenschaftliches Institut of the Hans Boeckler-Stiftung in Dusseldorf.

Michael Fichter is Lecturer in the Department of Political Science at the Free University of Berlin and Executive Director of its Centre for Labour Relations.

Ian Greer is a doctoral student in the School of Industrial and Labor Relations at Cornell University.

Kerstin Hamann is Associate Professor of Political Science at the University of Central Florida.

Edmund Heery is Professor of Human Resource Management at the Cardiff Business School.

Richard Hurd is Professor and Director of Labor Studies at Cornell University.

Nathan Lillie is a Research Associate in the School of Industrial and Labor Relations at Cornell University.

Miguel Martínez Lucio is Professor at the University of Bradford Management Centre.

Lowell Turner is Professor of International and Comparative Labor at Cornell University.

Jeremy Waddington is Reader in Industrial Relations at the University of Manchester Institute of Science and Technology and Project Coordinator at the European Trade Union Institute in Brussels.

Acknowledgements

We would like to acknowledge the financial support of a number of organizations throughout the course of our research: Ford Foundation, Friedrich-Ebert-Stiftung, Hans Boeckler Foundation, International Labour Organization, the Nuffield Foundation, School of Industrial and Labor Relations at Cornell University, Suntory-Toyota International Centre for Economics and Related Disciplines at the London School of Economics, and the US Department of Education. We would also like to thank those who commented on our work when we presented papers at a number of international conferences: the International Labour Organization, Geneva April 2001; the Industrial Relations Research Association, Atlanta January 2002 and again in Washington January 2003; the International Industrial Relations Association, Berlin September 2003; and the London School of Economics Workshop September 2002.

1

Why Revitalize? Labour's Urgent Mission in a Contested Global Economy

LOWELL TURNER

What looked like *carte blanche* for corporate-led globalization just a few years ago is now increasingly contested. The brave new vision of market fundamentalism has been challenged on several fronts, from massive demonstrations in Seattle and Genoa to contested trade and environmental summits at Johannesburg and Cancun. The critical insights of highly placed insiders have undermined the dominant neo-liberal ideology and given credence to mounting protests and opposition viewpoints (e.g. Soros 2002; Stiglitz 2002). Economic stagnation, inequality, desperate poverty and violence—whether in Japan, East Asia, Russia, Germany, or the United States and Latin America—have belied optimistic predictions of the positive effects of unbridled globalization. Economic policy makers from the rich countries are challenged both by domestic opposition and by a growing reluctance in the global South to acquiesce in one-sided trade deals. The future shape of the global economy and its international, as well as national and local economic policies, are now open to widespread and growing debate.

Yet, debate is clearly not enough. What is also required are strong organized actors to promote alternative viewpoints and to build the progressive coalitions—global, national, and local—that can turn policy around. While together they cannot yet match the power of multinational corporations (even if they could act together consistently), many such actors are already present, and many of them are increasingly ready to contest the dominant policies. Opposition forces include a broad range of international and domestic non-governmental organizations (NGOs), from environmental to health and human rights groups, swelling protest movements from global justice, and antiwar to land reform, from José-Bové-inspired farmers to religious and cultural defence movements, as well as increasingly independent governments across the global South (from Brazil and Argentina to South Africa, India, and China). And one clearly indispensable actor in present and future reform efforts is organized labour, the subject of this book.

THE URGENT NEED FOR LABOUR MOVEMENT
REVITALIZATION

Because unions represent—or seek to represent—vast numbers of the earth's 'have-nots' and a large number of 'have-somes' as well (e.g. workers in the global North), progressive coalitions and initiatives are greatly strengthened with the inclusion of labour. On the other hand, when unions operate as special interest groups, defending only their members and in some cases even opposing environmental, civil rights, or other reform efforts, the prospects for progressive economic policies are greatly diminished. Indeed, it is difficult to imagine transformation of global, national, and even local economies, including a reversal of the deep inequality that threatens both global and domestic peace, without the broad, proactive participation of labour in campaigns for reform. It is equally difficult to imagine preservation of the earth and a broadening of human rights unless unions join such coalitions as enthusiastic proponents and partners. This is why we believe that labour movement revitalization is such a critical contemporary task, one worthy of support through research that specifies the pros and cons of alternative strategies and points towards mutual learning and policy recommendations for unions, governments, and other actors.

Beyond recurrent employer and government opposition, there are at least two critical problems for a broadened labour participation in global, national, and local reform efforts. One is when unions take a narrow perspective and fail to develop the linkages, alliances, and broad reform vision required to build the necessary political power. The other is the widespread contemporary problem of union decline. Labour revitalization studies seek above all to identify strategies that can both broaden the perspective and reverse the decline. And our research persuades us of a close connection between the two, namely that a broadened perspective and more comprehensive strategic focus are necessary to reverse the decline of organized labour. With five country teams of researchers, our specific focus is on unions in the United Kingdom, the United States, Germany, Italy, and Spain. But we also believe that our findings and analysis have relevance throughout the global North, and that some of the same lessons could also be applied in the very different (and much more difficult) circumstances of the global South.

Our focus, therefore, is on actor strategies, and especially on the strategies of unions: national, sectoral, and local unions as well as national labour federations. Studies of union decline, of which there have been hundreds over the past two decades, are important, but this is not our task. We assume that the basic facts about union decline are no longer controversial; union leaders in all of our countries (and many more) acknowledge either the reality of protracted decline (the United States and United Kingdom) or the pressure from employers and neo-liberal economic policy that threatens decline (Germany, Italy, and Spain). And the causal factors driving decline have been specified, analysed, and widely debated (from Kochan, Katz, and McKersie 1986 to Kelly 1998 and beyond).

CONTEMPORARY PERSPECTIVES: FOCUS ON EMPLOYERS

Postwar labour scholarship, in the industrial relations and comparative political economy literatures, has emphasized institutional configurations and bargaining relationships (see also Baccaro, Hamann, and Turner 2003: 125–28). Two of the most recent and prominent of these perspectives—known to scholars as 'transformation of industrial relations' (Kochan, Katz, and McKersie 1986) and 'varieties of capitalism' (Hall and Soskice 2001)—illustrate where these literatures have arrived. Traditional industrial relations literature, especially but not only in the United States, talks about system stability, contracts and laws, and regularized bargaining relationships, but tells us little about what to do when the system approaches collapse (Kerr et al. 1960; Slichter, Healey, and Livernash 1960). The transformation literature of the 1980s and 1990s, by contrast, makes a valuable contribution in analysing collapse, especially in the United States, and identifying employer opposition as the driving causal force in system instability and union decline (Kochan, Katz, and McKersie 1986). The recent varieties of capitalism literature builds both on earlier institutional approaches and more recent transformation literature to show the very limited possibilities for union influence in liberal market economies (LMEs) such as the United States and the United Kingdom, in contrast to more substantial union roles in coordinated market economies (CMEs), although even here unions are either incorporated and weak (Japan) or under new pressure and in danger of decline (Germany) (Hall and Soskice 2001; Thelen 2001).

The problem with all of these views is that they assign union strategy a secondary place. Union strategies may matter, but they are either derivative of institutional frameworks or they are overwhelmed by opposing forces. Unions can adapt—to the institutions or the transformation, by collaborating with employers largely on management's terms—but they cannot pursue innovative strategies to promote a worker-friendly transformation of their own. This is true to a large extent in the varieties of literature even for CMEs (Hall and Soskice 2001; Swenson 2002); for LMEs there is little prospect for meaningful, independent union influence (Thelen 2001). Yet renewed transformation, to challenge employer dominance and broaden union influence, is precisely what innovative contemporary unions seek. For unions pursuing renewed influence both at work and in the broader society, proactive strategies matter a great deal. Today's revitalization literature aims to understand (and promote) the new proactive strategies, for which the received literature tells us all too little. Still in its early days, theoretically underdeveloped and incorporating conflicting currents, this recent work on union strategies offers rich promise for theoretical breakthroughs and policy prescriptions, based on new understandings of how unions can best influence contemporary developments (cf. Bronfenbrenner et al. 1998; Kelly 1998; Turner, Katz, and Hurd 2001; Nissen 2002; Turner 2003; Cornfield and McCammon 2003).[1] It is to this growing body of scholarship that we seek to contribute.

Ours is a synthetic view, in contrast to zero-sum debates between cooperationists and militants, between activism and participation, between social partners and organizers (cf. Kochan 1995; Moody 1997). Whether union strategies aim at promoting participation in the production of high value-added goods and services, political power for broad economic reform, or basic organization and dignity for low wage service workers, successful outcomes depend on union strength, and especially on renewed organizing and mobilizing capacity. Moreover, the institutional reform necessary to stabilize worker dignity and participation throughout the whole labour market—from labour law reform to corporate accountability and improved social policy—is inconceivable in the absence of sustained popular pressure from labour and its allies.

STRATEGIES FOR LABOUR MOVEMENT RENEWAL IN A GLOBAL ECONOMY

The most significant revitalization strategies identified in our country cases are *organizing, labour-management partnership, political action, reform of union structures, coalition-building,* and *international solidarity*. Strategies overlap and are combined in various ways (e.g. in comprehensive campaigns: see Hickey 2003), so that the interactions inevitably push their way into our analyses. Particular strategies are more or less important in different countries, and we attempt to analyse and explain the differences. Above all, we are interested in the ways in which these strategies combine to magnify the reform efforts of unions and their allies, as well as the conditions for success in different national and local settings.

The impact of globalization, and especially the market fundamentalist policies shaping contemporary world markets, means that unions are more often than not under pressure (if not open attack), from employers, governments, or both. Fighting back with one or two piecemeal strategies, no matter how innovative and intensive, is unlikely to reverse the tide. Nor is the panoply of conventional approaches. Unions, we argue, need a bigger tool kit, a range of strategies new and old that can be combined and recombined to escalate the counter-pressure and increase the prospects for resurgence and reform.

Partnership and mobilization, for example, can be (and often have been) dead-end strategies when taken alone. While they each tend to attract proponents who favour one and dislike the other (cf. Kochan 1995; Kelly 1998), both may well be necessary elements of sustained labour movement revitalization (Boxall and Haynes 1997). In intensified efforts to reverse decline, many unions today, building on broadened perspectives, seek 'virtuous linkages' among alternative strategies. Expanded coalition-building, for example, can broaden labour's political influence, which in turn can provide new support for union organizing.[2] Political and organizing success can then encourage rank-and-file mobilization and sustained relations of partnership. We look for the conditions under which such virtuous circles emerge, as well as the conditions that result in contrasting vicious circles—as when labour–management partnership results in workforce demobilization, undermining the prospects for both organizing success and political influence.

ACTORS AND STRATEGIES

The focus of this book is on actors and strategies: unions, coalitions, social movements, and related organizations, in politics and at the workplace, refocused on strategic innovations and renewed solidarity. Implicit in this perspective is the notion that unions must take responsibility for both internal reforms and innovative external strategies necessary to promote revitalization in today's extraordinarily difficult context. It will not do labour any good (beyond catharsis) to blame employers or governments—for everything from union decline to massive economic and social inequality (although employers and governments are very much responsible)—unless labour is also confronting the reality that new strategies and organizational reforms, new linkages and coalitions, are what unions require if present circumstances are to be turned around. The desired transformation is a task for mobilization, strategic participation, and a greatly broadened field of solidarity (from politics to local coalitions to international collaboration).

Our goal is to produce research and analysis that points towards policy implications for unions and their allies. In focusing on strategic innovations and campaigns, our hope is to assess the sources and relative merits of successful strategies and to demonstrate the conditions under which success and failure are likely, while at the same time capturing the very real drama and intensity of these events. The need for labour movement revitalization is urgent and we believe that researchers sympathetic to labour have an important contribution to make.

CASE SELECTION AND CENTRAL FINDINGS

In choosing the *United Kingdom,* the *United States, Germany, Italy, and Spain,* we have studied contemporary labour movement revitalization in all of the large advanced industrial societies with the exception of Japan and France. We have looked at two LMEs (the United Kingdom and the United States), one CME (Germany), and two 'Mediterranean' economies (Italy and Spain). And in this book we have moved beyond the conventional country case presentations to present cross-national comparative analysis of strategic innovation. As sketched out earlier, we have found six strategies that merit close consideration (organizing, labour–management partnership, political action, reform of union structures, coalition-building, and international solidarity). Repertoires of strategies vary significantly across both unions and countries. The book is organized around the strategies, one chapter for each, comparing their development, priority, use, and relative success across our five countries.

One lesson from this research collaboration is that unions have a broader range of strategic choice than most of us have imagined. In the *United Kingdom,* debates among resurgent militants, 'new unionism' organizers, and would-be social partners have only intensified under a Labour government, reflecting contending approaches to labour movement renewal (Heery, Kelly, and Waddington 2003). New union leadership in the *United States,* fighting the most serious decline of any of our country cases, has directed substantial resources towards innovative revitalization strategies, especially organizing, political action and coalition-building (Voss and Sherman 2000; Hurd, Milkman, and Turner 2003). Mobilization and coalition-building efforts have succeeded dramatically in some cases, from a UPS strike victory in 1997 to the Battle of Seattle in 1999, from Justice for Janitors to widespread living wage and anti-sweatshop campaigns. Yet, revitalization is concentrated in the strategies of the American Federation of Labor-Congress of Industrial Organizations (AFL-CIO) and several activist unions, with much of the labour movement as yet unreformed, even in the face of a renewed attack on labour from the Bush government and continuing union membership decline.

In *Germany*, unions have maintained their central position in the political economy by virtue of strong institutions, backed by mobilization capacity, in codetermination and comprehensive collective bargaining (Behrens, Fichter, and Frege 2003). Yet, intensified market competition, European integration, economic restructuring, and contemporary policy reform initiatives have challenged unions to move beyond traditional repertoires and institutional anchors to mobilize in innovative ways. The collapse of IG Metall's strike in eastern Germany in mid-2003 intensified debates between modernizers and traditionalists, perhaps opening the door for future organizational and strategic reform. The rise and fall and rise again of unions in *Italy*, from the Hot Autumn of 1969 through political transformation in the 1990s, has provided recurrent dramas of renewal (Baccaro, Carrieri, and Damiano 2003). The three major union confederations coalesced to play a leading role in the reconfiguration of Italian politics after the deep political crisis of 1993–94. While the Berlusconi government elected in 2001 brought union-led reform efforts to a halt, unions remained strong centres of opposition as well as entrenched actors in collective bargaining, shop floor representation, and workforce mobilization. In the newest democracy among our five country cases, *Spain*, where free trade unionism in its contemporary form is not yet 30 years old, opposing union confederations have collaborated to shore up their institutional position (Hamann and Martínez Lucio 2003). They have done this at the workplace, where they compete in works council elections, and in national politics, where they have bargained with parties, governments, and employers for institutional responsibilities. With some success at both levels, the result has been modest growth in union membership and stabilization of union influence.

INSTITUTIONS AND MOBILIZATION

Thus we find active efforts at labour movement revitalization everywhere in the global North, driven by globalization, intensified competition, neo-liberal economic policy (inspired by a US-led market fundamentalist ideology), employer and government opposition. In every case, there is experimentation, innovation, and wide-ranging internal debate regarding strategic direction and tactical choice. Because of fermentation and debate as well as contrasting institutional and political contexts, there is also great cross-national diversity of union strategy even in converging global and regional markets (Katz and Darbishire 2000). One useful distinction, at the broadest level of generalization, is between labour movements that focus revitalization effects on *mobilization*, and those that focus on *institutional position* and/or reform. Another look at our five country cases in this light reveals the following patterns.

The United Kingdom and the United States present the cases in which union strategies are most oriented towards mobilization—by no coincidence where the institutional position is weakest. *British unions* have acquired modest institutional support under the Blair government, without yet securing a position so entrenched that it could not be swept away by a Conservative government. Many activists focus on mobilization, either traditional militancy or innovative organizing, as the best route to institutional reform and influence. Others advocate social partnership with employers and/or collaboration with government, while the Trades Union Congress (TUC) struggles to maintain its umbrella over all of the contending parties. In spite of internal conflicts and limited government support (with gains for unions offset at least in part by ongoing privatization initiatives), union decline has been halted in the United Kingdom at around 30 per cent membership density amidst important signs of labour movement renewal and innovation. *American* unions have long advocated institutional reform (the 'labour law reform' debate), and see this as a prerequisite for broad growth in union membership. Yet, past reform efforts have failed in part because of weak mobilization of support. Current efforts in organizing, politics, and coalition-building seek to mobilize new support, with considerable promise and impressive success in particular areas (such as Las Vegas and Los Angeles) and particular industries (such as health care, building services, and telecommunications). The mobilization and political threshold beyond which meaningful institutional reform is possible remains nonetheless out of reach.

German unions have defended collective bargaining, codetermination, and the welfare state, under conservative and social-democratic governments alike, yet without the sustained mobilization necessary to promote a viable alternative vision for reform. The largest union, Ver.di, has consolidated through merger to defend public services and jobs, while the pattern-setting IG Metall appears divided and defensive in the wake of its first major strike defeat in 50 years. But German unions are now learning that when circumstances change—including intensified employer and government challenges in a context of globalization and European integration—established institutions may not be enough. To a certain extent, German unions have rested on their institutional laurels and lost touch with rank-and-file and broader social concerns. They may well be dependent now on renewed connections, grassroots leadership, and social coalitions to expand mobilization potential for the purpose of institutional reform, as the only viable alternative to institutional and organizational decline.

Italian unions have used political crisis and mobilization capacity to promote institutional reform, for both comprehensive collective bargaining and workplace representation, with considerable success over the past decade. Threats to hard-earned institutional position come from conservative economic policy as well as from union disunity (which the conservative government promotes in its labour market reform initiatives). Yet so far, Italian unions have maintained institutional strength while continuing to demonstrate vast mobilization capacity, helping to bring a million or more demonstrators out to protest against labour law reforms in 2002 and against the war in Iraq in 2003. Alongside new institutional stability, *Spanish unions* have also shown impressive mobilization capacity—bringing hundreds of thousands of demonstrators to Barcelona in 2002 to demand a stronger social Europe, and even larger numbers to Madrid in 2003 to protest against government support for war in Iraq. In doing so, unions have arguably deepened their popular base in Spain, at the same time underpinning and strengthening their enhanced institutional position.

While we are candid about the weaknesses and shortcomings of contemporary union strategies, everywhere we find experimentation and reform efforts, in many cases with new leadership and renewed vitality. There is widespread internal union debate, aimed at coalescing around appropriate strategies to renew mobilization and political influence, and to build, defend, or reform institutions of industrial relations. In all of our countries, for better and for worse, this is a time of contestation for labour unions, in the context of an urgent historical necessity for further strategic innovation. Such revitalization processes we would argue are exactly what unions need in the face of current challenges and uncertain outcomes and they are reflected in different combinations of strategies in different countries. While global capitalism skews the odds against labour, now and in the future, we nonetheless find cause for hope in the substantial union renewal efforts now underway in each of our country cases.

ACKNOWLEDGEMENT

This chapter was inspired by the work of a remarkable, collegial group of scholars engaged in comparative studies of labour movement revitalization, in several years of collaboration. For their comments and inspiration (although none of them I'm quite sure would agree with everything in this introductory chapter—contentious, critical thinkers that they are), many, many thanks to my project colleagues: Lee Adler, Lucio Baccaro, Martin Behrens, Brigid Beachler, Mike Fichter, Carola Frege, Ian Greer, Kerstin Hamann, Ed Heery, Rick Hurd, John Kelly, Nathan Lillie, Miguel Martínez Lucio, Ruth Milkman, Manfred Muster, Jeremy Waddington, and Kent Wong. A special thanks also to my research collaborators at Cornell University (the Global Democracy Research Group), including Beachler, Greer, and Lillie as well as Marco Hauptmeier, Ritu Jain, Heiwon Kwon, and Julie Sadler; and to several other colleagues who attended our conferences and commented on our papers, including Peter Auer, Reiner Hoffmann, Richard Hyman, Otto Jacobi, A.V. Jose, Nik Simon, Wolfgang Streeck, Robert Taylor, and Peter Unterweger. Specifically for this introductory chapter, book editors Frege and Kelly offered insightful (if not always heeded) comments and suggestions.

Notes

1. See also the March 2003 special issue of the *European Journal of Industrial Relations*, featuring a series of chapters by the authors of this book, presenting revitalization research from each of our five countries (Baccaro, Carrieri, and Damiano 2003; Behrens, Fichter,

and Frege 2003; Hamann and Martínez Lucio 2003; Heery, Kelly, and Waddington 2003; and Hurd, Milkman, and Turner 2003).

2. Unions in California, where legislative reforms have facilitated significant organizing successes in industries such as health care and agriculture, provide a contemporary case in point.

References

Baccaro, L., Carrieri, M., and Damiano, C. (2003). 'The Resurgence of Italian Confederal Unions: Will It Last?'. *European Journal of Industrial Relations*, 9/1: 43–60.

—— Hamann, K., and Turner, L. (2003). 'The Politics of Labour Movement Revitalization: The Need for a Revitalized Perspective'. *European Journal of Industrial Relations*, 9/1: 119–33.

Behrens, M., Fichter, M., and Frege, C. (2003). 'Unions in Germany: Regaining the Initiative?'. *European Journal of Industrial Relations*, 9/1: 25–42.

Boxall, P. and Haynes, P. (1997). 'Strategy and Trade Union Effectiveness in a Neo-liberal Environment'. *British Journal of Industrial Relations*, 35/4: 567–91.

Bronfenbrenner, K., Friedman, S., Hurd, R. W., Oswald, R. A., and Seeber, R. L. (eds.) (1998). *Organizing to Win: New Research on Union Strategies*. Ithaca, NY: ILR Press.

Cornfield, D. B. and McCammon, H. J. (eds.) (2003). *Labor Revitalization: Global Perspectives and New Initiatives*. Greenwich, CO: JAI Press.

Hall, P. A. and Soskice, D. (eds.) (2001). *Varieties of Capitalism: The Institutional Foundations of Comparative Advantage*. Oxford: Oxford University Press.

Hamann, K. and Lucio, M. M. (2003). 'Strategies of Union Revitalization in Spain: Negotiating Change and Fragmentation'. *European Journal of Industrial Relations*, 9/1: 61–78.

Heery, E., Kelly, J., and Waddington, J. (2003). 'Union Revitalization in Britain'. *European Journal of Industrial Relations*, 9/1: 79–98.

Hickey, R. (2003). *Collective Bargaining Ruptures: Conflict and Control in an Oil Refinery*. Ithaca, NY: Cornell University, Masters thesis.

Hurd, R., Milkman, R., and Turner, L. (2003). 'Reviving the American Labor Movement: Institutions and Mobilization'. *European Journal of Industrial Relations*, 9/1: 99–118.

Katz, H. C. and Darbishire, O. (2000). *Converging Divergences: Worldwide Changes in Employment Systems*. Ithaca, NY: Cornell University Press.

Kelly, J. (1998). *Rethinking Industrial Relations: Mobilization, Collectivism and Long Waves*. London: Routledge.

Kerr, C., Dunlop, J., Harbison, F., and Myers, C. (1960). *Industrialism and Industrial Man*. Cambridge, MA: Harvard University Press.

Kochan, T. A. (1995). 'Using the Dunlop Report'. *Industrial Relations*, 34/3: 350–66.

—— Katz, H. C., and McKersie, R. B. (1986). *The Transformation of American Industrial Relations*. New York: Basic Books.

Moody, K. (1997). *Workers in a Lean World: Unions in the International Economy*. New York: Verso.

Nissen, B. (ed.) (2002). *Unions in a Globalized Environment*. Armonk, NY: ME Sharpe.

Slichter, S., Healey, J., and Livernash, R. E. (1960). *The Impact of Collective Bargaining on Management*. Washington, DC: Brookings Institution.

Soros, G. (2002). *On Globalization*. New York: Public Affairs.

Stiglitz, J. (2002). *Globalization and its Discontents*. London: Penguin Books.

Swenson, P. (2002). *Capitalists Against Markets*. Oxford: Oxford University Press.

Thelen, K. (2001). 'Varieties of Labor Politics in the Developed Democracies', in P. A. Hall and D. Soskice (eds.), *Varieties of Capitalism: The Institutional Foundations of Comparative Advantage.* Oxford: Oxford University Press, 71–103.

Turner, L. (2003). 'Reviving the Labor Movement: A Comparative Perspective', in D. B. Cornfield and H. J. McCammon (eds.), *Labor Revitalization: Global Perspectives and New Initiatives.* Greenwich, CO: JAI Press, 23–58.

—— Katz, H. C., and Hurd, R. W. (eds.) (2001). *Rekindling the Movement: Labor's Quest for Relevance in the 21st Century.* Ithaca, NY: Cornell University Press.

Voss, K. and Sherman, R. (2000). 'Breaking the Iron Law of Oligarchy: Union Revitalization in the American Labor Movement'. *American Journal of Sociology,* 106/2: 303–49.

2

Conceptualizing Labour Union Revitalization

MARTIN BEHRENS, KERSTIN HAMANN,
AND RICHARD HURD

INTRODUCTION

Unions have engaged in revitalization efforts in all five country cases that form the basis of comparison of this book, though they differ in the strategies they have pursued and the level of success they have had. Some of the strategies have been promising or even successful in terms of their immediate outcomes; others are still waiting to be fully implemented; and still others have failed to live up to the original expectations. While in many countries union activists are eagerly developing strategies to turn their fate, they are also facing some doubt or even resistance by politicians and academics alike who question the need for a strong and unified representation of labour. Here, we set out to provide a conceptual framework to understand better these various efforts at revival of national union movements.

The following section discusses existing analyses of union revitalization and argues that a comparative perspective is well suited to shed light on unions' revitalization efforts. We then introduce different analytical perspectives on the role of labour in the economy, politics, and society to help identify the significance of unions in an ever more global economy. The next section outlines the parameters of crisis for unions by tracing indicators of union strength over time. We then suggest a framework for conceptualizing union revitalization as a multidimensional process and argue that revitalization has different meanings depending on the specific national context.

UNION REVITALIZATION: THE NEED FOR COMPARATIVE ANALYSIS

An emerging literature, assessing the strategies that union movements have adopted to stem their decline in membership and influence, can be categorized along two principal dimensions: first, whether the focus lies on a single country or multiple countries; and second whether it analyses one particular strategy or a range of strategies.

Examples of single strategy, one country studies include Bronfenbrenner et al. (1998) on organizing in the United States, Gall (2003) on organizing in Britain,

Clawson (2003) on coalition-building in the United States and the edited collections on international action by US unions from Gordon and Turner (2000) and Nissen (2002). The dominant research method in these collections is the qualitative case study of a single campaign, typically involving a 'thick description' of processes, events, and outcomes. Their results indicate, for example, that union success in boosting membership is more likely if an internal organizing committee exists and if the workforce shares a widespread sense of grievance (Bronfenbrenner and Juravich 1998; Taylor and Bain 2003). The volume of resources devoted to union organizing appears to depend heavily on union leadership commitment, and in some cases leadership change was a prerequisite to shifting union policy towards increased organizing (Voss and Sherman 2003).

However, the single-strategy, one country-approach is limited by three weaknesses. First, the case study method means that it is difficult to establish the contribution of a particular strategy, such as organizing, to aggregate union membership change. It is clear that under appropriate conditions union organizing can secure new members and new bargaining relations with employers. What is not clear is whether it can therefore revitalize a national union movement and notably boost total union membership. Second, the absence of comparative data on other strategies means that it is difficult to identify the relative costs and benefits of organizing as compared to social partnership or various forms of political action, for instance. Nor is it clear whether and how these strategies interact. For example, does organizing work better if used in conjunction with social partnership? Finally, the focus on a single country means that it is difficult to generalize to other countries and to identify the broader economic and political conditions that affect the success of specific strategies.

A second body of literature has also focused on a single country but examined a wide range of union strategies, both conventional and innovative (or 'field enlarging' to use Wever's 1997 term). Turner, Katz, and Hurd's (2001) collection on the United States is perhaps the best example (see also Kelly and Willman 2004 on the United Kingdom and Wheeler 2002 on the United States). It contains analyses of organizing, local and national political action, innovations in collective bargaining, joint city-level initiatives with employers' associations and union mergers and restructuring. It also examines different forms of union organization, including the union as individual servicing agency and as social movement. One strength of this approach is that it underlines the diversity of strategies pursued by US unions and shows that organizing is far from being the most significant or effective strategy of revitalization. A second strength flows from detailed case studies, which are able to bring out some of the constraints on the adoption of particular strategies. For example, a radical shift of resources into union organizing will encounter resistance from existing union officials and members because of a perceived deterioration in the quality of union service. Third, other studies use either the comparative method or time series evidence to analyse variation in union effectiveness. Milkman and Wong's (2001) comparison of successful and failed organizing drives shows that organizing across an entire industry, rather than a single firm, was more successful, other things equal. Shoch (2001) demonstrates that the declining political success of the American Federation of Labor-Congress of Industrial Organizations (AFL-CIO) in blocking free trade measures in the US Congress was a reflection of increased mobilization by the supporters of free trade, including the Democratic President, Bill Clinton. Yet, confining analyses of union strategy to a single country makes it very difficult to shed light on the impact of national institutions and to generalize results to other countries.

A third type of research has investigated a particular strategy across different countries. Although somewhat rare, the collection by Fairbrother and Yates (2003) on union organizing in five English-speaking countries is an example. One finding that emerges clearly from the comparison of the United States, the United Kingdom, Canada, Australia, and New Zealand is that union organizing takes different forms in different countries. In Britain and New Zealand, for example, it has been articulated through partnership with employers, whereas in the United States it has developed in a more adversarial form. One issue that arises from this research is that all five countries are examples of a single variety of capitalism, the 'liberal market economy'. The absence of either Coordinated or Mediterranean economies means that, as with single country studies, it is difficult to know whether findings can be generalized to other varieties of capitalism.

The approach adopted in this volume examines a wide range of strategies in diverse union movements across countries that vary along a range of variables. This method has also been used by Waddington and Hoffman (2000*a*) on the sixteen EU Member States, Martin and Ross (1999) on the United Kingdom, Germany, Sweden, France, Italy, and Spain, Ferner and Hyman's (1998) collected volume, and Harrod and O'Brien (2002) on unions in both the Southern and Northern Hemispheres. The essays in Waddington and Hoffman (2000*a*) provide detailed descriptions of union initiatives around membership recruitment and union mergers. The editors note substantial variation in the incidence and outcomes of merger activity across Europe. They also point out, however, that one common trend is towards the creation of large multi-occupational, multi-industry unions and away from any type of industrial union structure (Waddington and Hoffman 2000*b*). Ross and Martin (1999) carefully document the challenges to union membership and power arising out of developments in the economic, political, and industrial relations systems in their six countries. The growth of different forms of flexibility, of decentralized bargaining and of neo-liberal policies on the part of both left and right governments have, in their view, seriously curtailed the scope for a recovery of union membership and power back to the levels of the 'Golden Age' of postwar capitalism. Nonetheless they believe that recovery is possible in those countries where employers and the state still perceive a legitimate and useful role for unions. However, it remains unclear exactly what unions would have to do to consolidate their role as social partners or, in the case of Britain, to acquire such a role. In some countries, then, the continuing importance of unions is thus not taken for granted.

WHY UNION REVITALIZATION?

Much of the literature discussed above has one—frequently tacit and implicit—assumption: union revitalization is desirable and important. Yet, given the fact that unions in most countries are, to some degree, experiencing a crisis, the question of why one would care about union revitalization at all is a pertinent one. After all, maybe unions have become superfluous in a global economy where national boundaries appear to be of declining importance and where a shift to market regulation within many countries is clearly discernible (Held et al. 1999: 2–14). Thus, a fundamental question is: Does it matter whether and how unions are revitalizing? And, to what extent is union revitalization crucial for the functioning of capitalist economies or democratic polities given the generally accepted dominance of supply-side economic policies? In other words, does the strength of unions make any difference—and if so, for what and for whom? We argue that despite these shifts in the economy and in policies at both the global and national level, unions retain important functions for democracy as well as capitalist economies.

Conceivably, workers' interests could be represented and expressed (though not necessarily aggregated) through mechanisms that exclude labour unions. The model of the company union, non-union works councils, the provision of individual labour-market services and benefits to members or sophisticated human resource management procedures may each appear as an alternative to the collective representation of workers' interests through unions (see, for example, Kochan 1995: 363; Osterman et al. 2001: 18). If any of these models provide an alternative, then what is the value of unions?

Existing scholarship addresses several aspects of the contributions that unions make to society and the economy. One prominent function of unions is their role in producing macroeconomic outcomes. With respect to economic indicators, such as GDP growth or wage levels, the evidence of the impact of unions is mixed. For the 1970s, it has been argued that countries with encompassing union organizations exhibit better economic performance (Cameron 1984; Calmfors and Driffill 1988). Yet, for the 1990s, these correlations are not evident in cross-national comparisons; no clear links exist, for instance, between union strength and real wage growth or real wage share (Franzese and Hall 2000). However, evidence shows that higher union density is associated with a lower share of low-paid employment and a lower level of income dispersion, lending additional support to research suggesting that strong unions are linked to a compression of the wage structure (Organization for Economic Cooperation and Development (OECD) 2002: 270). Furthermore, union density and the generosity of the welfare state are related to a reduction in the proportion of the workers whose families live in poverty (OECD 2002: 269–70). Bargaining coverage is correlated with higher real wage growth, lower employment and higher unemployment, and higher inflation, but also with lower labour earnings inequality and wage dispersion (Aidt and Tzannatos 2002: 11). Hall and Soskice (2001: 21–2) find that in general, in liberal market economies (LMEs)—where unions are generally weaker—income inequality is higher and working hours are longer for a larger share of the population. To the extent that unions are in many countries involved in affecting welfare state provisions, one can infer an indirect and inverse link between strong, revitalized unions, and working poverty. If one of the functions of unions is considered to be balancing out the inequalities produced by market mechanisms, it appears that they may well make a valuable contribution in this area.

Furthermore, in many countries unions have begun to play a new role in social pacts of varying contents (see Hamann and Kelly, Chapter 6, this volume). This indicates that unions retain an important function in formulating and implementing various wage and welfare-related measures even when membership continues to fall and welfare state retrenchment is common. It appears that unions continue to exercise some measure of policy influence through their participation in these pacts. Powerful unions may also have some impact on the economic strategy a country adopts. For instance, in a country with high density and bargaining coverage, it would be difficult to base economic development on low-wage sectors with poor training (Streeck 1991, 1996). In that sense, strong unions are able to constrain the options for business and thus have some influence on countries' economic paths. However, it could be argued that this is a chicken-and-egg question. After all, strong unions are unlikely to develop in economies that are based on the 'low road' to growth. Given the idea of 'institutional complementarities' (Hall and Soskice 2001: 17), unions are more likely to develop a strong presence where conditions are more favourable.

A second body of literature links union strength to sector-specific economic outcomes, especially wages (Dunlop 1944; Ross 1948; Wallerstein and Golden 2000; Kaufman 2002). Here the evidence shows that in countries with a substantial non-union sector, such as the United Kingdom and the United States, unionized workers continue to enjoy a wage premium over their non-union counterparts from a low of 2–3 per cent to a high of 68 per cent (in the construction industry) (Mishel, Bernstein, and Schmitt 2001). In Britain the union wage premium is highest of all for the most disadvantaged groups in the labour market, such as women and ethnic minorities (Metcalf, Hansen, and Charlwood 2000).

Yet, unions are not just economic actors, but also have an important function as democratic actors both in society at large and in the workplace. Workplace democracy and workers' democratic participation rights in the workplace are intrinsically linked to the question of union presence in these workplaces. Workers are more able to influence workplace decisions, to exercise 'voice', where unions are recognized for collective bargaining (Freeman and Medoff 1984). Surveys in the United States and Britain have shown that approximately 50 per cent of employees enjoy less influence over work-related decisions than they would like and that figure has increased during the past 20 years as union density and bargaining coverage have fallen (Freeman and Rogers 1999: 48–9; Kelly 1998: 46). The question of how unions can enhance the citizenship rights of workers is especially relevant during times of economic hardship (Müller-Jentsch 1994). As market regulation replaces government regulation, the scope of the issues citizens exercise influence on is reduced, and democratic workplace representation might serve as a substitute. Unions can also help to overcome the power imbalance between the individual worker and employers endemic in capitalist systems.

Taking the idea of citizenship beyond the workplace, unions have also been established as integral parts of civil society because they have an important function in interest aggregation and representation in democratic societies (Hamann 2003). There is evidence, for example, that unions can be effective vehicles in boosting voter turnout (Hamann and Kelly, Chapter 6, this volume). The question here is not how successful unions are in getting their preferred party or candidate elected, but to what extent they contribute to the quality of democracy by increasing voter turnout in general and by stimulating political awareness and participation among citizens. While some authors bemoan a decline in civil society as Americans have forfeited bowling leagues and instead 'bowl alone' (Putnam 1995), unions in industrialized democracies are still one of the strongest interest associations where citizens 'bowl together' and thus perform an important democratic function.[1] Similarly unions can contribute to the stock of 'social capital' defined as 'features of social organizations, such as trust, norms and networks that can improve the efficiency of society by facilitating coordinated actions' (Putnam 1993: 167).

In addition, unions also have a political role, frequently serving as valuable allies of political parties in their competition for votes and policies (Stephens and Wallerstein 1991; Smith 1998). They also have a fundamental role in supporting or counterbalancing dominant political and economic ideas and ideologies and therefore broadening the spectrum of political discourse. Furthermore, they have been active participants in formulating policies in cross-class alliances with employers (e.g. Swenson 2002). The implications of unchecked union decline would thus extend to political processes and policy-making dynamics with extensive ramifications for policy outcomes.

Finally, unions form an integral part of industrial relations systems. Unions are part of the linkages between the actors and the institutions constituting the economic system, or 'institutional complementarities' (see Hall and Soskice 2001: 17). It follows that a fundamental weakening of the position of unions would have profound systemic implications. These would extend not just to unions as organizations or to the representation of workers' collective interests, but to the whole industrial relations and economic systems: production systems, training structures, wage setting and bargaining procedures, policy-making structures, and social welfare regimes would all be affected. If unions all but disappeared, a fundamental reorganization of the economic institutions might be a necessary consequence. This might not be a desirable undertaking in many economies, in particular in coordinated market economies (CMEs), which are based on high skill formation, low worker turnover, and principally cooperative relationships between unions and employers (Thelen 2000). If, however, a fundamental reorientation of economic institutions is deemed necessary in response to global economic pressures, this might be more easily undertaken in conjunction with unions (Thelen 2001: 79). Similarly, other studies have found that bargaining coordination is conducive to the labour market's capacity to absorb shocks quickly and at low employment cost; in addition, where bargaining coverage is high, real wages are more responsive to employment conditions (Aidt and Tzannatos 2002: 111). Maybe it is these kinds of far-reaching implications of a fundamental change in the strength and functions of unions that have led many Western European governments (with the UK liberal market being the exception) to include unions in processes of national concertation during times of economic adjustment (Pochet 1999; Berger and Compston 2002).

In sum, unions continue to be critical actors in capitalist democracies because they form an integral part of a democratic civil society, because they encourage participation in democratic processes, because they represent the interests of those that tend to be underrepresented, because they are able to overcome a crucial collective action problem, and because they add to the interest representation in pluralist societies. Margaret Levi's (2003: 45) claim that 'labor unions are important to American democracy and to the achievement of local, national, and global justice in the twenty-first century' and that 'organized labor is arguably the most effective popular vehicle for achieving a democratic and equitable society' can most likely be applied to our other country cases as well.

UNION DECLINE AND REVITALIZATION IN A GLOBAL WORLD

If unions retain important functions, what enables them to do so? Comparative research in industrial relations starting with Kerr et al.'s seminal work *Industrialism and Industrial Man* has pointed to differences in industrial relations systems and the ways in which key elements shape employment relations at the shop floor. While *Industrialism and Industrial Man* hypothesized the convergence of different national models towards a common system, more recent approaches, focusing on a wider set of key elements within the political economy, assume the perpetuation of three competing patterns of capitalism: CME, LME, and a less clearly defined Mediterranean economy (Hall and Soskice 2001). Besides this general differentiation, unions in the five countries analysed in this book vary not only in terms of their strength, an aspect that is crucial to estimate their chances of revitalization, but also in the institutional framework they are embedded in. Key elements of these institutional frameworks include the degree of coordination and centralization of collective bargaining (Calmfors and Driffil 1988; Soskice 1990; Traxler, Blaschke, and Kittel 2001); the strength, unity, and comprehensiveness of employers' associations (Swenson and Pontusson 2000; Thelen 2000; Traxler 2001); the existence of competent and powerful works councils (Turner 1991; Rogers and Streeck 1994; Frege 2002); the inclusion of labour into corporatist structures at the national or international level (Zagelmeyer 2000; Keller 2001; Baccaro 2002); or involvement in issues of training and skill development (Streeck 1996). In addition national and European employment law regulates strikes, the extension of collective bargaining agreements, and welfare rights, which also affect unions' scope for action (Esping-Andersen 1990; Stokke and Thörnqvist 2001; Traxler and Behrens 2002). Unions in our five countries thus operate under considerably different conditions.

First, the system of collective bargaining displays distinctive variation across the five cases. While the focus of collective bargaining is predominantly at the company level in the LMEs (the United Kingdom and United States), in Germany, collective agreements are mostly negotiated at the industry level. The same is true for Spain, where the sectoral–provincial level dominates with negotiations also occurring at the company and inter-sectoral level. Finally, in Italy a dual system of collective bargaining prevails where industry-wide agreements are complemented by negotiations at the company or territorial level. As emphasized in the varieties of capitalism literature, company-level bargaining strongly correlates with a low degree of bi- or tripartite concertation. As indicated in Table 2.1, unions in Germany, Italy, and Spain were involved in national-level social pacts. Finally, provisions for the extension of collective agreements are important to understand labour's capacity to determine wages, hours, and working conditions. Unions' capacity to set those standards is not exclusively determined by the size of their membership, and so extension provisions can potentially compensate for a low membership level. With differing degrees of effectiveness, such provisions exist in Germany and Spain, and in Italy, which features some functional equivalents to extension. British and American unions have no direct means of influencing the wages and working conditions of non-unionized workers.

As Table 2.1 shows, current levels of collective bargaining coverage vary widely with the two LME countries representing the lower end of the spectrum. If we focus on trends in coverage, Italy and Spain have remained fairly stable, but Germany,

Table 2.1. *Collective bargaining and social pacts 1990–2000*

	Scope of collective bargaining	CB coverage (2000)	CB coverage, trend, 1990–2000	Extension provisions	National-level tri-partite concertation/ social pacts
Germany	Industry level dominates, some company level	67%	Continued decline[a]	Yes	1995–96; 1998–2002
Italy	Two level bargaining, industry and either company or territorial level	Approx. 90% (for minimum wage levels only)	Relatively stable	No, but some functional equivalents	1992, 1993, 1996, 1998
Spain	Sectoral–provincial level dominates; also company level and intersectoral	80%	Relatively stable	Yes	1996 *ff.*
UK	Company level	36%	Continued decline	No	No
US	Company level	15%	Continued decline	No, some functional equivalents in some industries (construction)	No

[a] Data available for the time period 1994–2000 only.

Sources: Zagelmeyer (2000); Carley (2002); Hirsch and Macpherson (2003); Traxler and Behrens (2003).

the United States and the United Kingdom are witnessing decline. Union density exhibits divergent trends (Table 2.2). While density is declining in Germany and the United States, the United Kingdom, and Italy seem to have halted decline in the late 1990s. In Spain, in contrast, both density and membership grew steadily between 1990 and 2000. In 2000 union density fell into a rather narrow range between 13.5 per cent (the United States) and 31 per cent (Italy).

Patterns of inter-union competition also vary substantially across the five cases. In two countries (Spain and Italy) confederations, organized along political orientations, compete with each other, while in Germany, the United Kingdom, and the United States one major confederation heads the national labour movement even though other unions exist outside of these national peak organizations. As indicated in Table 2.3, variation is also notable in the field of industrial conflict with Spain being the most and Germany the least strike-prone country.

Table 2.2. *Union membership trends 1980–2000*

	Union membership (1980) in millions[a]	Union membership (1997) in millions[a]	Union density (1980)[b]	Union density (2000)[b]	Change in union density 1980/2000	Inter-union competition
Germany	9.484	10.278 (1998)[d]	33.6	21.6	−35.7	No
Italy	9.006	10.660[c]	44.4	31.0	−30.3	Yes
Spain	0.643 (1981)	1.457	5.7	13.3 (1997)	+133.3	Yes
UK	12.947	7.987 (1996)	52.2	29.5	−43.5	No
US	20.095	16.110	21.1	13.5	−36.0	No, some jurisdictional disputes

[a] Membership figures include pensioners and the unemployed.
[b] Germany, Italy, Spain: calculated as active union membership (excluding retired members)/working population (including unemployed); United Kingdom, United States: calculated as union members (including retired members)/working population (excluding unemployed).
[c] Including self-employed.
[d] Including east and west Germany.
Sources: Ebbinghaus and Visser (2000); Ebbinghaus (2003); Hirsch and McPherson (2003).

Table 2.3. *Working days lost through industrial action per 1,000 employees*

	1998	1999	2000	2001
Germany	0.6	2.6	0.4	0.9
Italy	28.2	43.6	41.7	40.6
Spain	119.4	129.6	292.5	151.0
UK	11.0	10.0	20.0	20.0
USA	42	16	163	N/A

Source: EIRO (2003).

As we show in the following section, this variation in key characteristics of the national institutions of industrial relations generate different degrees of urgency to the goal of union revitalization. It also has implications for union perspectives on revitalization and available resources.

FOUR DIMENSIONS OF UNION REVITALIZATION

The previous sections illustrate that union activity is multidimensional and extends to politics, society, and the market (see Hyman 2001 for a similar typology). Similarly, the nature of the crisis unions are facing differs across countries and between unions. Consequently, as union activity is multi-faceted, and unions also derive power resources from the various spheres they engage in, union revitalization can be conceptualized as (re)gaining power along the various dimensions that capture the main orientations or spheres of union activity.[2] We specify four dimensions along which revitalization can occur; three of these dimensions are derived inductively by observing patterns of union decline and revitalization. We identify the *membership* dimension, the *economic* dimension, and the *political* dimension as those that capture most clearly the different patterns of crisis and renewal. Yet, these dimensions together do not necessarily signal to what extent unions have made active and engaged efforts to revitalize their organizations. We thus add a fourth *institutional* dimension designed to encompass unions' internal structure, dynamics, and identity. We are interested in finding out to what extent the relationship between the institutional dimension and the other three dimensions is interactive. One could argue, for instance, that unions' identity and structures drive, to some extent, the choice of revitalization dimensions and strategies, but are also affected by them and can change in response to shifting emphases on the spheres of union activity (Hyman 1994: 119). However, in many cases it is difficult for unions to revitalize along one or more of these three core dimensions unless they also engage in fundamental organizational change.

Figure 2.1 represents the four dimensions of union revitalization as a pyramid. The graphic representation suggests that unions' revitalization efforts can either focus on one dimension, or can be a combination of more than one dimension. Thus, the revitalization efforts of a country's labour movement can be positioned within the space of the pyramid.

Membership Dimension

Union revitalization along the membership dimension consists of three measurable factors: an increase in membership numbers, an increase in membership density, and a change in the composition of union membership. Rising numbers of union members translate into increased resources for unions, including membership dues and people that can be mobilized in campaigns. Density is a commonly used indicator of union strength because it reflects the share of the workforce that is unionized and thereby has implications for legitimacy, representativeness, and bargaining power. It could be argued, though, that merely increasing membership and/or density by

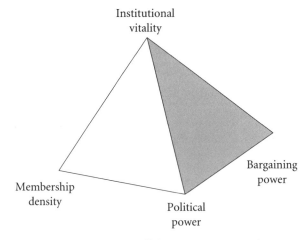

Figure 2.1. *Dimensions of labour movement revitalization*

recruiting a larger share of unions' traditional core constituencies does not present sufficient innovation to merit the label 'revitalization'. As the composition of the workforce changes, unions may no longer be able to boost their membership by targeting their traditional constituency, for example, male workers with stable employment. In most countries women, immigrants, part-time workers, and workers with temporary contracts constitute a growing share of the workforce. Successful union revitalization thus will include an increase both in membership and in union density, and also appropriate changes in the composition of union membership, thus embracing both a quantitative and qualitative element.

In addition to outreach to recruit additional members, the membership dimension also contains an internal component. Successful revitalization efforts may depend on changing the attitudes and expectations of existing membership. This may be especially true if external recruitment involves targeting new demographic groups that will change the membership composition and might be resented by the existing membership core. Regardless of which dimension of union revitalization takes priority, an engaged membership increases the potential for progress.

Economic Dimension

The economic dimension includes bargaining power, the ability to achieve wage and benefit improvements, and more broadly labour's impact on the distribution of wealth. Union revitalization along these lines implies the use of traditional and innovative methods to increase economic leverage. Under the latter heading unions may seek ways to boost their economic influence by developing new techniques outside of bargaining to increase leverage (e.g. corporate campaigns), by modifying deficient bargaining structures, or by redefining the union role in the bargaining process. Often detached from the direct power of union membership, revitalization within the economic realm materializes along different lines. This is because power might be 'derived' from employers' coordination and provisions for the extension of collective agreements. Based on law or on voluntary practice, extension rules broaden unions' direct ability to provide their members with decent wages, hours, and working conditions even where they fail to increase membership density. Ironically, to a substantial degree, unions' capacity for revitalization along the economic dimension depends on their adversaries' organizational strength. In terms of collectively agreed standards, it does not matter so much how many members a union has in a firm so long as the employer is a member of the appropriate employers' association.

Political Dimension

Revitalization along the political dimension implies that unions improve the effectiveness of their efforts to influence the policy-making process, either through traditional or innovative methods. This dimension involves union interaction with crucial actors at all levels of government—including supra-national bodies such as the European Union—and in three arenas of activity: elections, legislation, and implementation. Unions can seek to improve their leverage in the electoral process by working to secure victory for a political party they are allied with, or by participating more actively in the selection of candidates and in actual campaigns. In the legislative arena, unions may become more active in drafting or promoting legislation that alters regulation of the industrial relations framework, affects industries and markets where unions represent or are trying to recruit workers, or improves social conditions for union and non-union members alike. Unions may also seek to increase influence with government administration, particularly through enforcement of legislation relevant to union organizing or bargaining or the protection of workers' rights (the regulations in question may relate to the industrial relations framework or to a relevant product or labour market).

Institutional Dimension

The institutional dimension addresses unions' organizational structures and governance, as well as internal dynamics. It comprises unions' capacity to adjust to new contexts, internal enthusiasm to embrace new strategies, and a sense of introducing something new and 'fresh' to the union that is not adequately captured by the other three dimensions. A key aspect is the role of union leaders who promote new ideas and build internal political will to support change. Revitalization along the institutional dimension is sometimes spearheaded by changes in the other three dimensions. For instance, a new emphasis on organizing groups that were previously marginalized within union structures can lead to the creation of new departments (e.g. for women or immigrants), which can then influence the unions' larger goals and eventually lead to a redefinition of strategies. New bargaining approaches, such as corporate campaigns, may have similar effects—increasing the importance of research and public relations functions, for instance. Innovative leadership in unions can also reorient the union's identity, which subsequently has an impact on the choice of revitalization dimensions.

Revitalization along institutional lines does not clearly emerge out of observed indicators of union strength or decline as it is a concept that is difficult to measure. It is striking that unions overall seem to be rather reluctant to engage in profound organizational change that goes beyond adjusting particular strategies. In fact, an interesting question is why union organizations appear so reluctant to adapt and to innovate in the face of new external (and sometimes internal) pressures. Thinking more generally about how unions can be conceptualized theoretically improves our understanding of why the institutional dimension is crucial for union revitalization and at the same time so difficult to target. In particular, comprehending unions as organizations further illuminates the mechanisms that work within unions in their quest to identify new strategies for revitalization and offers some insights into the dynamics that may prevent unions from rapid internal adjustment to new circumstances.

Organizational theory identifies unions as formal interest organizations. While definitions of organizations vary widely, the core of any organization can be defined by two aspects.[3] 'First, the formal organization was seen as being directed towards explicit and clear goals. And second, the organization was seen as an instrument that was to be designed to achieve those goals with the greatest efficiency or economy of resources' (Nohria and Gulati 1994: 531). Weber (1980: 124) defines the 'ideal type' of the most efficient and stable organization as the modern bureaucracy with the following characteristics: a hierarchy, a management system based on written rules, a discrete set of jurisdictional areas and 'roles', an impersonal rule-governed environment and technical criteria for recruitment and promotion. The emphasis on rules, stability, and engrained culture may slow down initiatives for change and may also legitimate resistance to change on the grounds that it violates traditional cultural norms and threatens organizational stability (Voss and Sherman 2000).

Organizational analysis points to resource dependence and contingency theories to show that unions will use strategies that 'fit' their environment (Katz, Batt, and Keefe 2003). These approaches have demonstrated much potential when it comes to understanding why and how unions change to become revitalized. Other strands of organizational theory provide us with good reasons for why rapid change occurs only rarely. Scholars working in the tradition of 'population ecology' or 'ecological theory' (Hannan and Freeman 1989) as well as evolution theorists (Nelson and Winter 1982) argue that organizational change is limited by strong inertial pressures. From this perspective, rules, norms, and culture play an important role in the process of organizational change and thus determine, even more so than market competition, the selection of efficient organizational structures and processes.

The focus of these approaches on the intersection between organizations and their environment is potentially of high value to understanding labour's specific space for maneuver. Organizational theory contributes to deepening our understanding of how unions may employ resources internal to the union organization—in particular to reduce their dependence on external resources—and how they adapt their internal organizational structure to fit their external environment.[4] This illustrates the problems union movements have evidenced in reforming their identities and structures that are sometimes a precondition and at other times a consequence of the changes that accompany revitalization efforts.

CONCLUSION: REVITALIZATION AS A CONTEXT-DEPENDENT PROCESS

Revitalization can be conceptualized in terms of either an ongoing, and incomplete, process, or as an outcome, along four dimensions. We posit that in our country cases, it is the former use of the term that is more meaningful. We can observe revitalization efforts of various types in all five countries, maybe more timid in some than in others, but we shy away from calling any of the national union movements successfully 'revitalized'. In their endeavour to revitalize, unions may well reshape their identities and goals, and may fundamentally redefine their role in society, politics, and the marketplace (Hyman 2001). Such changes indicate the need for flexibility in our indicators of union strength and success.

While all four dimensions of union revitalization are of significance for all five countries, the relative import of each of these dimensions varies across the cases. This is hardly surprising given that the position of unions is context-dependent, that is, hinges on the specific political, economic, and legal provisions that regulate union activity and places unions in the larger political and economic system. The differential focus of national union movements on these dimensions is also shaped by the nature of the crisis that unions find themselves in. For instance, if membership has fallen drastically but has not substantially affected unions' power in the marketplace (e.g. bargaining coverage rates have remained constant), we would probably not expect the same priority on membership as a revitalization strategy as in a case where dwindling membership rates have resulted in similarly reduced bargaining coverage rates. Where unions' rights on the shop floor are supplemented by the parallel existence of works councils, they might similarly find that the membership dimension is of less immediacy for revitalization than in cases where they are the only intermediary between workers and management.

The specific national context does matter, but we do not mean to imply that the dimensions of revitalization unions target are entirely determined by their position in their national industrial relations, political, or economic systems. Instead, we view these exogenous variables as influential and constraining, but not determinant. Unions, as organizations, have some leeway in deciding whether they want to focus their efforts and resources on gaining political or market power or both, whether pursuing internal organizational or leadership changes is vital to their renewal efforts, and how crucial the membership dimension is. Union leaders can, within the constraints of their national contexts and union organizations, decide on the most promising revitalization dimensions and pick strategies they identify as conducive to furthering revitalization along those dimensions. We thus introduce the element of strategic choice (see Child, Loveridge, and Warner 1973; Kochan, Katz, and McKersie 1986; Swenson 1989; Johnston 1994) to our explanation of the variation in importance of revitalization dimensions in our cases.

The following chapter outlines further the strategies unions in the different countries have engaged in to regain strength. Subsequent chapters analyse the efforts of major unions in five countries by comparing how, why, and to what effect they have employed these strategies of union revitalization.

Notes

1. In Britain, for example, approximately 200,000 workers acted as unpaid union representatives at their workplace in 1998 (Millward et al. 2000: 155).
2. Although we label these different aspects of union activity 'dimensions', no one term can fully capture our intent. On the one hand the four aspects are indicators of revitalization, on the other hand they are power resources that drive revitalization. Our adoption of the term 'dimensions' should not be interpreted as limiting the importance of these four factors.
3. As Powell and DiMaggio (1991) have shown, the same plurality of concepts and definition is also true for institutions in the case of defining institutions.
4. Nonetheless, despite their merits, organizational theories also have limits in their application and explanatory power. For instance, they cannot account for cases of vibrant labour protest, short and punctuated periods of time where labour movements are born. While resource dependence and contingency theories help to understand how labour (as an organization) handles a complex and uncertain environment by way of diversification, they do not tell us why—at certain times and at certain places—labour is capable of challenging powerholders by mobilizing thousands of people on the streets.

References

Aidt, T. and Tzannatos, Z. (2002). *Unions and Collective Bargaining: Economic Effects in a Global Environment*. Washington, DC: The World Bank.

Baccaro, L. (2002). 'Negotiating the Italian Pension Reform with the Unions: Lessons for Corporatist Theory'. *Industrial and Labor Relations Review*, 66/3: 579–601.

Berger, S. and Compston, H. (2002). *Policy Concertation and Social Partnership in Western Europe: Lessons for the 21st Century*. New York: Berghahn.

Bronfenbrenner, K. and Juravich, T. (1998). 'It takes more than House Calls: Organizing to Win with a Comprehensive Union-Building Strategy', in K. Bronfenbrenner, S. Friedman, R. W. Hurd, R. A. Oswald, and R. L. Seeber (eds.), *Organizing to Win: New Research on Union Strategies*. Ithaca, NY: ILR Press, 19–36.

—— Friedman, S., Hurd, R. W., Oswald, R. A., and Seeber, R. L. (eds.) (1998). *Organizing to Win: New Research on Union Strategies*. Ithaca, NY: ILR Press.

Calmfors, L. and Driffill, J. (1988). 'Bargaining Structure, Corporatism, and Macroeconomic Performance'. *Economic Policy*, 6: 13–61.

Cameron, D. (1984). 'Social Democracy, Corporatism, Labour Quiescence, and the Representation of Economic Interest in Advanced Capitalist Societies', in J. Goldthorpe (ed.), *Order and Conflict in Contemporary Capitalism*. Oxford: Clarendon Press, 143–78.

Carley, M. (2002). 'Industrial relations in the EU, Japan and USA, 2001'. EIRO, www.eiro. eurofound.ie/2002/12/feature/TN0212101F.html.

Child, J., Loveridge, R., and Warner M. (1973). 'Towards an Organizational Study of Trade Unions'. *Sociology*, 7/1: 71–99.

Clawson, D. (2003). *The Next Upsurge: Labor and the New Social Movements*. Ithaca, NY: ILR Press.

Dunlop, J. T. (1944). *Wage Determination Under Trade Unions*. New York: Macmillan.

Ebbinghaus, B. (2003). 'Die Mitgliederentwicklung deutscher Gewerkschaften im historischen und internationalen Vergleich', in W. Schröder and B. Weßels (eds.), *Die Gewerkschaften in Politik und Gesellschaft der Bundesrepublik Deutschland. Ein Handbuch*. Wiesbaden: Westdeutscher Verlag, 74–203.

—— and Visser, J. (2000). *Trade Unions in Western Europe since 1945*. London: Macmillan.

EIRO (2003). *Developments in Industrial Action 1998–2002*, www.eiro.eurofound.ie/ 2003/03/Update/TN0303104U.html.

Esping-Andersen, G. (1990). *The Three Worlds of Welfare Capitalism*. Princeton, NJ: Princeton University Press.

Franzese, R. J. and Hall, P. A. (2000). 'Institutional Dimensions of Coordinating Wage Bargaining and Monetary Policy', in T. Iversen, J. Pontusson, and D. Soskice (eds.), *Unions, Employers, and Central Banks: Macroeconomic Coordination and Institutional Change in Social Market Economies*. New York: Cambridge University Press, 173–204.

Fairbrother, P. and Yates, C. A. B. (eds.) (2003). *Trade Unions in Renewal: A Comparative Study*. London: Continuum.

Ferner, A. and Hyman, R. (eds.) (1998). *Changing Industrial Relations in Europe*, 2nd edn. Oxford: Blackwell.

Freeman, R. B. and Medoff, J. L (1984). *What do Unions Do?* New York: Basic Books.

—— and Rogers, J. (1999). *What Workers Want*. Ithaca, NY: ILR Press.

Frege, C. (2002). 'A Critical Assessment of Theoretical and Empirical Research on German Works Councils'. *British Journal of Industrial Relations*, 40/2: 221–48.

Gall, G. (ed.) (2003). *Union Organizing: Campaigning for Trade Union Recognition*. London: Routledge.

Gordon, M. E. and Turner, L. (eds.) (2000). *Transnational Cooperation Among Labor Unions*. Ithaca, NY: ILR Press.

Hall, P. A. and Soskice, D. (2001). 'An Introduction to the Varieties of Capitalism', in P. A. Hall and D. Soskice (eds.), *Varieties of Capitalism: The Institutional Foundations of Comparative Advantage*. Oxford: Oxford University Press, 1–70.

Hamann, K. (2003). 'European Integration and Civil Society in Spain'. *South European Society and Politics*. 8/1: 47–68.

Hannan, M. T. and Freeman, J. (1989). *Organizational Ecology*. Cambridge: Harvard University Press.

Harrod, J. and O'Brien, R. (eds.) (2002). *Global Unions? Theory and Strategies of Organized Labour in the Global Political Economy*. London: Routledge.

Held, D., McGrew, A., Goldblatt, D., and Perraton, J. (1999). *Global Transformations: Politics, Economics and Culture*. Cambridge: Polity Press.

Hirsch, B. and McPherson, D. (2003). *Union Membership and Coverage Database from the Current Population Survey*, www.unionstats.com.

Hyman, R. (1994). 'Changing Trade Union Identities and Strategies', in R. Hyman and A. Ferner (eds.), *New Frontiers in European Industrial Relations*. Oxford: Basil Blackwell, 108–39.

—— (2001). *Understanding European Trade Unionism: Between Market Class and Society.* London: Sage.

Johnston, P. (1994). *Success while others Fail. Social Movement Unionism and the Public Workplace.* Ithaca, NY: ILR Press.

Katz, H. C., Batt, R., and Keefe, J. H. (2003). 'The Revitalization of the CWA: Integrating Collective Bargaining, Political Action, and Organizing' *Industrial and Labor Relations Review,* 56/4: 573–89.

Kaufman, B. E. (2002). 'Models of Union Wage Determination: What have we Learned since Dunlop and Ross?'. *Industrial Relations,* 41/1: 110–58.

Keller, B. (2001). 'Social Partners and Social Partnership at the European Level', in C. Kjaergaard, and S.-Ä. Westphalen (eds.) *From Collective Bargaining to Social Partnerships: New Roles of the Social Partners in Europe.* Copenhagen: The Copenhagen Centre.

Kelly, J. (1998). *Rethinking Industrial Relations: Mobilization, Collectivism and Long Waves.* London: Routledge.

—— and Willman, P. (eds.) (2004). *Union Organization and Activity.* London: Routledge.

Kochan, T. A. (1995). 'Using the Dunlop Report to Achieve Mutual Gains'. *Industrial Relations,* 34/3: 350–66.

—— Katz, H., and McKersie, R. (1986). *The Transformation of American Industrial Relations.* New York: Basic Books.

Levi, M. (2003). 'Organizing Power: The Prospects for an American Labor Movement'. *Perspectives on Politics,* 1/1: 45–68.

Martin, A. and Ross, G. (eds.) (1999). *The Brave New World of European Labor: European Trade Unions at the Millennium.* New York: Berghahn Books.

Metcalf, D., Hansen, K., and Charlwood, A. (2000). *Unions and the Sword of Justice: Unions and Pay Systems, Pay Inequality, Pay Discrimination and Low Pay.* London: London School of Economics, Centre for Economic Performance, Discussion Paper 452.

Milkman, R. and Wong, K. (2001). 'Organizing Immigrant Workers: Case Studies from Southern California', in L. Turner, H. C. Katz, and R. W. Hurd (eds.), *Rekindling the Movement: Labor's Quest for Relevance in the 21st Century.* Ithaca, NY: ILR Press, 99–128.

Millward, N., Bryson, A., and Forth, J. (2000). *All Change at Work? British Employment Relations 1980–1998, as Portrayed by the Workplace Industrial Relations Survey Series.* London: Routledge.

Mishel, L., Bernstein, J., and Schmitt, J. (eds.) (2001). *The State of Working America 2000–01.* Ithaca, NY: Cornell University Press.

Müller-Jentsch, W. (1994). 'Über Produktivkräfte und Bürgerrechte', in N. Beckenbach and W. van Treeck (eds.), *Umbrüche gesellschaftlicher Arbeit.* Göttingen: Sonderband 9 Soziale Welt, 643–61.

Nelson, R. and Winter, S. (1982). *An Evolutionary Theory of Economic Change.* Cambridge: Harvard University Press.

Nissen, B. (ed.) (2002). *Unions in a Globalized Environment: Changing Borders, Organizational Boundaries, and Social Roles.* New York: ME Sharpe.

Nohria, N. and Gulati, R. (1994). 'Firms and Their Environments', in N. Smelser and R. Swedberg (eds.), *The Handbook of Economic Sociology.* Princeton, NJ: Princeton University Press, 529–55.

OECD (2002). *Employment Outlook.* Paris: OECD.

Osterman, P., Kochan, T. A., Locke, R. M., and Piore, M. J. (2001). *Working in America. A Blueprint for the New Labor Market.* Cambridge and London: MIT Press.

Pochet, P. (ed.) (1999). *Monetary Union and Collective Bargaining in Europe.* Brussels: Peter Lang.

Powell, W. W. and DiMaggio, P. J. (1991). 'Introduction', in W. W. Powell and P. J. DiMaggio (eds.), *The New Institutionalism in Organizational Analysis*. Chicago and London: University of Chicago Press, 1–38.

Putnam R. (1993). *Making Democracy Work: Civic Traditions in Modern Italy*. Princeton, NJ: Princeton University Press.

——(1995). 'Bowling Alone: America's Declining Social Capital'. *Journal of Democracy*, 6/1: 65–78.

Rogers, J. and Streeck, W. (eds.) (1994). *Works Councils*. Chicago IL: University of Chicago Press.

Ross, A. (1948). *Trade Union Wage Policy*. Berkeley CA: University of California Press.

Ross, G. and Martin, A. (1999). 'Through a Glass Darkly', in A. Martin and G. Ross (eds.), *The Brave New World of European Labor: European Trade Unions at the Millennium*. New York: Berghahn Books, 368–99.

Shoch, J. (2001). 'Organized Labor Versus Globalization: NAFTA, Fast Track and PNT with China', in L. Turner, H. C. Katz, and R. W. Hurd (eds.), *Rekindling the Movement: Labor's Quest for Relevance in the 21st Century*. Ithaca, NY: ILR Press, 275–313.

Smith, W. R. (1998). *The Left's Dirty Job: The Politics of Industrial Restructuring in France and Spain*. Pittsburgh PA: University of Pittsburgh Press.

Soskice, D. (1990). 'Wage Determination: The Changing Role of Institutions in Advanced Industrialized Countries'. *Oxford Review of Economic Policy*, 6: 36–61.

Stephens, J. D. and Wallerstein, M. (1991). 'Industrial Concentration, Country Size, and Trade Union Membership'. *American Political Science Review*, 85/3: 941–54.

Stokke, T. A. and Thörnqvist, C. (2001). *Industrial Conflict in the Nordic Countries: Convergence or Divergence?* Paper presented at the 6th European IIRA Congress, Oslo, June 2001.

Streeck, W. (1991). 'On the Institutional Conditions of Diversified Quality Production', in E. Matzner, and W. Streeck, (eds.), *Beyond Keynesianism: The Socio-Economics of Production and Employment*. London: Edward Elgar, 21–61.

——(1996). 'Lean Production in the German Automobile Industry: A Test Case for Convergence Theory', in S. Berger and R. Dore (eds.), *National Diversity and Global Capitalism*. Ithaca, NY: Cornell University Press, 138–70.

Swenson, P. (1989). *Fair Shares. Unions, Pay, and Politics in Sweden and West Germany*. Ithaca, NY: Cornell University Press.

——(2002). *Capitalists Against Markets*. New York: Oxford University Press.

——and Pontusson, J. (2000). 'The Swedish Employer Offensive against Centralized Bargaining', in T. Iversen, J. Pontusson, and D. Soskice, (eds.), *Unions, Employers, and Central Banks. Macroeconomic Coordination and Institutional Change in Social Market Economies*. New York: Cambridge University Press, 77–106.

Taylor, P. and Bain, P. (2003). 'Call Centre Organizing in Adversity: From Excell to Vertex', in G. Gall (ed.), *Union Organizing: Campaigning for Trade Union Recognition*. London: Routledge, 153–72.

Thelen, K. (2000). 'Why German Employers Cannot Bring Themselves to Dismantle the German Model', in I. Torben, J. Pontusson, and D. Soskice (eds.), *Unions, Employers and Central Banks: Macroeconomic Coordination and Institutional Change in Social Market Economies*. New York: Cambridge University Press, 138–172.

——(2001). 'Varieties of Labor Politics in the Developed Democracies', in P. A. Hall and D. Soskice (eds.), *Varieties of Capitalism: The Institutional Foundations of Comparative Advantage*. Oxford: Oxford University Press, 71–103.

Traxler, F. (2001.) 'Der verbandliche Organisationsgrad der Arbeitgeber: ein internationaler Vergleich', in J. Abel, and H. J. Sperling (eds.), *Umbrüche und Kontinuitäten. Perspektiven nationaler und internationaler Arbeitsbeziehungen.* Munich and Mering: Rainer Hampp Verlag, 315–30.

——and Behrens, M. (2003). 'Collective bargaining coverage and extension procedures'. *EIRObserver*, 2/2003: i–viii.

—— Blaschke, S., and Kittel, B. (2001). *National Labour Relations in Internationalized Markets. A Comparative Study of Institutions, Change, and Performance.* Oxford: Oxford University Press.

Turner, L. (1991). *Democracy at Work. Changing World Markets and the Future of Labor Unions.* Ithaca, NY: Cornell University Press.

—— Katz, H. C., and Hurd, R. W. (eds.) (2001). *Rekindling the Movement: Labor's Quest for Relevance in the 21st Century.* Ithaca, NY: ILR Press.

Voss, K. and Sherman, R. (2000). 'Breaking the Iron Law of Oligarchy: Union Revitalization in the American Labor Movement'. *American Journal of Sociology*, 106/2: 303–49.

—————— (2003). 'You Just can't do it Automatically: The Transition to Social Movement Unionism in the United States', in P. Fairbrother and C. A. B. Yates (eds.), *Trade Unions in Renewal: A Comparative Study.* London: Continuum, 51–77.

Waddington, J. and Hoffman, R. (eds.) (2000*a*). *Trade Unions in Europe: Facing Challenges and Searching for Solutions.* Brussels: European Trade Union Institute.

—————— (2000*b*). 'Trade Unions in Europe: Reform, Organisation and Restructuring', in J. Waddington and R. Hoffman (eds.), *Trade Unions in Europe: Facing Challenges and Searching for Solutions.* Brussels: European Trade Union Institute, 27–79.

Wallerstein, M. and Golden, M. (2000). 'Postwar Wage Setting in the Nordic Countries', in T. Iversen, J. Pontusson, and D. Soskice (eds.), *Unions, Employers, and Central Banks: Macroeconomic Coordination and Institutional Change in Social Market Economies.* New York: Cambridge University Press, 107–37.

Weber, M. (1980, first published 1922) *Wirtschaft und Gesellschaft. Grundriss der verstehenden Soziologie*, 5th rev. edn. Tübingen: J. C. B. Mohr.

Wever, K. (1997). 'International Labor Revitalization: Enlarging the Playing Field', *Industrial Relations*, 37/3: 388–407.

Wheeler, H. N. (2002). *The Future of the American Labor Movement.* New York: Cambridge University Press.

Zagelmeyer, S. (2000). *Innovative Agreements on Employment and Competitiveness in the European Union and Norway.* Dublin: European Foundation for the Improvement of Living and Working Conditions.

3

Union Strategies in Comparative Context

CAROLA FREGE AND JOHN KELLY

INTRODUCTION

The previous chapter outlined the concept of union revitalization and explored the social, political, and economic significance of union decline and revival. The purpose of this chapter is to take the analysis a step further by exploring the strategies used by union movements to recover their influence. While all four dimensions of union revitalization are significant for all five countries, the relative importance of each of these dimensions varies across the cases. This is hardly surprising given that the position of unions is context-dependent, that is, hinges on the specific political, economic, and legal provisions that regulate union activity and place unions in the larger political and economic system. The differential focus of national union movements on these dimensions is also shaped by the nature of the crisis in which unions find themselves. For instance, if membership has fallen drastically but has not substantially affected unions' economic power (e.g. bargaining coverage rates have remained constant), we would probably not expect the same priority on membership as a revitalization strategy as in a case where dwindling membership rates have resulted in equally reduced bargaining coverage rates. Where unions' rights on the shop floor are supplemented by the parallel existence of works councils, they might similarly find that the membership dimension is of less immediacy for revitalization than in cases where they are the only intermediary between workers and management.

The specific national context does matter, but we do not mean to imply that the dimensions of revitalization unions target are entirely determined by their position in their national industrial relations, political, or economic systems. Instead, we view these exogenous variables as influential and constraining, but not determinant. Unions, as organizations, have some leeway in deciding whether they want to focus their efforts and resources on gaining political or economic power or both, whether pursuing internal organizational or leadership changes is vital to their renewal efforts, and how crucial is the membership dimension. Union leaders can, within the constraints of their national contexts and union organizations, decide on the most promising revitalization dimensions and choose strategies they identify as conducive to furthering revitalization along those dimensions. We thus introduce the element of strategic choice (see Child, Loveridge, and Warner 1973; Kochan, Katz, and McKersie 1986; Swenson 1989; Johnston 1994) to our explanation of the variation in importance of revitalization dimensions in our cases.

In the opening section, we set out six different strategies that unions might employ and briefly comment on each. We also explain how and why we came to focus on these strategies as they comprise the core of the book and we explore their relative salience in the five countries. In the next section, we consider the variables necessary to address two key questions that will run throughout the book: why do different union movements adopt different mixes of strategies? And how can we account for the varying success of different strategies in revitalizing trade unionism?

UNION REVITALIZATION STRATEGIES

Theoretically, we started from the premise that one of the key differences between a union movement in labour decline and one that is revitalizing is the degree of power to influence other relevant actors such as employers or the state (see also Turner, Chapter 1, this volume). As discussed in the previous chapter, it is difficult to establish precise benchmarks to measure success in union revitalization. In particular, how much of revitalization is due to unions' own efforts? Unions may profit from 'uncontrollable' external factors, such as the change of the governing political party or the improvement of the economy and labour market conditions. However, improved external conditions do not automatically lead to union revitalization. Unions still need to actively translate these potential resources into revitalization. Some unions are more successful than others in similar socioeconomic and political conditions, and it is these strategic differences and their possible outcomes we are interested in.

Why use the term 'strategy' rather than say 'actions' or 'policies'? The term strategy is primarily about delimiting the subject matter of our research. We wanted to focus on initiatives by unions that were reasonably substantial and which were intended as means for the achievement of specified union goals. Unions and union confederations are continually engaged in a wide range of actions of many different kinds. Rather than try to embrace all of these, however ephemeral, we aimed to concentrate on those actions we took to be relatively enduring and which seemed to be reasonably well thought out means for contributing to one or more of our dimensions of revitalization. For example, unions may engage in coalition-building with various social movements as a way of expressing core values of the union's identity or they may construct coalitions strategically in order to facilitate revitalization and it is the latter in which we are interested. The next question becomes: How do the strategies relate to the four revitalization dimensions described in the previous chapter? In other words, what sources of power are used by unions? As outlined in Turner (Chapter 1, this volume) the most significant revitalization strategies identified in our country cases are: organizing, partnership relations with employers, political action, union restructuring, coalition-building, and international solidarity. These six strategies embrace all major relations between the union and the other key actors within the economy, political system, and civil society, namely workers, employers, the state, social movements, and labour movements in other countries. Restructuring embraces relations within and between unions as organizations. There are three other areas we might have examined but chose not to do so. Strike action has tended to accompany union revival in earlier periods of economic recovery from recession or war, such as the 1940s and the 1890s (Kelly 1998: 89–94). However, the strike has typically been used as part of the process of collective bargaining with employers or as a means of influencing state policy. The sharp decline in economic strike activity since 1980 suggested there was little to be gained from an empirical examination of the contribution of strike activity to union revitalization (although the issue will be returned to in the Conclusion to the book (Chapter 10)) (Bordogna and Cella 2002). However, we did decide to incorporate political or general strikes, into the study of union political action since they are typically targeted at the state as a means of exercising political power. Membership education is another significant area of union activity but we decided to touch on that part of the union education programme most closely related to revitalization, in particular therefore on the training of union organizers. Finally we decided not to examine individual servicing, through legal representation for instance, except where such representation comprised part of a political strategy to change the law or was part of a union restructuring programme directed towards revitalization and not just maintenance of the current membership (see Hamann and Kelly, Chapter 6, and Behrens, Hurd, and Waddington, Chapter 7, this volume).

On first sight, the link between strategies and dimensions of revitalization or power resources is straightforward: organizing relates to the membership dimension, labour–management partnership relates to economic power resources, political action relates to the political dimension, and the remaining three strategies, union restructuring, coalition-building, and international solidarity relate to institutional power resources. However, there is not a linear relationship between one strategy and one revitalization dimension because strategies can address multiple dimensions. For example, although our first strategy, *union organizing*, is most clearly directed at union membership recovery, in principle, as we shall see, it can also help political lobbying, because larger unions are taken more seriously. In addition, organizing could create and strengthen workplace representation; this in turn might increase the union's mobilizing capacity and therefore its economic bargaining power.

Second, we explored strategies in which unions exploit favourable labour and product market conditions to bargain with employers. Unions may seek to increase bargaining coverage, alter the structure of collective bargaining, or expand the bargaining agenda. On the other hand, employers can seriously undermine union effectiveness by refusing to negotiate at all, by negotiating in bad faith, or by leaving the employers' association. By agreeing to negotiate and consult on a wide range of issues, employers can enhance union effectiveness. Much of the literature on this topic in recent years has centred around the pitfalls and potentials of *partnership relations with employers* as a means of union revitalization and it therefore constitutes our second strategy. These labour–management relations are clearly directed towards improving the economic power resources of unions but they also have a potential impact on their political capabilities: social partnership arrangements at enterprise or sector level may help to establish corporatist arrangements at the national level. Partnerships with employers at national, industrial, or workplace level may also allow unions to protect or develop bargaining institutions and allow them to pursue new kinds of interests. If partnership were to improve workers' terms and conditions of employment, then it might increase perceptions of union instrumentality amongst non-union employees and assist union organizing (Clark 2000). Insofar as they embody a union desire to cooperate with employers, they may erode the negative image that unions are associated with militancy and conflict (Cohen and Hurd 1998). This in turn could reduce potential employee, employer, and political antagonism to unions.

Third, unions can attempt to access the power of the state through *political action.* Successful political action could consolidate or increase union political power as union movements exert influence over government, resulting in more favourable labour legislation or in corporatist labour market regulation. In addition, political action can also have an impact on the level of union membership. Countries with corporatist institutions through the postwar period usually had higher union density than non-corporatist countries and suffered less density decline during the 1980s (Western 1997: 24). Moreover, political action, such as lobbying for broader social issues can help to enlarge institutional power resources such as facilitating coalitions with other social movements.

Fourth, there is union restructuring, which occurs in three forms: mergers between individual unions, closer relations between union confederations, and internal restructuring of union organization. Mergers between two unions may be thought of as a form of 'market share unionism' which merely redistributes existing union members amongst a smaller number of organizations (Willman 1989). However, the merger is often presented by union leaders as a means of augmenting institutional union power because it overcomes divisions between unions that can sometimes be very damaging (see Waddington 1995). In countries with a single or dominant union centre—in our sample the United Kingdom, the United States, and Germany—inter-union competition and merger take the form of relations between individual unions. However, in Italy and Spain there are powerful and competing union confederations. In these countries, greater cooperation between unions therefore mainly takes the form of closer links between the confederations. Finally, the union as an organization can also be thought of as a source of power, quite apart from its membership, because of its financial wealth and its personnel (Willman, Morris, and Aston 1993). Both of these organizational sources of power are tied up to a very large degree in representing existing union members. In the UK, for example, around 80 per cent of union expenditure goes on the salaries of union officials and the overwhelming majority of their time is spent servicing members (Kelly and Heery 1994). If unions could restructure themselves and become more efficient organizations they might be able to divert some of these resources to activities that could be focused on union revitalization while continuing to service their members at the same time. In sum, union restructuring could have the following positive impacts: it could strengthen union organization through economies of scale and through rationalization; it could increase both economic and political power by eliminating inter-union competition and division; the combination of additional resources and increased power, for example, through mergers, could encourage more workers to join unions and boost membership; and finally decentralization of union organization could also encourage more grassroots involvement by rank-and-file members, which again could increase membership density.

Fifth, the literature on social movements and mobilization has highlighted strategies linking unions with civil society, where there is an abundance of groups and social movements representing a diverse range of interests, identities, and issues (cf. Kelly 1998; McAdam, Tarrow, and Tilly 2001). The antiwar, environmental, and gay rights organizations are perhaps the best-known examples in recent years. In theory, unions might be able to increase their institutional power by accessing the power of social movements in civil society through building coalitions with these groups and therefore *coalition-building* is our fifth union strategy.

Coalition-building with other social movements, such as the anti-globalization or environmental movements, could help unions acquire power resources, such as access to key individuals and networks within specific communities who could assist with organizing campaigns. Such links might also serve to broaden the range of interests pursued by unions and make them into more relevant civil actors as well as broadening their appeal to poorly represented segments of the labour force (Hyman 1997).

Finally, we need to consider the increased globalization of production, investment, and trade, which has become especially prominent during the past 20 years or so. Globalization has posed new problems for unions through the increased mobility of capital, especially in parts of manufacturing and financial services (Dicken 2003). At the same time, problems and contradictions within international production chains may also create opportunities for unions to reconstruct forms of *international union action* and this category therefore comprises our sixth, and final, union strategy (e.g. see Gordon and Turner 2000). International union action can also improve the exchange of information about multinational corporations, enhancing unions' bargaining power, and also facilitating the mobilization of members in campaigns. International links could also enhance union political power through the lobbying efforts of union bodies within institutions such as the EU (Ross and Martin 1999*a*).

EXPLAINING UNION CHOICES AND OUTCOMES

How do we explain the different ways in which union movements choose among these strategies? In particular, what explains different strategic choices across countries? Why, for example, does the organizing approach appear to be more prevalent in the United States and the United Kingdom than in Germany, Italy, or Spain? Unions differ also within national movements but only a cross-country comparison allows us to take into account national parameters such as the political system and its impact on unions' strategies.

Closely related is the question of how we can measure and account for variations in the success of these strategies across countries. One possibility would be to compare the success of different strategies within or across countries. For example, is organizing a more successful strategy for revitalization than coalition-building? There is, for instance, a strong bias in the current US literature towards organizing as perhaps the best revitalization strategy (cf. Bronfenbrenner et al. 1998). However, the literature is usually not very specific about the precise measure of success. Nor is there necessarily much virtue in ranking strategies in order of effectiveness because such an exercise assumes that strategies are independent when in fact they may be interdependent. In the United States, for example, organizing is frequently dependent on coalition-building at community level. What may be more useful is to compare the success of a single strategy in different countries, such as organizing in the United States and in Britain. The purpose here is not to adjudicate between different strategies but to explore the contextual conditions, which shape differing degrees of success. We start to examine theses issues by reviewing what the literature tells us about the factors influencing strategic choices of unions in responding to crisis, and on this basis, we develop a more comprehensive framework for analysis.

It is surprising that although Kochan, Katz, and McKersie (1986) introduced the concept of 'strategic choice' to the industrial relations literature in the mid-1980s there is very little research on the different strategic choices made by unions and on their consequences (Heery 2003: 295). A number of authors have proposed typologies of union strategic choices, such as Boxall and Haynes (1997) who argue unions can choose one of two orientations to their membership (servicing vs. organizing) and either of two orientations to the employer (cooperative vs. adversarial). As we shall see in later chapters, unions often try and pursue all of these simultaneously, sometimes in different segments of their job territories (Heery and Adler, Fichter and Greer, Chapters 4 and 5, this volume). Nonetheless, although multi-country studies of industrial relations are increasingly popular there has been little truly comparative research on union strategies in different countries (Hyman 2001a). Most comparative studies have focused on one of two issues: The explanation of cross-country variation in quantitative indices such as union density or strike rates (e.g. Price 1991; Blanchflower and Freeman 1992; Shalev 1992; Western 1997); or the classification and explanation of different union types, structures, or identities (Maurice and Sellier 1979; Poole 1986; Martin 1989; Visser 1994; Hyman 2001b). Examples of work in the second category include Maurice and Sellier (1979) who drew comparisons between what they termed the charismatic character of French unionism, appealing to elements of 'emotional commonality' with the accent on class struggle, and the more functional (bureaucratic and professionalized) nature of unions in Germany. Poole (1986) observed that the role of employers, management, and the state had been decisive in the genesis of labour strategies. For example, militant employer strategies, which precluded trade union recognition, often promoted labour radicalism, and a powerful role of the state in the industrial relations system almost invariably promoted a politically active labour movement. In similar vein, Geary (1981) argued that state and employer repression was associated with greater political and industrial militancy on the part of labour. This viewpoint is clearly rooted in the classic understanding of the trade union as the less powerful labour market actor, largely responding to employer initiatives rather than becoming proactive and exercising strategic choice (cf. also Crouch and Streeck 1997; Kitschelt et al. 1999).

Clegg (1976) on the other hand tried, to establish a link between union organization and industrial relations institutions in different countries. He argued that key features of unions such as membership density, structural form, internal distribution of power, and strike behaviour were determined by the collective bargaining system in each country. For example, low union density in France was explained by the limited depth of collective bargaining, whereas high density in Sweden was due to the strength of collective bargaining at all levels. His approach has been criticized by some as almost tautological; moreover, the direction of causality is not always clear. For example, does widespread collective bargaining lead to high union density, does unionization encourage collective bargaining or are the two phenomena reciprocally connected (Shalev 1980; Hyman 1994: 174)? From a comparative perspective, Clegg's emphasis on collective bargaining seems too embedded in an Anglo-American understanding of industrial relations to be able to account for the political role of unions, common throughout much of Europe. In other words, the 'institutions' of industrial relations should not be confined to collective bargaining structures but can also include legal and arbitration procedures and the political system including corporatist structures (Peters 1999). In addition, as we are trying to account for union strategic choices, we can think of union structure as an independent variable. Nonetheless, his study alerts us to the powerful argument that industrial relations institutions shape the structures and behaviours of the actors, in other words 'institutions matter'. One important refinement we can add to Clegg's approach is to categorize union structure as part of the institutional environment within which union strategic choices are formulated, alongside the structure of bargaining. Although institutions can be changed, they often persist for long periods (Ebbinghaus and Visser 2000) and thus in the short-term influence actors' strategies to a greater degree than vice versa. Union structures comprise the horizontal and hierarchical organization of the union movement (centralized or decentralized union organization, unitary or multiple peak federations). Also included are national union leaderships and their relations with other union officials and rank-and-file union members, relations that are likely to vary across countries. Union leadership is differently organized in different countries and this will have an impact on how unions frame their opportunities and threats and their choices of action. In similar vein, Ross and Martin (1999*b*) refer to the 'national industrial relations system' as an explanation of differences in union structures and policies; unfortunately, they do not show a clear link between these variables. Western (1997) provides convincing evidence that labour movements survived best through the 1980s when they were involved in 'Ghent' systems of unemployment insurance, a national trademark of the northern European industrial relations systems.

A more recent and sophisticated account of institutions goes beyond the industrial relations system to embrace the structure of the economy, centred around the firm. According to Hall and Soskice (2001) there are five basic institutions at the heart of capitalist economies: the industrial relations system, the training system, the structures of worker motivation and reward, the structures of corporate governance, and the networks of relations between firms. These institutions can be configured in different ways to generate several 'varieties of capitalism' each with its own dynamics and economic outcomes. Liberal Market Economies (LMEs), such as the United Kingdom and the United States, typically have decentralized industrial relations systems in which bargaining coverage closely mirrors union density and where pay inequality is relatively high. Coordinated market economies (CMEs), such as Germany and the Netherlands, by contrast, typically have more centralized bargaining, higher bargaining coverage (even if union density is relatively low), and lower earnings inequality. Mediterranean economies, such as Italy and Spain, are normally thought of as hybrids of the LME and CME types, but their precise characteristics are the subject of considerable debate.

One implication of this classification is that different varieties of capitalism may be associated with different types of union problem and differing degrees of union crisis. For example, the most severe declines in union membership since the early 1980s have been observed in some of the LMEs, especially the United Kingdom, the United States, Australia, and New Zealand (although German union density has declined just as steeply since the early 1990s: Behrens, Hamann, and Hurd, Chapter 2 this volume; Kelly 2003). A further implication is that in their efforts to deal with problems, unions will face different types of constraints and opportunities. For example, within the CMEs employers are typically well organized in employers' associations, which are generally quite supportive of collective bargaining. By contrast, employers in the LMEs tend to be poorly organized, less capable of acting collectively, and less supportive of bargaining with unions. These differences in turn will impact on union strategies. Alternatively, to express this more formally, union movements face different 'opportunity structures' across the different varieties of capitalism, different sets of channels through which demands can be placed on employers and governments.

One further implication of the 'varieties of capitalism' approach arises from the persistence of economic institutions through time. Because these institutions are relatively enduring, union movements come to develop ways of organizing and representing workers that are adapted to their institutional environment and which also persist through time, reflecting what are sometimes referred to as 'path dependencies'. For example, the general strike against government policy is a familiar component of the 'repertoires of contention' (McAdam, Tarrow, and Tilly 2001) within Spanish trade unionism but is almost unknown in the American labour movement. In other words while union actions are shaped by contemporary institutions they also reflect histories of action that developed within particular national institutional environments. Ebbinghaus and Visser (2000) also emphasize the historical embeddedness of labour institutions. They argue that the character and context of national union movements can be traced back to historic, social, and political cleavages which generate 'cross-national variation and historical contingency'. Union movements in some countries are divided along political lines, for example, France, Italy, while in other countries there emerged separate Catholic and Protestant confederations, for example, Netherlands, Switzerland. However, despite the obvious analytical importance of 'institutions' and path dependencies, we argue that explaining actors' strategies by their institutional context alone is too simplistic and deterministic, downplaying the mutual dependency and the interrelationships between actors and institutions. Actors both influence and are influenced by institutions; what is important is to trace out the reciprocal interconnections between the two. In addition, the structure and character of institutions themselves need to be explained (Peters 1999).

Finally, Hyman (1994, 2001*b*) introduced union identities as another potential determinant of union strategies. 'Identities may be viewed as inherited traditions which shape current choices, which in normal circumstances in turn reinforce and confirm identities.' Thus, union identities produce path dependencies for union strategic decisions. In Hyman's (2001*b*) terms, union identity is oriented to class, market, or society and it can have an impact on how unions perceive opportunities and threats. For example, Italian or Spanish unions are embedded in a more militant, mobilizing tradition whereas German unions operate within a long social partnership tradition, which shapes union leaders perceptions and strategies. In the language of social movement theory, identities constitute the collective world view of union leaders, shaping the ways in which they 'frame' issues and problems (Hunt, Benford, and Snow 1994). These same world views also structure the 'repertoires of collective action', the forms of action which union leaders consider to be legitimate and feasible (Tilly 1978: 151–59). Unions in different countries have different identities, which shape their behaviour although this link can be 'disturbed' by outside factors:

> Yet in a period of crisis, trade unions . . . may be driven to choices (redefinition of interests, new systems of internal relations, broadening or narrowing of agenda, altered power tactics) at least partly at odds with traditional identities. . . . To the extent that old beliefs, slogans and commitments—the ideological supports of union self-conceptions—are undermined, an explicit and plausible redefinition of trade union purpose is essential if 'the capacity itself of labour movements to pursue the social and political construction of solidarity' (Regini 1992: 13) is to be salvaged. (Hyman 1994: 132)

One interesting issue flowing from the notion of identity concerns the conditions under which unions are likely to repeat well-worn behavioural patterns in responding to new challenges rather than risking new strategies. Rigid organizational structures, weak leaders, and outdated collective identities may all play a part in predisposing unions towards a conservative rather than an innovative response. One potential problem with the identity concept, however, is the need to make a convincing argument that union identities are independent, and not entirely shaped by the institutional setting of industrial relations, including the actions of employers and the state. There is also room for debate about what constitutes a 'crisis' for trade unionism sufficient to call into question traditional identities.

In summary, our reading of the comparative literature suggests that neither *institutions, state, and employer strategies* nor *union structures and identities* alone will be able to account for union strategic choices. Rather it is the combination of these variables that is likely to prove important in accounting for the choices made by unions.

The institutional context of industrial relations comprises collective bargaining structures, legal and arbitration procedures, and the political system including corporatist institutions (Peters 1999); but in contrast to labour economists, we define unions and employers as actors rather than as institutions. 'State and employer strategies' derive from the other key actors within the industrial relations system. As the political economy literature convincingly shows, employers and governments have different strategies over time and across different countries, and these help shape union responses (Crouch and Streeck 1997; Kitschelt et al. 1999). Union identity refers to the collective identity of the union movement, defined as the shared definition among its members of what the organization stands for, an attribute that is shaped by the historical legacies of the labour movement. Identity becomes embodied in structures, that is, the horizontal and hierarchical organization of the union movement. Likewise, the identity of a union movement will often be reflected in its national union leaderships and their relations with other union officials and rank-and-file union members, relations that are likely to vary across countries.

Before proceeding further, we should clarify a number of features of this model. Its form reflects our interest in explaining variations in union strategies so that institutions, state, and employer strategies, and union identities are therefore independent variables. If our concern had been to explain variations in institutional contexts then union strategies may have featured as an independent variable, since union strategic choices will themselves shape the behaviour of governments and employers. Clearly the relative explanatory power of these variables will differ over time and from one country to another. Moreover, there are likely to be complex interactions between them. State and employer strategies of union exclusion, for example, may reinforce union identities constructed around ideas of class identity and class antagonism (Geary 1981). Finally, by arguing that all three independent variables coexist we want to highlight that in contrast to the mainstream literature, structural variables—though useful in providing a primary explanation of cross-country variation—are insufficient to explore the deeper dynamics of union revitalization. For cross-country comparisons it is essential to take national union identities into account. We show that by looking at the historical embeddedness of union movements' identities we obtain a better understanding of why national unions perceive and react differently to similar external challenges. In the following section, we discuss how our six union strategies can be shaped by these explanatory variables.

THE RELATIVE SALIENCE OF DIFFERENT UNION STRATEGIES AND OUTCOMES IN DIFFERENT COUNTRIES

The previous chapter has already outlined a multidimensional approach to union revitalization and explained the reasons behind this. In essence, and in line with the logic of comparative analysis, union power and influence is secured in different ways in different national systems. A power resource that is critical in one system, say membership in the United Kingdom, may not be so critical in a different context, such as Spain or Italy, where unions rely more heavily on other power resources, whether votes in works council elections or mobilizing capacity. In other words when we compare the strategic choices and the outcomes of union strategies across a range of countries we shall endeavour to make 'contextualized comparisons' (cf. Locke and Thelen 1995).

Union organizing is likely to feature as a principal method of union revitalization where bargaining coverage is closely tied to membership density, as in the LMEs of the United Kingdom and the United States. The salience of organizing may also depend on unions' identities. Within a more militant class-based union movement, for example, as in Spain, recruiting members to pay union subscriptions may be less important than recruiting activists.

The construction of *partnerships with employers* can be understood as a form of labour–management cooperation. It may therefore be found where unions are weak and unable to mobilize members for collective action or conversely where unions are strong and employers have a powerful incentive to cooperate with labour. In the United Kingdom and the United States, for example, the absence of extension clauses agreed with encompassing employer associations means that unions which lose members and bargaining power may have a powerful incentive to elicit employer support by offering some form of cooperation at the level of the individual enterprise or workplace. By contrast, in economies where there is coordinated or centralized bargaining and enterprise works councils, partnership or labour–management cooperation may take a different form, centred on measures that affect an entire sector. Under these conditions, both sides have incentives to adhere to their collective agreements and possess the capacity to detect and punish free-riding and defection (Baccaro 2003).

Certain forms of *political action* are more likely to be found where there is a high degree of state regulation of the economy so that unions have a clear incentive to engage the state in consultation or negotiation. However, union movements may also seek to engage in political action to compensate for labour market weakness. The degree to which they succeed will depend heavily on the incentives for governments to negotiate with unions and therefore to constitute them as major political actors. In other words, union success may depend on the policies of the major political parties as well as on the attributes of the institutions of political power (e.g. a centralized vs. decentralized political system, strong vs. weak state or proportional vs. non-proportional voting systems). For example, the Spanish and Italian governments both faced general strikes in 2002 in protest at labour market and welfare reforms. The Spanish government chose to adopt a conciliatory approach and offered concessions sufficient to engage both union confederations in negotiations. By contrast, the Italian government took a much tougher line and managed to split the three union confederations, signing a national agreement in July 2002 with two of them and isolating the CGIL.

It is harder to analyse the conditions under which unions are more or less likely to engage in restructuring, coalition-building, or international action, for reasons that will become clear in the course of the respective chapters dealing with those topics. The most straightforward argument is that outside of a crisis of historic proportions union movements are likely, as all social movements, to respond to problems by drawing on familiar modes of action, whether it be organizing non-union workers, offering concessions in collective bargaining or seeking to engage the state in dialogue. More novel forms of action, such as coalition-building or international action are therefore less likely to be deployed.

However, we can think of certain conditions, which make unions more likely to engage in these activities. For example, unions facing a heavy financial crisis or experiencing a steep decline of membership are more likely to merge with other unions and may be more likely to focus on organizational change. Or again, unions may be more likely to engage in international action in economic systems which are strongly export oriented and where companies are transferring production into countries with lower labour costs. Such action may also be more likely where there are well-developed political opportunity structures within regional free market zones such as the European Union or to a much lesser degree in North American Free Trade Agreement (NAFTA) and where unions are already organized in regional bodies such as the European Trade Union Confederation (ETUC). Finally, unions may also be more likely to engage in coalition-building with new social movements if they are not encompassing social movements themselves. By contrast unions, which operate primarily as bargaining agents—as in the United States, for example, may therefore need to link up with other movements to broaden their agenda.

In sum, the degree to which national unions engage in the six strategies, as well as their degree of success, depends on the varying interplay of the three factors, employer and state strategies, IR institutions, and union identities in each national setting. Throughout the rest of this book, we shall be looking in turn at the union strategies we have outlined and their impact, paying particular attention to the different dimensions of revitalization.

References

Baccaro, L. (2003). 'What is Alive and What is Dead in the Theory of Corporatism'. *British Journal of Industrial Relations*, 41/4: 683–706.

Blanchflower, D. G. and Freeman, R. B. (1992). 'Unionism in the United States and other Advanced OECD Countries'. *Industrial Relations*, 31: 56–79.

Bordogna, L. and Cella, G. P. (2002). 'Decline or Transformation? Changes in Industrial Conflict and its Challenges'. *Transfer*, 8/4: 585–607.

Boxall, P. and Haynes, P. (1997). 'Strategy and Trade Union Effectiveness in a Neo-liberal Environment'. *British Journal of Industrial Relations*, 35/4: 567–91.

Bronfenbrenner, K., Friedman, S., Hurd, R. W., Oswald, R. A., and Seeber, R. L. (eds.) (1998). *Organizing to Win: New Research on Union Strategies*. Ithaca, NY: ILR Press.

Child, J., Loveridge, R., and Warner, M. (1973). 'Towards an Organisational Study of Trade Unions'. *Sociology*, 7: 71–91.

Clark, P. (2000). *Making Unions More Effective*. Ithaca, NY: ILR Press.

Clegg, H. (1976). *Trade Unionism Under Collective Bargaining*. Oxford: Blackwell.

Cohen, L. and Hurd, R. W. (1998). 'Fear, Conflict, and Organizing', in K. Bronfenbrenner, S. Friedman, R. W. Hurd, R. A. Oswald, and R. L. Seeber (eds.), *Organizing To Win: New Research On Union Strategies*. Ithaca, NY: ILR Press, 181–96.

Crouch, C. and Streeck, W. (eds.) (1997). *Political Economy of Modern Capitalism*. London: Sage.

Dicken, P. (2003). *Global Shift: Reshaping the Global Economic Map in the 21st Century 4e*. London: Sage.

Ebbinghaus, B. and Visser, J. (2000). 'A Comparative Profile', in B. Ebbinghaus and J. Visser (eds.), *Trade Unions in Western Europe Since 1945*. London: Macmillan, 33–74.

Geary, D. (1981). *European Labour Protest 1848–1939*. London: Croom Helm.

Gordon, M. E. and Turner, L. (eds.) (2000). *Transnational Cooperation Among Labor Unions*. Ithaca, NY: ILR Press.

Hall, P. A. and Soskice, D. (2001). 'An Introduction to Varieties of Capitalism', in P. A. Hall and D. Soskice (eds.), *Varieties of Capitalism: The Institutional Foundations of Comparative Advantage*. Oxford: Oxford University Press, 1–68.

Heery, E. (2003). 'Trade Unions and Industrial Relations', in P. Ackers and A. Wilkinson (eds.), *Understanding Work and Employment: Industrial Relations in Transition*. Oxford: Oxford University Press, 278–304.

Hunt, S. A., Benford, R. D., and Snow, D. A. (1994). 'Identity Fields: Framing Processes and the Social Construction of Movement Identities', in E. Larana, H. Johnston, and J. R. Gusfield. (eds.), *New Social Movements: From Ideology to Identity*. Philadelphia, PA: Temple University Press, 185–208.

Hyman, R. (1994). 'Changing Trade Union Identities and Strategies', in R. Hyman and A. Ferner (eds.), *New Frontiers in European Industrial Relations*. Oxford: Blackwell, 108–39.

——(1997). 'The Future of Employee Representation'. *British Journal of Industrial Relations*, 35/3: 309–31.

——(2001*a*). 'Trade Union Research and Cross-national Comparison', *European Journal of Industrial Relations*, 7/2: 203–32.

——(2001*b*). *Understanding European Trade Unionism*. London: Sage.

Johnston, P. (1994). *Success While others Fail: Social Movement Unionism and the Public Workplace*. Ithaca, NY: ILR Press.

Kelly, J. (1998). *Rethinking Industrial Relations: Mobilization, Collectivism and Long Waves*. London: Routledge.

——(2003). *Labour Movement Revitalization in Comparative Perspective*. Dublin: Countess Markievicz Memorial Lecture.

——and Heery, E. (1994). *Working for the Union: British Trade Union Officers*. Cambridge: Cambridge University Press.

Kitschelt, H., Lange, P., Marks, G., and Stephens, J. D. (eds.) (1999). *Continuity and Change in Contemporary Capitalism*. New York: Cambridge University Press.

Kochan, T. A., Katz, H. C., and McKersie, R. B. (1986). *The Transformation of American Industrial Relations*. New York: Basic Books.

Locke, R. and Thelen, K. (1995). 'Apples and Oranges Revisited: Contextualized Comparisons and the Study of Comparative Labor Politics'. *Politics and Society*, 23/3: 337–67.

McAdam, D., Tarrow, S., and Tilly, C. (2001). *Dynamics of Contention*. Cambridge: Cambridge University Press.

Martin, R. M. (1989). *Trade Unionism: Purposes and Forms*. Oxford: Clarendon Press.

Maurice, M. and Sellier, F. (1979). 'Societal Analysis of Industrial Relations. A Comparison between France and West Germany'. *British Journal of Industrial Relations*, 17: 322–36.

Peters, B. G. (1999). *Institutional Theory in Political Science: The 'New Institutionalism'*. London: Pinter.

Poole, M. (1986). *Industrial Relations. Origins and Patterns of National Diversity*. London: Routledge.

Price, R. (1991). 'The Comparative Analysis of Union Growth', in R. Adams (ed.), *Comparative Industrial Relations: Contemporary Research and Theory*. London: Harper Collins, 37–55.

Ross, G. and Martin, A. (1999*a*). 'Through a Glass Darkly', in A. Martin and G. Ross (eds.), *The Brave New World of European Labor: European Trade Unions at the* Millennium. New York: Berghahn, 368–97.

—— (1999*b*). 'European Unions Face the Millennium', in A. Martin and G. Ross (eds.), *The Brave New World of European Labor: European Trade Unions at the* Millennium. New York: Berghahn, 1–25.

Shalev, M. (1980). 'Industrial Relations Theory and the Comparative Study of Industrial Relations and Industrial Conflict'. *British Journal of Industrial Relations*, 18: 26–43.

—— (1992). 'The Resurgence of Labour Quiescence', in M. Regini (ed.), *The Future of Labour Movements*. London: Sage, 102–32.

Swenson, P. (1989). *Fair Shares: Unions, Pay and Politics in Sweden and West Germany*. Ithaca, NY: Cornell University Press.

Tilly, C. (1978). *From Mobilization to Revolution*. New York: McGraw Hill.

Visser, J. (1994). 'European Trade Unions: The Transition Years', in R. Hyman and A. Ferner (eds.), *New Frontiers in European Industrial Relations*. Oxford: Blackwell, 87–107.

Waddington, J. (1995). *The Politics of Bargaining: The Merger Process and British Trade Union Structural Development 1892–1987*. London: Mansell.

Western, B. (1997). *Between Class and Market: Postwar Unionization in the Capitalist Democracies*. Princeton, NJ: Princeton University Press.

Willman, P. (1989). 'The Logic of Market-Share Trade Unionism: Is Membership Decline Inevitable?'. *Industrial Relations Journal*, 20/4: 260–70.

—— Morris, T., and Aston, B. (1993). *Union Business: Trade Union Organization and Financial Reform in the Thatcher Years*. Cambridge: Cambridge University Press.

4

Organizing the Unorganized

EDMUND HEERY AND LEE ADLER

INTRODUCTION

The trade unions in all five countries considered in this book have experienced membership decline (see Chapter 2), albeit with some counter-movement in individual cases. Spanish trade unions experienced a revival in the 1990s, but that has since petered out and the aggregate level of membership in Spain is low (Van der Meer 2000: 599). British unions have stabilized membership since New Labour's election in 1997 but density has continued to fall and Britain, like all of the other countries, has experienced declining membership amongst the young and a failure to unionize much of the private service sector (Brook 2002: 344, 346–48). Despite this shared experience the reaction of the union movement has differed across the five countries. In the United States and the United Kingdom organizing the unorganized has become a priority for national leaders and a focus of policy, as seen in the creation of the Organizing Institute by the American Federation of Labor-Congress of Industrial Organizations (AFL-CIO) and the Organizing Academy by the Trades Union Congress (TUC) (Heery et al. 2000a; Hurd, Milkman, and Turner 2003: 101). In the three other countries, there have been recruitment initiatives but organizing has been less central to the project of revitalization (Baccaro, Carrieri, and Damiano 2003; Behrens, Fichter, and Frege 2003; Hamann and Martínez Lucio 2003).

This disjuncture is reflected in academic commentary on unions across the five cases. Union organizing has made only a faint appearance in the main journals that survey developments in trade unionism in continental Europe, the *European Journal of Industrial Relations* and *Transfer*, but articles on organizing are recurrent in those that cover Britain and North America (cf. Fiorito, Jarley, and Delaney 1995; Bronfenbrenner 1997; Hurd 1998; Carter 2000; Heery et al. 2000a; Findlay and McKinlay 2003b). The same is true of books. Fairbrother and Griffin's (2002) recent edited collection that surveys unions in English-speaking countries accords prominence to the theme of organizing, while it makes only a fleeting visitation, and then primarily in the chapter on Britain, in Martin and Ross's (1999) equivalent volume on unions in Europe. Moreover, books dedicated to the theme of organizing have become a feature of recent publishing on trade unions in Britain and America (cf. Bronfenbrenner et al. 1998; Milkman 2000; Gall 2003) but are virtually absent from Germany, Spain, and Italy. Dribbusch's (2002) comparative analysis of union organizing in the retail sector in Britain and Germany and Behrens' (2002) comparison of US and German construction unions provide the only exceptions.

The purpose of this chapter is to explain this seeming anomaly: Why is it that organizing the unorganized is central to the attempts at revitalization in Britain and the United States but is less of a priority in continental Europe? This task is performed in two main stages. In the first stage, an analytical framework is presented to help map the pattern of organizing in the five countries. The focus here is on the approach that unions use to recruit non-union workers in membership, a basic function of all trade unions arising from their status as membership organizations. The framework contains indicators of the level of organizing activity, the direction of organizing policy, and the primary methods used by unions. In the second stage, an explanation is offered of variation in national patterns of organizing that draws upon theories of comparative industrial relations. This explanation emphasizes the opportunity structure presented to unions by the institutions of industrial relations, the strategies of governments and employers, and the meanings attached to membership in countries with different union identities. Necessarily it is tentative. Research on organizing to date has been largely restricted to the countries of the English-speaking world and, while there are excellent international surveys of union membership, systematic data on the steps unions take to build membership are lacking. Given this lacuna, the analysis that follows presents an agenda for comparative research, as much as a summary of current knowledge.

THE PATTERN OF ORGANIZING

Before comparison can begin it is necessary to establish what is being compared. A useful framework that can help answer this question has been developed by Hyman (2001*a*: 211–20) who identifies different types of comparative project. The type that is adopted here is a comparative examination of a particular issue or process, which is common across a range of national cases but which is handled in a variety of ways. The issue with which we are concerned is the approach of national trade union movements to the organizing of new members. This task, in turn, comprises the selection of organizing targets, the adoption of organizing methods, and the allocation of resources to organizing: activities in which any trade union movement must engage if it is to reproduce itself. Reflecting the interest in revitalization, we are also concerned with change over time; whether organizing is becoming a more important sphere of activity, attracting greater resources, in each of the case-study countries.

While our comparison is issue-based, we also have regard to a second type of analysis identified by Hyman. Comparative analysis can be functional, addressing the question of how common or equivalent outcomes are secured in different national contexts. In Britain and the United States, organizing serves several functional needs of trade unions. It is a means of generating income through subscriptions, of securing legitimacy and recognition from employers and government and of creating bargaining power: where membership is high and interlaced with a network of activists, unions are better able to secure concessions from employers and state. In other countries, however, these functions of organizing may be fulfilled through other processes. In Germany, Italy, and Spain the legitimacy of unions in large part rests on their ability to compete in elections to works councils or equivalent bodies and is less dependent on levels of membership. In what follows, therefore, we will also have regard to this second form of comparison and consider processes analogous to organizing that serve the same functional needs.

The first component of organizing is that of resource allocation. National trade union movements can differ in terms of their level of commitment to organizing the unorganized and the level of investment they make in the process. Such commitment, itself, can be manifested on three dimensions: formalization, specialization, and the degree of centrality accorded to organizing in union strategies for revitalization. Formalization refers to the development and refinement, either by central union confederations or individual unions of written organizing policies, plans, budgets, objectives, targets, and procedures for review. Mechanisms of this kind can be viewed as channelling union resources towards organizing though it cannot be assumed that this will be achieved in all cases; in unions, as in other organizations, policy may fail at the point of implementation. Specialization is likely to be associated with the development of formal organizing policy and can take the form of the creation of a dedicated organizing function, consisting of committees, staff, and representative roles that are focused on organizing activity. Centrality refers to the relative priority given to organizing in union attempts at revitalization. Hard indicators of centrality include the proportion of union finance that is allocated to organizing activity and the relative size of the organizing function. Softer indicators include the prominence accorded to organizing policy compared to other spheres of activity and the extent to which unions have undergone 'culture change' or attained the status of an 'organizing union', which defines its central purpose in terms of extending trade unionism (Fletcher and Hurd 1998).

The second component of organizing is the targeting of activity. Again, there are three dimensions. Along the first, unions can choose to consolidate membership through 'internal' organizing, through attempts to raise density where they already have a presence. The alternative is to concentrate resources on expansion, on attempts to build membership in hitherto unorganized sectors, employing organizations and sites (Kelly and Heery 1989: 198–9). Attempts at expansion can be further divided into those aimed at 'close' and 'distant' expansion, the former embracing the targeting of workers in the same occupations as existing members and the latter targeting groups with no prior union tradition. A second, and in many cases intersecting dimension, refers to attempts by unions to develop 'field-enlarging strategies' (Wever 1998: 392). Unions can pursue a recruitment policy that reproduces the demographic and contractual status of their existing members or they can strive for field enlargement, in which women, minority, younger, contingent, and part-time workers are accorded organizing priority. The final dimension of targeting refers to the depth of organizing, an element that is captured to a degree in the distinction between organizing and servicing unionism (Hurd 1998). Unions can pursue a policy that seeks simply to build membership or they can engage in 'union-building' (Bronfenbrenner and Juravich 1998) that strives to create collective organization within and between workplaces and provides a basis for reproducing membership over time.

The third component of organizing comprises the methods used. One dimension of method is the degree to which recruitment is a diffuse or concentrated activity. Where recruitment is diffuse, union joining will be ongoing and conducted through relatively routine activities, such as a presence at induction for new employees, and stress will be placed on making the union available to those wishing to join through advertising, the regular mailing of membership forms and union websites. Where recruitment is concentrated, in contrast, it will be conducted through planned, dedicated campaigns that may last for a considerable period of time, absorb considerable resources, and rely upon specialist organizers. A second distinction is that between attempts at organizing that target the employer and those that target employees (Willman 2001: 99). Under the former, the union seeks in the first instance to win recognition from or the support of the employer and uses this as a basis for organizing the workforce, while under the latter, there is a stress on building membership before approaching the employer. Approaches to employees can also vary, with the clearest distinction between those that seek to recruit individual members on the basis of union representation and other services and those that seek to collectivize workers through a 'rank and file organizing strategy' (Bronfenbrenner 1997: 211). This, in turn, returns matters to the distinction between organizing and servicing: Unions can approach workers as a provider of protective and labour market services or they can assume the characteristics of a social movement and approach workers as potential activists.

NATIONAL PATTERNS

United States

Across the five case study countries, the American labour movement is clearly distinctive in its degree of formal commitment to organizing (see Table 4.1 below, pp. 50–51). Particularly since the election of John Sweeney's New Voice leadership, but even before (Nissen 1999: 12–13), the AFL-CIO has prioritized organizing and sought to direct resources towards it. Formal programmes launched by the AFL-CIO have included the creation of the Organizing Institute in 1989 and the launching of the Union Summer and Union Cities programmes in 1996 (Foerster 2001; Kriesky 2001). There have also been significant initiatives by individual unions. These have included the well-known Justice for Janitors programme of the SEIU and less publicized developments elsewhere, such as the succession of organizing initiatives that have been launched by US construction unions since the early 1980s (Behrens 2002: 142–78). American unions have long operated with specialist organizing departments but a feature of recent policy has been the attempt to strengthen the organizing function. Initiatives have included restructuring organizing departments, appointing more specialist organizers, drawing lay activists into organizing activity, and launching training programmes, like the AFL-CIO Elected Leaders' programme (Hurd 1998: 19–20; Foerster 2001: 160–66). These developments have formed part of a wider purpose, to make organizing central to the revitalization of American labour. Reflecting this increased priority, there has been an increase in financial resources committed to organizing by the AFL-CIO and several of its affiliates, together with the re-deployment of union officers to organizing activity (Fletcher and Hurd 2001: 202; Jarley 2002: 224; Hurd, Milkman, and Turner 2003: 110). The scale of these changes should not be exaggerated (Fiorito 2003: 206) and they are concentrated in particular unions. Nevertheless, at both confederal level and in major unions, like CWA, HERE, SEIU, and UNITE, organizing the unorganized has become a central task, absorbing considerable resources.

In states with 'right to work' laws and in the public sector, US unions must engage in consolidating on-going recruitment to maintain density (Jarley 2002: 206). The main focus of organizing, however, is expansion and there is evidence of some US unions broadening their job territories in response to decline and targeting a wider range of potential members (Jarley 2002: 216). Field-enlargement is also a priority for a proportion of US unions, including SEIU, UNITE, and HERE, which have deliberately targeted low wage, immigrant workers and workers with non-standard contracts, including the 74,000 Californian home-care workers organized by SEIU in 1999 (Frege, Heery, and Turner, Chapter 8, this volume; Milkman and Wong 2001). The decentralized structure of industrial relations in the United States creates a need for strong local organization and recruiting activists, promoting organizing depth, is also a feature of American unionism. Interest in the organizing model, moreover, has strengthened commitment to this objective: there is a desire to promote self-sufficient lay organization at unionized sites in order to release resources for new organizing activity elsewhere (Fiorito 2003: 194).

Most American organizing is concentrated in the sense that it is conducted through certification campaigns under the National Labor Relations Act (NLRA). Even when unions organize outside the framework of the NLRA, an increasing trend, they tend to do so through focused campaigns. Indeed, there has been a recent experiment with 'strategic campaigns', directed at lead employers or groups of employers in key industries. Whether beyond or within the NLRA framework, organizing campaigns seek majority support and use a variety of, often imaginative, tactics to contact, persuade, collectivize, and mobilize workers (Bronfenbrenner and Juravich 1998; Fiorito 2003: 201). Occasionally, they spill out into the wider community and involve coalition-building with other organizations in support of unionization (Milkman and Wong 2001; Frege, Heery, and Turner, Chapter 8, this volume). American unions do target individual workers, through initiatives like the AFL-CIO's associate member programme (Jarley and Fiorito 1990), and in sectors like construction or through 'neutrality agreements', the employer may be the initial target (Fletcher and Hurd 2001: 200–2; Safford and Locke 2001: 29). The primary method, however, is for unions to organize collectively, often in the face of intense employer opposition.

United Kingdom

Many of the themes present in American organizing are also manifest in Britain, particularly since the mid-1990s. In 1996, the TUC launched its New Unionism initiative

Table 4.1. *Patterns of union organizing*

Dimensions of organizing	USA	UK	Germany	Spain	Italy
Commitment Formalization	High and increasing Adoption of formal organizing policies by AFL–CIO and individual unions	Moderate and increasing Recent adoption of organizing policies by TUC and affiliated unions	Low and increasing Recent development of organizing policies by German unions facing decline and competition	Low Limited development of organizing policy	Low Limited development of organizing policy
Specialization	Tradition of dedicated organizing departments with recent investment in organizing skills	Creation of specialist organizing function by unions in recent years; creation of Organizing Academy	Low status attached to organizing but recent strengthening of function in some unions	Specialization has taken the form of 'extension teams' to ensure union candidates stand in 'works council' elections	No evidence of specialization or separating out of organizing function
Centrality	Increased investment in organizing; organizing central priority of AFL–CIO and some unions	Increasing priority to organizing but other elements of revitalization, such as partnership, have higher profile	Organizing has increasing priority but is not yet central to revitalization policy of most unions	Organizing has low centrality; primary union focus is on developing relations with government	Organizing has low centrality; primary union focus has been on relations with state and employers
Objectives					
Expansion	Focus on expansion other than in right to work states and public sector where 'internal organizing' has priority	Increased focus on expansion to exploit new statutory recognition procedure; the primary organizing effort is directed at 'in-fill' consolidation	Following successful extension of unions to the east, there is little emphasis on expansion; main focus is consolidation	Expansion is a priority in the sense of using extension teams to create works councils in smaller companies; focus on consolidating membership where unions are strong	Primary focus is on consolidation of membership where unions have a presence
Enlargement	High profile attempts in recent years to extend unionization to contingent, low paid, and immigrant workers	Higher emphasis attached in recent years to recruitment of women, part-timers, young, and ethnic minority workers	Increasing emphasis on the recruitment of women, young workers, and workers in the new service sector	Increasing emphasis on the recruitment of women, immigrant workers, and workers in casual employment	Increasing emphasis on the recruitment of contingent workers alongside traditional attempts to recruit retired and unemployed workers

Depth	Organizing depth pursued through union-building tactics in organizing campaigns	Depth pursued by application of an organizing model that accords with traditional reliance on workplace activists	Depth pursued by capture of works councils and extension of works councils to the small firm and new economy sectors	Depth pursued by initiating and winning works council elections	Depth pursued by initiating and winning works council elections
Methods					
Concentration	Emphasis on concentrated organizing campaigns to secure certification; experiment with community and strategic campaigns	Diffuse organizing coupled to campaigns aimed at winning recognition and 'reorganizing' unionized sites	Diffuse organizing with heavy reliance on advertising and on-going recruitment by works councillors; concentrated works council election campaigns	Diffuse organizing through advertising and electronic media; concentrated works council election campaigns	Diffuse organizing through strong activist base of Italian unions; concentrated works council election campaigns
Focus	Focus on workers supplemented by attempts to secure employer support neutrality and other concessions	Focus on workers supplemented by attempts to organize by offering partnership; heavy reliance on employer backing for consolidating recruitment	Focus on workers with isolated attempts to organize anti-union firms through offer of partnership	Focus on workers; partnership developing but not as a vehicle for organizing	Focus on workers; partnership developing but not as a vehicle for organizing
Collectivism	Some reliance on recruitment through individual member benefits but collective organization to the fore; experiment with union-building methods and attempts to launch social movement unionism	Individual recruitment through consumer and advisory services common but also widespread use of union-building methods; experiment with 'organizing model'	Individual recruitment to the fore on the basis of benefits and traditional solidarity; use of incentives to encourage recruitment and joining	Traditional reliance on class solidarity and left ideology supplemented by individualized recruitment on the basis of advisory and consumer services; discourse of 'modernization'	Traditional reliance on strong workplace trade unionism and left ideology supplemented by individualized recruitment on the basis of advisory and consumer services

to promote organizing, which gave rise to the Organizing Academy and which has been followed by associated programmes to encourage lay organizing and the strengthening of workplace representation (Heery 1998: 343). In the same period, a considerable number of individual unions have adopted formal organizing strategies, complete with objectives, targets, plans, budgets, and training programmes (Carter 2000; Waddington and Kerr 2000; Heery et al. 2000*b*: 988–90). There has also been a process of specialization and the creation, for the first time in many UK unions, of a dedicated organizing function. The TUC has established a New Unionism Task Group, with representation from its major affiliates, has used the Academy to train specialist organizers, and established a series of annual organizing conferences. Within its member unions there has been a drive to establish organizing units and create new organizing roles amongst activists and paid staff: in 2001, 50 per cent of UK unions reported they employed specialist organizers (Heery et al. 2003: 67). Despite these changes, organizing has not become as central to attempts at revitalization as it has in the United States. The proportion of TUC and union funding allocated to organizing remains modest and specialist organizers remain a small minority amongst paid staff (Heery et al. 2003: 13). Moreover, the unions that have undergone the most thorough-going transformation, allocating most resources to organizing, are small or medium-sized, such as Connect, GPMU, ISTC, TSSA, and USDAW (Heery et al. 2000*a*: 411–13; Wills 2003: 134–6). While these and others aspire to the status of 'an organizing union', other themes are prominent in the quest for revitalization in Britain and have occasionally eclipsed or exist in tension with organizing (Carter and Cooper 2003: 717). The most important of these is partnership with employers: in 2000, the TUC created a Partnership Institute to sit alongside its Organizing Academy (see Fichter and Greer, Chapter 5, this volume).

As in the United States, there is a growing focus on both expansion and enlargement in union organizing activity in Britain. The former is apparent in the several hundred recognition agreements signed over the past 5 years, which have brought tens of thousands of members into the union fold (Wood et al. 2003: 138–41). The latter is apparent in recruitment campaigns targeted at women, part-timers, working students, and ethnic minorities (Heery et al. 2000*a*: 406). It remains though that the bulk of union organizing in Britain is directed at consolidation, at raising density where the union is already recognized by the employer (Heery et al. 2003: 61). In attempts at both consolidation and expansion, a third objective is typically to deepen union organization. In the British union lexicon, 'organizing' refers to the promotion of activism and the creation of collective organization, typically at workplace level. It is often contrasted with 'recruitment', simply attracting workers into membership. A concern to organize, not just recruit, has long been a feature of UK unions, reflecting their dependence on lay activism. But it has been accentuated in recent years as a result of the desire of the TUC and individual unions to apply an 'organizing model' (Waddington and Kerr 2000; Heery et al. 2003: 7–8; Wills 2003; Findlay and MacKinlay 2003*b*).

Much organizing activity in Britain is diffuse and is carried out by lay representatives at their place of work. There has been a movement towards concentrated campaigning, however, as unions have sought new recognition agreements in the shadow of Labour's Employment Relations Act 1999 (Simms 2003; Wills 2003; Taylor and Bain 2003; Findlay and MacKinlay 2003*a*; Oxenbridge et al. 2003: 320). This activity has also spilled over into 're-organizing' campaigns, directed at restoring membership and systems of lay representation where they have fallen into disrepair (Heery et al. 2000*c*: 46–50). Reflecting the interest in the 'organizing model' there has been fairly widespread experiment by British unions in recent years with a variety of 'union-building' techniques, including workplace mapping, use of representative organizing committees, issue-based organizing, house-calling, and recruitment on a one-to-one and like-to-like basis (Heery et al. 2003: 64). Such practices can be viewed as systematizing traditional elements of union organizing in Britain, which have long cultivated workplace activism. They exist in occasional tension, however, with other methods. Top-down organizing through approaches to employers continues to be significant and is associated with offers of partnership working (Taylor and Bain 2003: 168–70). Many unions in Britain, moreover, continue to appeal to individual joiners through the offer of representational, labour market, and consumer services. The TUC has withdrawn somewhat from its earlier advocacy of 'consumer unionism' but, for many unions with a professional membership or organizing contingent workers, this method of recruitment remains important.

Germany

In Germany, the degree of formalization, specialization, and centrality of organizing activity are generally lower than they are in both Britain and the United States. Organizing has tended not to be a major focus of formal policy, organizing departments tend to be small, employing few specialist organizers, and organizing has tended to have low status as a field of activity, attracting few resources (Silvia 1999: 113; Behrens 2002: 190). Changes to union structure through merger and the relaxation of jurisdictional rules have been the primary union response to decline and financial stringency, not organizing (Ebbinghaus, Armingeon, and Hassel 2002: 294). Nevertheless, there has been a switch towards greater concern with organizing in recent years. The key developments have been at individual union level. DPG (now ver.di), IG BCE, IG Metall, and IG BAU have all launched formal organizing initiatives, which have embraced both the appointment of specialist organizers and organizational changes to encourage union staff to commit more time to organizing (Behrens 2002: 198–208; Behrens, Fichter, and Frege 2003: 28–9).

As in Britain, much organizing in Germany is directed at maintaining and raising density at sites with a union presence. The early 1990s, however, witnessed the successful extension of union membership to the eastern *Lander* and subsequently there have been campaigns to establish a presence at companies that have remained aloof or detached themselves from industry-wide bargaining (Turner 1998: 129–32). There is also evidence of German unions pursuing field enlargement, including attempts to recruit younger workers and provide dedicated structures for workers in non-traditional employment in private services (Behrens 2002: 195; Jacobi 2003: 217). The main thrust of attempts to re-position trade unionism, however, has been through substantive policies that accommodate the interests of new groups rather than through organizing as such. Workplace trade unionism in Germany typically rests upon statutory works councils. Concern at the declining coverage of works councils has led unions to promote the revival of statutory participation, an objective that is analogous to UK and US unions pursuing organizing depth. The prime method has been political action to reform the Works Constitution Act in order to facilitate the establishment of works councils in small and medium enterprises and subsidiary companies (Jacobi 2003: 220).

Dedicated organizing campaigns are increasingly common in Germany but the bulk of organizing is diffuse, consisting of recruitment by works councillors at the point of entry into unionized firms or when strike action is threatened (Behrens 2002: 190–91). Head office initiatives also tend to be diffuse and take the form of advertising campaigns, designed to promote trade unionism (Behrens, Fichter, and Frege 2003: 28). There are cases of German unions seeking to organize the employer through offers of cooperative relations, particularly in a context of inter-union competition (Turner 1998: 132; Royle 2000: 100–1). However, the main focus of organizing is the employee, chiefly through individualistic approaches that emphasize service provision and offer incentives to existing members to recruit colleagues (Behrens 2002: 196, 202). Union-building of the kind seen in US and some UK campaigns is relatively rare.

Spain

Attempts at union revitalization in Spain have centred on 'political action, directed towards the state...rather than...organizing and membership' (Hamann 2001: 157). The centrality of organizing has been low and the kind of high profile, formal organizing initiatives, apparent in other countries, have not been launched in Spain. Nevertheless, the salience of organizing has risen and the main confederations, CC.OO and UGT, cooperated in the 1990s to counteract declining membership. As part of this increased focus on membership, Spanish unions have developed a specialist organizing function. 'Extension' or 'campaign' teams have been created to ensure that union sections are established in companies where they have been absent and elections to works councils are contested by candidates from the main confederations (Fraile 1999: 303; Hamann and Martínez Lucio 2003: 70). Lay activists from well-organized sectors and plants have played an important role in these teams, using paid time-off under works council legislation to engage in remote organizing.

It follows that Spanish unions have adopted a policy of expansion in recent years, seeking to extend union organization beyond their heartlands and into the service and small-firm sectors. There have also been attempts at field enlargement. The unions have tried to raise membership amongst women, young workers, immigrants, and the large proportion of employees engaged on temporary contracts (Miguélez Lobo 2000: 499). Initiatives of this kind, however, have often taken the form of creating representative structures and secretariats at confederation-level with limited resonance at the workplace (Hamann and Martínez Lucio 2003: 72). To date, they have not been very successful. The unions have also pursued organizing depth, though in a manner that reflects the peculiarities of Spanish labour law. The 1980 Workers' Statute allows unions to establish workplace sections, the members of which have the right to collect union dues. Of greater importance, however, is its second core provision, which allows for the appointment of 'personnel delegates' in small firms and the election of works councils in larger companies (Van der Meer 2000: 578–9). The pursuit of organizing depth, in a Spanish context involves ensuring these various representative positions are held by union delegates, and the function of 'campaign teams' is to ensure that union activists stand for office. The degree of achieved depth should not be exaggerated, however. According to Hamann and Martínez Lucio (2003: 70), the level of continuing activism of newly elected works councillors and the degree of external support they receive are often limited, especially in smaller workplaces.

In the immediate aftermath of the Franco era Spanish unions, and especially Comisiones Obreras (CC.OO) had a pronounced social movement character (Martínez Lucio 1992: 490). Recent attempts at revitalization, however, have stressed the 'modernization' of union functions and the 'professionalization' of union activity. Associated with the latter, has been an emphasis on individual recruitment through the offer of member services, including tax advice, legal services, organized holidays, and the provision of housing (Van der Meer 2000: 588; Hamann and Martínez Lucio 2003: 70). Much recruitment is concentrated around the periodic works council elections but associated with the movement to 'professionalization' has been an emphasis on diffuse, ongoing recruitment (Fraile 1999: 302). At workplace level, this is undertaken by union sections and works councillors, while at national level union websites and other electronic means of communication have assumed increasing importance (Hamann and Martínez Lucio 2003: 70).

Italy

The pattern of organizing seen in Italy shares many of the characteristics of that in Spain. Organizing has not been central to the revitalization project of Italian unions, which instead has focused on the revival of concertation in the political sphere (Baccaro, Carrieri, and Damiano 2003: 44). Neither has there been the launch of formal organizing policies, akin to those in Britain and the United States, or the development of a specialist organizing function. Investment in processes analogous to organizing has nevertheless increased in Italy over the past decade. Concern at declining bargaining power and at the challenge to their authority from independent unions led the three main union confederations, CGIL, CISL, and UIL, to promote the reform of plant-level representative structures in the early 1990s (Locke and Baccaro 1999: 253–4). Under the new system, union-nominated representatives can be elected to workplace committees, *Rappresentatanze Sindicali Unitarie* (RSU), provided they have the support of 5 per cent of the workforce and unions can thereby achieve 'representational' status with attendant legitimacy and acceptance as bargaining agents and social partners. The result has been that, 'the three confederations…are forced to spend ever more resources on proselytising' to win votes (Visser 2000: 395). This investment has paid off. In the 1990s, the main confederations won 96 per cent of votes cast in the private sector and in the public sector, where non-confederal unions have traditionally been stronger, they have achieved 70 per cent (Baccaro, Carrieri, and Damiano 2003: 45–7).

This focus on strengthening organization through contesting workplace elections is shared with Spain. Also shared with Spain is an attempt at field enlargement through establishing new union sections for groups targeted for recruitment. Italian unions have established sections for pensioners, the unemployed, and most recently for contingent workers, 'parasubordinates'—skilled workers who work continuously for a single employer but who have self-employed status in law (Baccaro, Carrieri, and Damiano 2003: 45). Success on this dimension is more mixed. Italian unions have substantial membership amongst pensioners, fully half the membership of Italian unions was retired by 1997 (Visser 2000: 395). The numbers of unemployed and contingent workers that have been recruited, however, remain low (Visser 2000: 395; Baccaro, Carrieri, and Damiano 2003: 45). The other main focus of policy has been organizing depth. The creation of RSUs was aimed at reinvigorating workplace union organization, in a similar manner to the recent works council reform in Germany. Again, there is evidence of success with the new system drawing thousands of previously inactive workers into union representative positions since its inception (Regini and Regalia 2000: 382).

Concentrated organizing campaigns to extend membership to non-union enterprises appear to be rare in Italy. The biennial elections to RSUs, however, do provide a focus for concentrated activity where unions have a presence, which is supplemented by more diffuse recruitment through the relatively strong activist network maintained by Italian unions at workplace level. Italian unions have developed partnership arrangements with individual employers since the early 1980s (Regini 1997: 262) but this trend has not been driven by pressure to organize. Strong legal support for workplace unionism since the introduction of the Workers' Statute of 1970 and *de facto* extension provisions mean that Italian unions are not heavily dependent on employer cooperation to establish union organization within the enterprise (Visser 2000: 390; Baccaro, Carrieri, and Damiano 2003: 45). Despite the tradition of workplace organization, recent organizing has stressed the provision of selective benefits to both pensioner and employed members (Chiarini 1999: 587; Baccaro, Carrieri, and Damiano 2003: 45). Italian unions rest on a platform of strong collective organization at workplace level, and they have reinvigorated this tradition through the creation of RSUs. But alongside this collectivist strand in policy there is increased reliance on individualized methods of recruitment.

The five countries fall roughly into three clusters. The first cluster comprises the United Kingdom and the United States and is characterized by relatively high organizing centrality, which finds expression in the development of formal policies and the specialization of organizing activities. Unions in these two countries are also distinctive in their focus on expansion and in the methods they use: rather paradoxically attempts to organize the employer through offers of partnership and union-building through application of an 'organizing model' are both found more frequently in these two cases. At the other extreme lie Spain and Italy, where organizing has relatively low centrality, where there is an emphasis on consolidation and organizing methods are relatively diffuse and rely particularly on the offer of member services. Germany occupies a middling position between these poles. There is a growing interest in organizing that has led to the adoption of formal policies and some specialization of functions but this is coupled with a stress on consolidation, diffuse methods, and recruitment through member services.

These broad-brush differences must be qualified in three important ways. First, there is variation within each cluster. The pattern of organizing in the United Kingdom shares some characteristics with that in the United States but is also distinctive. In Britain, organizing is less central, formal policy less developed, and organizing practice is more diffuse and more orientated towards consolidation. There are also differences between Italy and Spain, with unions in the latter placing greater emphasis on expansion through attempts to establish a union presence at smaller companies via extension teams. Second, while there are striking differences between the five countries there are also some common themes, the most notable of which is a shared emphasis on field enlargement. This has taken different forms in the five cases but it is apparent that each national labour movement has taken steps to broaden its membership among workers with 'non-traditional' characteristics. Finally, it is important to stress that in the three continental European countries there are functional equivalents to organizing, which have been the subject of policy development in recent years in a manner that parallels the revival of organizing in Britain and the United States. Continental initiatives have focused particularly on strengthening works councils to provide a basis for union organization in the workplace. Attempts to increase the depth of union organization in this manner, moreover, have often taken the form of periodic election campaigns that resemble the intensive recognition and certification campaigns seen in Britain and the United States.

EXPLAINING NATIONAL PATTERNS

In comparative industrial relations there is a long tradition of explaining variation in union behaviour in terms of the institutions of industrial relations. In Clegg's (1976) classic statement of this position, the primary institutional influence on patterns of union behaviour was the structure of collective bargaining. As bargaining varied, Clegg argued, so did the adaptive response of trade unions, leading to varying patterns of membership, structure, government, workplace organization, and strikes. In this line of reasoning, the institutional structure that unions face presents itself as a set of opportunities and constraints, to which unions adapt through rational calculation. Applied to organizing, this suggests that the level, direction, and form of activity in a specific national context will reflect a specific set of institutionally derived incentives, an opportunity structure.

Institutions

Three features of the institutions of industrial relations appear to underlie the patterns of organizing described above. These are the structure of collective bargaining, and its degree of centralization or decentralization in particular, the legal procedures that exist to allow unions to form bargaining relationships with employers and the framework of worker participation: whether or not union voice is supplemented with participation through works councils. Each of these institutional structures presents incentives to trade unions, which serve to raise or depress organizing activity. They also influence the form of organizing, encouraging unions to select particular organizing targets or objectives and to use particular methods (see Table 4.2).

Bargaining structure can also influence the form of organizing. Where bargaining is centralized, organizing tends to emphasize the consolidation of membership through diffuse activity and recruitment methods that offer selective incentives for joining to the individual free-rider. In Italy and Germany, the function of a great deal of organizing is to close the wide gap that exists between the level of union density and the level of coverage by collective bargaining and diffuse, individualized methods serve this purpose. In Britain and the United States, in contrast, decentralized bargaining means that organizing is the means to create new bargaining relationships. The result is that expansion is a much stronger feature of organizing activity, particularly in the United States.

Table 4.2. *The influence of institutions on union organizing*

Institutions	Elements of organizing		
	Incentive	Direction	Method
Bargaining structure			
Centralized	Low incentive: high bargaining coverage	Consolidation	Diffuse; individualized
Decentralized	High incentive: low bargaining coverage	Expansion	
Union recognition			
Supportive	Low incentive: alternative means to establish bargaining	Consolidation	
Certification	High incentive: majority required for bargaining	Expansion plus consolidation of open shop	Concentrated; organizing the employer
Worker participation			
Dual channel	Low incentive: reliance on works councils	Depth achieved by triggering and winning elections	Concentrated extension/election campaigns
Single channel	High incentive: reliance on union recognition	Depth achieved by union-building	Concentrated union-building campaigns

The second institutional influence on organizing activity is the set of regulations and procedures that states have created to allow unions to form bargaining relationships. In the three continental European countries the level of support is high and consists of measures that allow the extension of collective agreements to non-conforming employers, laws that allow unions access to the workplace and to form workplace sections, and relatively strong obligations on employers to bargain with unions (Ebbinghaus and Visser 1999: 144; Calmfors et al. 2001: 80). Arguably, this supportive context reduces the incentive to organize: there are alternative, institutional mechanisms in place to establish a union presence and form bargaining relationships (Baccaro, Carrieri, and Damiano 2003: 45; Behrens, Fichter, and Frege 2003: 26). In Britain and the United States, regulations governing union access to workers and the forming of bargaining relationships is governed by certification law, the essential component of which is a requirement on unions to demonstrate majority support before they can be 'certified' or 'recognized' as a bargaining agent. Law of this kind acts as a stimulus to organizing activity in general and attempts at expansion in particular. It also encourages unions to rely on concentrated organizing campaigns. These may have a militant tenor, particularly where the employer is hostile. Certification law, however, also encourages unions to 'organize the employer' by offering partnership in return for voluntary recognition. A deal of this kind can short-circuit the costly and high-risk route to recognition via the legal process.

Although certification law provides an incentive for both American and British unions to engage in expansion, in the latter case this sits alongside a requirement to consolidate membership where recognition has already been achieved. In Britain, the closed shop is outlawed, requiring unions to invest continually in maintaining membership where they have a presence in order to preserve recognition. In this regard British unions are at one with their European counterparts. In much of the American private sector economy, in contrast, the closed or union shop is lawful, thereby reducing the need for consolidation and freeing union resources for expansion. The strength of legislation providing security to unions therefore interacts with legislation on recognition to shape the direction of organizing activity and produces different patterns in the two liberal-market cases.

The final set of institutions that shape the level and form of organizing is that governing worker participation in the enterprise. In countries with a dual-channel system of worker representation, in which unions and collective bargaining exist alongside works councils, there is a reduced incentive to organize. Unions can use the second channel to secure their objectives and are thereby less dependent on membership and organizational strength. In Germany, Italy, and Spain, unions can capture works councils by winning elections and by doing so gain access to the kinds of resource that unions in Britain and the United States obtain by winning recognition. These include legitimacy, rights to information, consultation, and codetermination, acceptance by the state as a 'representative' union and resulting access to state funds that can substitute, to a degree, for income from subscriptions (Hamann and Martínez Lucio 2003: 69). Moreover, where a second channel exists unions are drawn to activities that are analogous to organizing but which have as their focus the creation and strengthening of works councils. Organizing depth is pursued by triggering and winning works council elections often through concentrated extension and election campaigns. In countries where the second channel is absent, like the United States, or under-developed, like Britain, the pattern of incentives is different. Organizing is required to ensure the single channel is put in place and operates effectively and organizing depth is pursued by attempts to build workplace trade union organization. This, in turn, may be attempted through concentrated union-building campaigns that identify and develop workplace activists.

Strategic Choice

While 'institutions matter' and shape patterns of organizing, so too do other factors including the strategies of actors. A strategic choice perspective on organizing would suggest that patterns reflect the strategies of unions themselves and those of employers and state. Indeed the latter may be regarded as exerting the dominant influence because of their greater resources of power and the necessarily reactive nature of much union behaviour. Government strategy probably exerts the strongest influence on the level of organizing activity. The relative neglect of organizing by the Spanish and Italian unions arises in part from their relations with the state (Baccaro, Carrieri, and Damiano 2003; Hamann and Martínez Lucio 2003). In both countries in the recent past the state has bolstered the role of central union confederations as authoritative social partners, thereby reducing their need to rely on internal sources of strength, developed through organizing. In Germany, similar processes are discernible. The concern of German unions at their declining presence in parts of the economy has led to organizing activity but also to successful pressure on the government to reform the Works Constitution Act to make it easier to establish works councils in subsidiaries and smaller enterprises (Jacobi 2003: 219–21). In the United States, in contrast, the state continues to pursue an effective policy of 'union exclusion' and so the labour movement is thrust back on its own capacities, with the result that organizing is central to attempts at revitalization. Public policy is less hostile to trade unionism in Britain, particularly since New Labour's coming to power, but relations still fall short of social partnership rendering unions dependent on organizing activity.

The strategies of employers arguably exert most influence on the form of organizing and here the most instructive comparison is between Britain and the United States. In the latter, near universal employer opposition to unions and the development of sophisticated union-busting services create an extremely hostile environment for organizing. The result has been the continual refinement of union tactics and the emergence of sophisticated techniques for countering employer opposition. American unions have trained organizers, planned campaigns and use methods like house-calling, representative organizing committees, community coalitions, and corporate campaigning because they need them to cope with a harsh environment (Hurd, Milkman, and Turner 2003: 102–3). In Britain, employers can be intensely hostile and some have begun to use US union-busting consultants. Where employer resistance is intense in Britain then unions are more likely to adopt methods, like house-calling, that have been developed in the United States (Heery and Simms 2003). The overall degree of hostility is less, however, leading some unions to rely on partnership approaches to organizing or to rely on employer support and encouragement of union joining when building up membership through a strategy of consolidation.

Union Identity

While unions tailor activity to institutional incentives and react to the strategies of employers and state, they are not bereft of independent influence. What unions do matters and this is most apparent when change occurs and unions develop new organizing strategies as a result of internal processes of renewal (Voss and Sherman 2000). The pattern of organizing in the five national cases bears the stamp of unions' own activity in two senses. In each case, 'union identity' is an influence in the sense of unions continuing with an inherited or customary approach to organizing that reflects core assumptions about the meaning of trade unionism (Hyman 2001*b*: 3). The very meaning of union membership varies across the national cases and inherited meaning shapes the organizing activities chosen to build membership. In this sense, organizing can become institutionalized within unions. Second, in each case there has been recent change in patterns of organizing, which are traceable to internal processes of reform. Unions across the five countries have developed new policies as a result of political change, leadership transformation, the emergence of new cohorts of activists and attempts to learn deliberately from other national union movements, and indeed other social movements beyond organized labour. It is this latter process that is emphasized below. Change in organizing, it is suggested, has been driven by national union movements, with the notable exception of Germany, identifying models of desirable practice beyond their own boundaries.

In Hyman's terms (2001*b*: 6–13), the dominant identity in the United States and Britain has been 'market-oriented unionism' though this has existed in tension in both countries with alternative, more radical conceptions of union purpose. The prime purpose of market-oriented unionism is to raise the economic condition of its members through collective bargaining, which in turn requires the development of bargaining strength through organizing. For unions in these two countries therefore organizing has always had relatively high priority because it is integral to their central purpose of collective bargaining. The basis of organizing has also reflected unions' market orientation. It has tended to be instrumental, stressing the immediate benefits of membership to potential joiners, and it is notable that the initial response to decline in both countries was the accentuation of this rationale through the provision of selective benefits (Jarley and Fiorito 1990; Bassett and Cave 1993). More recent attempts at organizing, however, have challenged this tradition and have emanated primarily from the radical wing of each country's labour movement. They have emphasized the need to raise investment in organizing but also to change its form in three distinctive ways. First, new organizing has been associated with a broadening of union purpose to stress both qualitative demands—dignity and respect at work—and the need for unions to act, not just as membership organizations, but to secure social change—to act on behalf of 'working people' in the code used in America. Second, there has been a renewed emphasis on field enlargement, on extending unionization to those at the 'rough end of the labour market', in the terms used by the TUC's Organizing Academy. Third, there has been an emphasis on mobilizing, union-building tactics, which in the most developed cases has embraced community coalitions. Particularly in the United States, reformers have been influenced by the notion of social movement unionism and have tried to use organizing to recreate labour as a social movement (Turner and Hurd 2001). In the United Kingdom, there has been an echo of this influence but for many the recreation of British trade unions as a European social partner has been equally beguiling and has lessened the impulse to experiment with new organizing methods.

The challenge to market-oriented unionism and its conservative organizing style gathered force as the crisis of unionism deepened in Britain and the United States but it has also been driven by internal change. In the United States, leadership change at the AFL-CIO and in several unions has been critical. But so too has the renewal of the activist and officer tier as those with experience of social movements beyond labour have emerged as a key constituency within union ranks (Turner and Hurd 2001: 17). The civil rights, women's and other social movements have not just provided activists for unions in the United States they have provided new methods—a repertoire of contention—that have been incorporated into organizing practice (Voss and Sherman 2000). In the United Kingdom, tutelage from social movements beyond labour is less apparent but the example of renewed organizing vigour in the United States, and Australia, has provided an alternative model. This has served to justify increased investment in organizing, yielded new techniques and has provided a new language through which organizing initiatives can be framed (Heery et al. 2000c).

In Italy and Spain the traditional, dominant identity has been 'class unionism', with a conception of purpose that stresses mobilization and social transformation through a challenge to the power of capital (Hyman 2001b: 20–8). This identity continues to influence the pattern of organizing in these countries. Thus, members have tradition- ally been regarded as activists, part of a socialist or communist cadre, and this has reduced the salience of organizing per se. Provided workers support unions in the crit- ical context of a call to strike action, it is not essential that they join (Miguélez Lobo 2000: 503). Moreover, the fracturing of union structure along ideological lines has created a situation in which unions compete for legitimacy by contesting workplace elections. It is the relative performance of ideologically founded union confederations in these elections, rather than trends in aggregate membership, that provides the cen- tral indicator of organizational success for union leaders. This again, serves to depress the salience of organizing.

As in Britain and the United States, traditional union identity has been challenged in Italy and Spain. In Spain a discourse of 'modernization' and 'professionalization' has informed a redefinition of union purpose (Hamann and Martínez Lucio 2003: 70), while in Italy there has been a steady distancing of unions from their syndicalist past (Hyman 2001b: 165). The prime model that has informed these developments is European social partnership and Italian and Spanish unions have looked to their counterparts in northern Europe as a source of fresh identity. This, in turn, has led to an emphasis on the development of more cooperative relations with government and employers as key elements of revitalization with a consequent de-centring of organizing. Moreover, when new organizing initiatives have been launched they have tended to emphasize improved service delivery and selective benefits.

In Germany, the dominant conception of union purpose has emphasized social dialogue and the role of unions in integrating working people within civil society and the political process (Hyman 2001*b*: 116–23). Partly for this reason, German unions have often not actively recruited members: membership should arise organically from socialization into the world of work. The emphasis on social partnership, more-over, has discouraged German unions from adopting the aggressive, mobilizing tac-tics seen particularly in US organizing campaigns. Union decline, however, has prompted German unions to change. To update their integrative function in the face of labour market change, there has been an embrace of field enlargement with attempts to attract 'non-traditional' workers into membership. There is also a fresh emphasis on the instrumental benefits of union membership through the introduc-tion of consumer services and other incentives to join. Arguably, this development betokens a stronger market orientation on the part of German trade unionism (Hyman 2001*b*: 140). This might imply an attempt to learn from the experience of unions in Britain and the United States, where organizing is a component of a mar-ket orientation, but as yet there are few signs of German unions looking beyond their ranks for lessons in revitalization. In this, German unions are distinctive amongst the five cases examined.

CONCLUSION

Organizing is a necessary function of trade unions that arises from their status as membership organizations. Despite the common requirement to organize, however, national labour movements differ in the priority they accord to organizing with the result that for some it has been central to the project of revitalization while for others it is secondary. This is the first conclusion that can be drawn from our five-country survey. National union movements differ in the centrality of organizing, which in turn results in substantial variation in the formalization and specialization of organ-izing policy. They also differ in their form of organizing, in the targeting of policy and the methods used. On our three dimensions of commitment, direction, and method it has been possible to develop five distinct organizing profiles for our national cases, albeit with substantial convergence between the two liberal-market and the two Mediterranean-economy cases.

Our second conclusion is that much of this variation can be explained in terms of the established theoretical repertoire of comparative industrial relations. National organizing profiles reflect the structure of incentives provided by the formal institu-tions of industrial relations, which stimulate organizing activity in some cases but not in others and encourage it to assume a particular form. They also reflect the strategies of state and employers. Where states accord the status of social partner to unions and allocate resources to support their functions there is less incentive to organize but where states pursue a policy of union exclusion the need to cultivate internal resources of power through organizing is correspondingly stronger. Employers, for their part, shape the character of organizing, pushing unions towards innovation and use of more sophisticated techniques where their own resistance assumes an acute form. Finally, organizing bears the stamp of union identity and the inherited meanings attached to membership and union functions within national labour movements. Identities are not fixed, however, and change in organizing profiles can be viewed as part of a broader renegotiation of union identity. Central to this change, we believe, is a mimetic process through which repertoires of practice have been imported from new social movements or other national labour movements in order to reinforce internally directed change.

In short, profiles of union organizing, and the place of organizing in attempts at revitalization, are a function of institution, strategy, and identity. But if these factors can explain organizing, what contribution can organizing itself make to the revitalization of labour movements? We want to conclude by considering this question, first for the two countries where organizing has had greatest centrality, Britain and the United States, and second for the three continental European countries, where unions have relied on functional equivalents to organizing to secure their objectives.

Notwithstanding greater centrality, the contribution that organizing has made to the revitalization of the American and British labour movements, has been decidedly mixed. There is evidence of organizing activity proving to be highly effective, particularly at a micro-level (Bronfenbrenner 1997) and for the British case it is likely that increased investment organizing has helped unions stabilize aggregate membership (Heery et al. 2003). It remains though that the turn towards organizing has not yet transformed the fortunes of either movement. A possible explanation is that, despite the strong relative commitment to organizing in these cases, the absolute size of the organizing effort is insufficient (Carter and Cooper 2002; Fiorito 2003; Heery et al. 2003). There are islands of organizing innovation in Britain and the United States but the aggregate effort is not at a level to overcome the constraints of a difficult organizing environment.

This failure might be explained in two ways. It could be due to the continuing presence of a cautious leadership at the centre of the union movement, anxious about the disruptive consequences, particularly of aggressive organizing based on rank-and-file mobilization (Fairbrother 2002: 88). On this view, union failure to organize to a sufficient degree is symptomatic of union oligarchy, of unions opting not to pursue a necessary course because it is contrary to the interests of union officialdom. An alternative view is that the structure of the British and American labour movements constrains investment in organizing. Such investment implies taxing existing members, covered by mature bargaining arrangements and, in the shorter term at least, may lead to a reduction in the quality of representation they receive from their unions. For this reason they are likely to resist, if not organizing, then at least the reallocation of resources it implies (Willman 2001). The decentralized structure of both movements, moreover, with their relatively weak confederations and the high degree of autonomy accorded to local branches gives scope for existing members to retain control of resources and thereby frustrate organizing. Both explanations of the limits to organizing may have validity. In combination, they suggest that the release of further organizing effort, which seemingly is required in both cases, may depend on further changes in union leadership but also on the reconfiguration of the national union movement to allow greater coordination and cross-subsidy of activities.

In Italy, Spain, and Germany the incentives to organize are less acute, in part because there are functional equivalents that allow unions to secure legitimacy, control resources, and represent their members. The system of dual channel representation based on works councils is particularly important in this regard. The question that arises for these cases is whether the alternative supports of trade unionism are a true functional equivalent, fully justifying the relatively low centrality of organizing. It is questionable whether they are. Of the three, only Spain has been able to maintain aggregate membership and it is widely believed that 'voters' unionism' in Spain provides insufficient organizing depth to provide for effective representation of much of the workforce (Hamann 2001: 156). Reliance on institutional and political support, moreover, can make unions vulnerable when governments change as with the recent lurch to the right in Italy. Although immediate incentives to organize are lower in these three cases, we believe in the longer term all three national movements will come under increasing pressure to re-build membership and organization. If they do, they may face fewer constraints than their liberal-market counterparts. The German, Spanish, and Italian trade union movements are more centralized with a stronger capacity to coordinate their activities. Our final observation is to note this paradox: that the capacity and incentive to renew trade unionism through organizing seems inversely related across the five national cases.

ACKNOWLEDGEMENT

We would like to thank Martin Behrens, Carola Frege, Kerstin Hamann, Miguel Martínez Lucio, Peter Turnbull, and Lowell Turner for helpful comments on earlier versions of this chapter.

References

Baccaro, L., Carrieri, M., and Damiano, C. (2003). 'Resurgence of the Italian Confederal Unions: Will it Last?'. *European Journal of Industrial Relations*, 9/1: 43–59.

Bassett, P. and Cave, A. (1993). *All for One: The Future of Unions*. London: Fabian Society Pamphlet 559.

Behrens, M. (2002). *Learning from the Enemy? Internal Union Restructuring and the Imitation of Management Strategies*. Ithaca, NY: Cornell University, PhD Dissertation.

——Fichter, M., and Frege, C. M. (2003). 'Unions in Germany: Regaining the Initiative'. *European Journal of Industrial Relations*, 9/1: 25–42.

Bronfenbrenner, K. (1997). 'The Role of Union Strategies in NLRB Certification Elections'. *Industrial and Labor Relations Review*, 50/2: 195–212.

——and Juravich, T. (1998). 'It Takes more than House Calls: Organizing to win with a Comprehensive Union-Building Strategy', in K. Bronfenbrenner, S. Friedman, R. W. Hurd, R. A. Oswald, and R. L. Seeber (eds.), *Organizing to Win: New Research on Union Strategies*. Ithaca, NY: ILR Press, 19–36.

——Friedman, S., Hurd, R. W., Oswald, R. A., and Seeber, R. L. (eds.), (1998). *Organizing to Win: New Research on Union Strategies*. Ithaca, NY: ILR Press.

Brook, K. (2002). 'Trade Union Membership: An Analysis of Data from the Autumn 2001 LFS'. *Labour Market Trends*, July: 343–54.

Calmfors, L., Booth, A., Burda, M., Checchi, D., Naylor, R., and Visser, J. (2001). 'The Future of Collective Bargaining in Europe', in T. Boeri, A. Brugiavini, and L. Calmfors (eds.), *The Role of Unions in the Twenty-First Century*. Oxford: Oxford University Press. 1–155.

Carter, B. (2000). 'Adoption of the Organising Model in British Trade Unions: Some Evidence from Manufacturing, Science and Finance (MSF)'. *Work, Employment and Society*, 14/1: 117–36.

——and Cooper, R. (2002). 'The Organizing Model and the Management of Change: A Comparative Study of Unions in Australia and Britain'. *Relationes Industrielles*, 57/4: 712–42.

Chiarini, B. (1999). 'The Composition of Union Membership: The Role of Pensioners in Italy'. *British Journal of Industrial Relations*, 37/4: 577–600.

Clegg, H. A. (1976). *Trade Unionism under Collective Bargaining: A Theory Based on Comparisons of Six Countries*. Oxford: Basil Blackwell.

Dribbusch, H. (2002). *Gewerkschaftliche Mitgliedergewinnung im Dienstleistungssektor*. Berlin: Edition Sigma.

Ebbinghaus, B. and Visser, J. (1999). 'When Institutions Matter: Union Growth and Decline in Western Europe, 1950–1995'. *European Sociological Review*, 15/2: 135–58.

——Armingeon, K., and Hassel, A. (2000). 'Germany', in B. Ebbinghaus and J. Visser (eds.), *Trade Unions in Western Europe since 1945*. London: Macmillan, 279–337.

Fairbrother, P. (2002). 'Unions in Britain: Towards a New Unionism?', in P. Fairbrother and G. Griffin (eds.), *Changing Prospects of Trade Unionism: Comparisons between Six Countries*. London: Continuum, 56–92.

——and Griffin, G. (eds.) (2002). *Changing Prospects for Trade Unionism: Comparisons between Six Countries*. London: Continuum.

Findlay, P. and McKinlay, A. (2003a). 'Organizing in Electronics: Recruitment, Recognition and Representation—Shadow Shop Stewards in Scotland's "Silicon Glen" ', in G. Gall (ed.), *Union Organizing: Campaigning for Trade Union Recognition*. London: Routledge, 114–32.

————(2003b). 'Union Organizing in "Big Blue's" Backyard'. *Industrial Relations Journal*, 34/1: 52–66.

Fiorito, J. (2003). 'Union Organizing in the United States', in G. Gall (ed.), *Union Organizing: Campaigning for Trade Union Recognition*. London: Routledge, 191–210.

——Jarley, P., and Delaney, J. T. (1995). 'National Union Effectiveness in Organizing: Measures and Influences'. *Industrial and Labor Relations Review*, 48/4: 613–35.

Fletcher Jr., B. and Hurd, R. W. (1998). 'Beyond the Organizing Model: The Transformation Process in Local Unions', in K. Bronfenbrenner, S. Friedman, R. W. Hurd, R. A. Oswald, and R. L. Seeber (eds.), *Organizing to Win: New Research on Union Strategies*. Ithaca, NY: ILR Press, 37–53.

————(2001). 'Overcoming Obstacles to Transformation: Challenges on the Way to a New Unionism', in L. Turner, H. C. Katz, and R. W. Hurd (eds.), *Rekindling the Movement: Labor's Quest for Relevance in the 21st Century*. Ithaca, NY: ILR Press, 182–208.

Foerster, A. (2001). 'Confronting the dilemmas of Organizing: Obstacles and Innovations at the AFL-CIO Organizing Institute', in L. Turner, H. C. Katz, and R. W. Hurd (eds.), *Rekindling the Movement: Labor's Quest for Relevance in the 21st Century*, Ithaca, NY: ILR Press, 155–81.

Fraile, L. (1999). 'Tightrope: Spanish Unions and Labor Market Segmentation', in A. Martin and G. Ross (eds.), *The Brave New World of European Labor: European Trade Unions at the Millennium*. New York and Oxford: Berghahn Books, 269–311.

Gall, G. (ed.) (2003) *Union Organizing: Campaigning for Trade Union Recognition*. London: Routledge.

Hamann, K. (2001). 'The Resurgence of National-Level Bargaining: Union Strategies in Spain'. *Industrial Relations Journal*, 32/2: 154–72.

——and Martínez Lucio, M. (2003). 'Strategies of Union Revitalization in Spain: Negotiating Change and Fragmentation'. *European Journal of Industrial Relations*, 9/1: 61–78.

Heery, E. (1998). 'The Re-launch of the Trades Union Congress'. *British Journal of Industrial Relations*, 36/3: 339–60.

——and Simms, M. (2003). *Bargain or Bust? Employer Responses to Union Organizing*. London: Trades Union Congress.

——Simms, M., Delbridge, R., Salmon, J., and Simpson, D. (2000*a*). 'The TUC's Organising Academy: An Assessment'. *Industrial Relations Journal*, 31/5: 400–15.

——Simms, M., Delbridge, R., Salmon, J., and Simpson, D. (2000*b*). 'Union Organizing in Britain: A Survey of Policy and Practice'. *International Journal of Human Resource Management*, 11/5: 986–1007.

——Simms, M., Simpson, D., Delbridge, R., and Salmon, J. (2000*c*). 'Organizing Unionism Comes to the UK'. *Employee Relations*, 22/1, 2: 38–57.

——Simms, M., Delbridge, R., Salmon, J., and Simpson, D. (2003). 'Trade Union Recruitment Policy in Britain: Form and Effects', in G. Gall (ed.), *Union Organizing: Campaigning for Trade Union Recognition*. London: Routledge, 56–78.

Hurd, R. W. (1998). 'Contesting the Dinosaur Image: The Labor Movement's Search for A Future'. *Labor Studies Journal*, 23/4: 5–30.

——Milkman, R., and Turner, L. (2003). 'Reviving the American Labour Movement: Institutions and Mobilization'. *European Journal of Industrial Relations*, 9/1: 99–117.

Hyman, R. (2001*a*). 'Trade Union Research and Cross-National Comparison'. *European Journal of Industrial Relations*, 7/2: 203–32.

——(2001*b*). *Understanding European Trade Unionism: Between Market, Class and Society*. London: Sage Publications.

Jacobi, O. (2003). 'Union Recognition in Germany: A Dual System of Industrial Relations with Two Recognition Problems', in G. Gall (ed.), *Union Organizing: Campaigning for Trade Union Recognition*, London: Routledge, 211–27.

Jarley, P. (2002). 'American Unions at the Start of the Twenty-First Century: Going Back to the Future?', in P. Fairbrother and G. Griffin (eds.), *Changing Prospects for Trade Unionism: Comparisons between Six Countries*, London and New York: Continuum, 200–37.

——and Fiorito, J. (1990). 'Associate Membership: Unionism or Consumerism?'. *Industrial and Labor Relations Review*, 43/2: 209–24.

Kelly, J. and Heery, E. (1989). 'Full-Time Officers and Trade Union Recruitment'. *British Journal of Industrial Relations*, 27/2: 196–213.

Kriesky, J. (2001). 'Structural Change in the AFL-CIO: A Regional Study of Union Cities' Impact', in L. Turner, H. C. Katz, and R. W. Hurd (eds.), *Rekindling the Movement: Labor's Quest for Relevance in the 21st Century*. Ithaca, NY: ILR Press, 129–54.

Locke, R. M. and Baccaro, L. (1999). 'The Resurgence of Italian Unions?', in A. Martin and G. Ross (eds.), *The Brave New World of European Labor: European Trade Unions at the Millennium*. New York: Berghahn Books, 217–68.

Martin, A. and Ross, G. (eds) (1999). *The Brave New World of European Labor: European Trade Unions at the Millennium*. New York: Berghahn Books.

Martínez Lucio, M. (1992). 'Spain: Constructing Institutions and Actors in a Context of Change', in A. Ferner and R. Hyman (eds.), *Industrial Relations in the New Europe*. Oxford: Blackwell, 482–523.

Miguélez Lobo, M. (2000). 'The Modernization of Trade Unions in Spain', in J. Waddington and R. Hoffman (eds.), *Trade Unions in Europe: Facing Challenges and Searching for Solutions*. Brussels: European Trade Union Institute, 499–527.

Milkman, R. (ed.) (2000). *Organizing Immigrants: The Challenge for Unions in Contemporary California*. Ithaca, NY: ILR Press.

——and Wong, K. (2001). 'Organizing Immigrant Workers: Case Studies from Southern California', in L. Turner, H. C. Katz, and R. W. Hurd (eds.), *Rekindling the Movement: Labor's Quest for Relevance in the 21st Century*. Ithaca, NY: ILR Press, 99–128.

Nissen, B. (1999). 'Introduction', in B. Nissen (ed.), *Which Direction for Organized Labor? Essays on Organizing, Outreach, and Internal Transformation*. Detroit, MI: Wayne State University Press, 11–17.

Oxenbridge, S., Brown, W., Deakin, S., and Pratten, C. (2003). 'Initial Responses to the Statutory Recognition Provisions of the Employment Relations Act 1999'. *British Journal of Industrial Relations*, 41/2: 315–34.

Regini, M. (1997). 'Still Engaging in Corporatism? Recent Italian Experience in Comparative Perspective'. *European Journal of Industrial Relations*, 3/3: 259–78.

——and Regalia, I. (2000). 'The Prospects for Italian Trade Unions in a Phase of Concertation', in J. Waddington and R. Hoffman (eds.), *Trade Unions in Europe: Facing Challenges and Searching for Solutions*. Brussels: European Trade Union Institute, 365–92.

Royle, T. (2000). *Working for McDonald's in Europe: The Unequal Struggle?*. London: Routledge.

Safford, S. C. and Locke, R. M. (2001). *Unions on the Rebound: Social Embeddedness and the Transformation of Building Trades Locals*. Boston, MA: MIT Sloan School of Management, Sloan Working Paper 4175–01.

Silvia, S. J. (1999). 'Every which way but Loose: German Industrial Relations Since 1980', in A. Martin and G. Ross (eds.), *The Brave New World of European Labor: European Trade Unions at the Millennium*. New York: Berghahn Books, 75–124.

Simms, M. (2003). 'Union Organizing in a Not-For-Profit Organization', in G. Gall (ed.), *Union Organizing: Campaigning for Trade Union Recognition*. London: Routledge, 97–113.

Taylor, P. and Bain, P. (2003). 'Call Center Organizing in Adversity: From Excell to Vertex', in G. Gall (ed.), *Union Organizing: Campaigning for Trade Union Recognition*. London: Routledge, 153–72.

Turner, L. (1998). *Fighting for Partnership: Labor and Politics in a Unified Germany*. Ithaca, NY: ILR Press.

——and Hurd, R. W. (2001). 'Building Social Movement Unionism: The Transformation of the American Labor Movement', in L. Turner, H. C. Katz, and R. W. Hurd (eds.), *Rekindling the Movement: Labor's Quest for Relevance in the 21st Century*. Ithaca, NY: Cornell University Press, 9–26.

Van der Meer, M. (2000). 'Spain', in B. Ebbinghaus and J. Visser (eds.), *Trade Unions in Western Europe since 1945*. London: Macmillan, 573–603.

Visser, J. (2000). 'Italy', in B. Ebbinghaus and J. Visser (eds.), *Trade Unions in Western Europe since 1945*. London: Macmillan, 371–428.

Voss, K. and Sherman, R. (2000). 'Breaking The Iron Law of Oligarchy: Union Revitalization in the American Labor Movement'. *American Journal of Sociology*, 106/2: 303–49.

Waddington, J. and Kerr, A. (2000). 'Towards an Organizing Model in UNISON: A Trade Union Membership Strategy in Transition', in M. Terry (ed.), *Redefining Public Sector Unionism: UNISON and the Future of Trade Unions*. London: Routledge, 231–62.

Wever, K. S. (1998). 'International Labor Revitalization: Enlarging the Playing Field'. *Industrial Relations*, 37/3: 388–407.

Willman, P. (2001). 'The Viability of Trade Union Organization: A Bargaining Unit Analysis'. *British Journal of Industrial Relations*, 39/1: 97–117.

Wills, J. (2003). 'Organizing in Transport and Travel: Learning Lessons from TSSA's Seacat Campaign', in G. Gall (ed.), *Union Organizing: Campaigning for Trade Union Recognition*. London: Routledge, 133–52.

Wood, S., Moore, S., and Ewing, K. (2003). 'The Impact of the Trade Union Recognition Procedure Under the Employment Relations Act, 2000–2', in H. Gospel and S. Wood (eds.), *Representing Workers: Union Recognition and Membership in Britain*. London: Routledge, 119–43.

5

Analysing Social Partnership: A Tool of Union Revitalization?

MICHAEL FICHTER AND IAN GREER

INTRODUCTION

Recently, much has been written about social partnership. Especially in Europe, the spread of national social pacts, the introduction of tripartite institutions to the Central and Eastern European accession countries, and the implementation of the Social Dialogue in the European Union have created a new interest in the effects and effectiveness of such arrangements. In the United States, the meaning of labour–management partnership is developing further, as revitalized unions of service and construction workers have applied this instrument to extend and consolidate gains (Mills 2001; WAI 2002).

This chapter focuses on one issue among many with regard to social partnership: When can it be a tool of union revitalization? In the past, critics close to the labour movement associated social partnership with a stagnant and defensive brand of unionism that was out of touch with the working class, overly concerned about ongoing relations with the state and capital, and incapable of carrying out a contentious role in class struggle and pluralist industrial relations (Parker and Slaughter 1994; Kelly 1998). More recently, critical voices have taken a more contingent approach by using different union capacities (Parker and Slaughter 1997) and differing product and labour market conditions (Kelly 2004) to explain varying outcomes of partnership experiences for unions and their members. Using evidence from five countries, we find that social partnership contributes to revitalization, when it is institutionalized, integrated with other union strategies, and, most importantly, when it is pursued in the interest of a broader social agenda.

Just what do we mean when we use the term 'social partnership'? For one, we define it as a kind of interaction between unions and employers (Turner 1998) and not as Kjaergaard (2001: 9) does, as including the whole range of other civil society organizations. While other organizations often play important roles, the core of the partnerships we are discussing consists of formally structured, ongoing relations of cooperation[1] between unions and employers, whether at the national, regional, or sectoral level between unions and employer associations, or within enterprises between worker and management representatives. Second, social partnership has a policy agenda, which can cover a wide range of issues, usually including 'mutual gains'. These may be part of efforts to reform collective bargaining itself (such as setting up frameworks for continuous 'integrative bargaining' inside or beyond the workplace), but the agenda can also include issues outside the usual focus of collective bargaining (i.e. in-house training or political issues) as well as social policy goals that extend beyond the two social partners (such as labour market integration, equality of opportunity, regional economic development, and welfare state reform). Lastly, social partnership requires that labour and management be able and willing to apply sanctions on unilateral violations of cooperation by the other side. To this end, unions can use partnership, when part of a larger repertoire of strategies, to bolster their own bargaining position, especially of local unionists participating in workplace change. Social partnership relations, then, can satisfy our basic definition and feed into union revitalization while differing across structural, functional, and strategic dimensions.

Historically, strong union movements have been able to use their organizational and mobilization capacities to work with employers and government and institutionalize their successes. The *institutional framework* of social partnership, which they have helped to create, can include codetermination legislation at workplace level, national corporatist structures, or cooperative collective bargaining arrangements at industry or regional level. This framework has not only served union-specific agendas, but has also been the foundation for implementing wider public policy goals such as solidaristic welfare and labour market re-integration programmes as well as company/workplace-level employee participation. A strong institutional framework with extended union participation is, we argue, a prerequisite for functioning social partnership. However, it is not sufficient and can sometimes even prevent unions from developing or implementing innovative strategies. Therefore, social partnership is more likely to contribute to union revitalization when it is complementary to the strategies and *autonomous organizational capacities* of unions. In other words, unions should use their own resources and skills to counter or prevent attacks from governments and employers as well as to pursue partnership proactively and strategically. Institutionalized partnership activities in conjunction with the broader array of union activities, however, are not enough; 'doing it alone' with management can strengthen unions in their old strongholds but it can also engender particularism in political action or bargaining activity. For an integrated strategy to promote revitalization, the partnership also has to serve *a broad social agenda* that appeals to allies both in particular communities and in the general socio-political arena. Examples of such agenda-setting would include efforts to combat unemployment at the national level or to eliminate discrimination against immigrant workers.

Social partnership arrangements are most conducive, we argue, to furthering union revitalization in cases that meet these three criteria. In other words, they need to be institutionally embedded, they must be integrated into a proactive union strategy, and they should pursue a broader social agenda rather than focusing on narrow union-specific issues alone. In terms of Behrens, Hamann, and Hurd's (Chapter 2, this volume) definition of union revitalization, these kinds of partnerships may strengthen labour's political influence, its bargaining power, membership density, and other indicators of organizational 'vitality'. By contrast, absent a solid anchor of supportive institutions and union strategies and a link to broader social initiatives, social partnerships usually strengthen the interdependence between unions and specific firms, thus remaining particularistic, thwarting the embeddedness of partnership in a broader social environment. While we find our argument applicable in the five national contexts, it is based on a reading of evidence in which cases meeting our three preconditions are few and far between. This is as much a statement about the still limited occurrence of union revitalization as it is a reflection of the limited use of social partnership as a tool to this end.

In Italy, Spain, and Germany, confirmation of this argument comes not only from the historical accomplishments of labour and management establishing widely valued policies for welfare provision and worker participation, but also from recent stumbling blocks with national-level social partnership. Our argument helps to understand organized labour's reaction to more recent neo-liberal policy orientations in these countries. The neo-liberal turn in national policy-making may have weakened labour's supportive institutional environment, and has certainly stirred debate over the pitfalls of continued cooperation with capital in national competitiveness pacts. At the same time, labour movements have learned to focus partnership activities in other arenas, such as firms and regions. This shifting paradigm raises two possibilities. First, labour's institutional embeddedness may be, paradoxically, both a prerequisite for, and retardant of, union revitalization, in the sense that unionists may be finding that the heavy reliance on institutionalized social partnership has led to the neglect of other strategies (Baccaro, Hamann, and Turner 2003), and an isolation in broader society. Second, new subnational loci of action have their own limitations from the point of view of union strategy, by only being useful within existing union strongholds and by increasing the problems of decentralization (Schroeder and Weinert 1999; Artiles Martin, and Moner 2003).

After a short review of the literature on social partnership and union revitalization, the chapter goes on to analyse the evidence on social partnership in five countries.

PARTNERSHIP, UNIONS, AND UNION REVITALIZATION: AN OVERVIEW OF THE LITERATURE IN ENGLISH

Analyses of the prospects and dimensions of social partnerships in countries without an institutionalized tradition of cooperative labour relations (such as the United States and the United Kingdom) have provided insights into the problems unions face under such conditions when the balance of power between labour and management is notably unequal.[2] The 1980s marked the appearance of a great number of new publications on labour–management partnerships in the United States. Initial findings showed that management was increasingly able to define 'cooperation' on its own terms based on a new strategy to decentralize bargaining and make labour–management relations more flexible and differentiated by sector, firm, and by workplace (Katz 1993). Changes in industrial relations systems were driven by the 'strategic choices' of management (Kochan, Katz, and McKersie 1986; Walton, Cutcher-Gershenfeld, and McKersie 1994). Unions faced with demands for wage concessions and cooperation in the upgrading of production methods were obliged to accept the implementation of new human resource practices emphasizing cooperation and de-emphasizing protective shop-floor rules. Although this literature pointed to union role changes (Katz 1985) and to how union members could benefit from linking local labour–management partnerships to national policies (Frost 2001), it did not systematically follow up on how unions could transform choices made in hard times into opportunities for renewal. At the same time, another segment of the literature argued that partnerships reinforced the subordination of union organizations to management (Wells 1987; Parker and Slaughter 1994). The discontent with partnership as a union strategy resonated with the British literature, beginning in the early Blair years, which focused on a wave of firm-based partnerships (Guest and Peccei 2001). Critics further asked whether unions were being forced into partnership by economic trends beyond their control (Klare 1988); how partnership could serve a strategic purpose on the new 'terrain' of modern production organization (Banks and Metzgar 1989); and how, specifically, unions could harness partnership activities to support other goals such as member involvement (Juravich 1998). As such, the Anglo-American literature pointed out the problems of partnership for unions without being able to conclude whether unions could reverse their decline in partnership with employers.

In contrast, the literature on Europe brought out important national differences in the extent to which firms could implement change unilaterally and in the ability of unions to work strategically with social partnership. The case of Germany in particular, with its dual system of interest representation, showed how different institutions could promote social partnership and lead to better outcomes, both for workers and for the economic vitality of the country (Streeck 1984; Turner 1991). Subsequent developments in the comparative political economy literature suggested that industrial relations institutions (and hence patterns of partnership and conflict) were closely related to other features of national political economies, such as financial markets, welfare states, and skill provision (Hall and Soskice 2001). But as Turner (Chapter 1, this volume) has noted, these authors tend to see union strategy as unimportant and overlook the importance of subnational arenas that constitute union activity in a given country (Christopherson and Storper 1987; Locke 1992). The comparative industrial relations literature thus found national variation in union strategies linked to a broader institutional context, without being able to conclude the extent to which essentially subnational phenomena driven by unions, such as instances of union revitalization, could be explained by national characteristics. Moreover, it seemed that the applicability of traditional comparative political economic theory outside of 'corporatist' or 'coordinated market economies' such as Germany, was questionable (Thelen 2001; Baccaro 2002).

Union revitalization as a central concern has only recently been addressed in the literature. To be sure, the revitalization literature has not systematically assessed the impact of labour–management partnership on the vitality of unions. But its presentation of the many and diverse instances of the revitalization phenomenon (Mills 2001) allows us to analyse the concrete actions of unions in partnership, such as building new institutions, seeking new allies, pursuing new policies, and strategizing in ways that link the array of activities. On this basis, we can change the question from 'is partnership good or bad' to 'under what conditions do partnerships feed into or frustrate revitalization' and look beyond broad national trends to phenomena in specific firms and local sectors. The cases below illustrate how our argument, based on this actor-centred re-reading of industrial relations literature, helps us to understand the dynamics of partnership and union renewal.

US AND BRITISH PARTNERSHIP AGREEMENTS AS ISOLATED PROJECTS

In the United States, where the term 'labour–management partnership' is generally used, most writings on this topic have little to say about union strategy, because unions have usually signed on to cooperative projects with management when they had no other options. During the 1980s and 1990s, for example, unions in troubled auto, aircraft, and steel firms sought out and developed surprisingly strong relations of partnership with firms. Such arrangements, shaped by firm-level collective bargaining frameworks and supplemented with in-plant agreements, benefited some union members by paying for skill development for both internal and external labour markets, by modernizing human resource policies, and increasing job security (Gray, Myers, and Myers 1999). Such partnerships have, in some cases, included 'neutrality' provisions that extend new organizing rights to workers in some non-union plants (Eaton and Kriesky 2001) and recognize a union role in the introduction of 'sensitive' or 'lean' systems of production. As the 1998 General Motors strike showed, this put massive disruptive power in the hands of some workers (Herod 2001).

This kind of 'new industrial relations', however, did not usually protect unions from membership loss or stop the decline of unionized industries. Employers used bankruptcy proceedings and the creation of non-union subsidiaries to negotiate further concessions and cuts, shrinking the number of workers who benefited from partnership. As such, labour–management partnerships were not the main cause of union organizational decline, but at least in the manufacturing sector, they also did not turn the tide in favour of revitalization. Most commentators within the labour movement have accepted partnerships as a fact of life, and a few have begun to ask how unions can develop the kinds of rule-based partnership that could protect participants and feed into other strategies (Banks and Metzgar 1989; Juravich 1998).

In other sectors, such as construction, health care, hotels, and entertainment, unions have begun to shift towards a more strategic use of partnership by incorporating partnerships with employers into local political action, coalitions with communities of immigrants and racial minorities, and other revitalization strategies (WAI 2000, 2002). Construction unions, for example, suffered considerable membership losses during the recessions of the 1970s and 1980s when hundreds of thousands of unemployed union members accepted lower-paid jobs in the non-union sector, the growth of which had been abetted by public and private owners of construction projects seeking lower prices (Erlich 1986; Linder 1999). Attempts since the 1990s to organize increasingly non-white construction workers have benefited from more favourable market conditions, but have also had to overcome a history of racial exclusion from the unionized trades. By the late 1990s, construction unions throughout the country had begun to heal relations with urban community groups and become important players in local politics, able to influence contract awards over construction projects and real estate development. In this way they succeeded in increasing their membership while most unions were in decline. Employers played a supporting role in these efforts by contributing to the modernization of recruitment and training structures and the development of supportive public policy instruments.

The union-led labour-management partnership in Seattle's construction industry illustrates this approach. Beginning in the 1990s, a consortium of local craft unions organized collectively as the local building and construction trades council and—together with unionized contractors, who had an interest in expanding their share of the market and improving jointly administered apprenticeship programmes—approached private and public customers of building contractors, asking them to sign project labour agreements (PLAs). These were designed to reduce cost overruns and delays while upholding specified minimum standards for working conditions (e.g. wages, health and safety) defining procedures to resolve jurisdictional disputes between craft unions, and eliminating inefficient work rules. Through the widespread recognition of PLAs, the unions sought to prevent non-union contractors from being able to win contracts through wage dumping (Northrup 1997). When opponents attacked PLAs and put pressure on government officials to reject or cancel such agreements, the unions built community support by expanding the rationale for PLAs beyond that of mutual gains for the union, contractors, and customers, to promote racial and gender diversity in the workplace and investment in skills training.

By advocating rules to include 'labour market outsiders' in relatively well-paid construction jobs, Seattle unions have built community pressure for PLAs while healing old wounds with the black and Latino communities. Unlike most workers in the United States, unionized construction workers normally undergo formal occupational apprenticeships, combining on-the-job with classroom training; accordingly, the PLAs mandate the use of apprentices on large construction sites. By coupling apprenticeship rules with racial and gender diversity targets, the agreements open job opportunities for traditionally excluded groups. Organizations of minority groups helped to convince authorities to sign PLAs by testifying at public hearings that the agreements would create first-rate training opportunities for minority workers who had until then been consigned to second-rate jobs in the non-union sector. The unions pushed the concept further by including an on-the-job mentorship programme to protect new workers from the usual 'sink or swim' demands, which usually lead to high dropout rates from apprenticeships.

Since the early 1990s, PLAs have been successfully implemented at several large projects in Seattle (and many other major cities),[3] including a new airport runway, new public buildings, and even some private projects (WAI 2002). By linking their own partnership and market expansion strategy with workplace diversity, broadly recognized as a valuable public policy goal, Seattle's construction unions have extended the bounds of typical labour–management partnerships beyond the achievement of 'mutual gains' for employers and unions by recruiting, training, and providing on-the-job supports for new workers. Downward wage pressure has been reduced as non-union firms, although not formally excluded from contract bidding under PLAs, have lost their ability to win contracts through low bids based on low pay. As PLAs have become more widespread and union contractors have sought more employees, we can assume that union density on large building projects has increased, although exact numbers are not available. Furthermore, healing old wounds with minority groups and the establishment of a network of public policy experts working in union offices, who specialize in framing, passing, and implementing union-driven upgrading-directed local economic development projects, has helped strengthen the unions' influence in local politics. This is superimposed on top of decades-old practices of sectoral collective bargaining and jointly governed training institutions. Broadening the agenda, integrating partnership with other strategies, and using a longstanding role in training have led to more political influence and more union members, both of which indicate union revitalization, although quantitative measures are not available.

The link between social partnership and broader coalition politics is unusual in the United States, especially outside the building trades, primarily due to the focus on arrangements for achieving 'mutual gains' within a specific firm. Manufacturing unions could follow the coalition approach as well to overcome their inability to integrate partnership with other strategies and to attract and retain high wage, eco-friendly 'good jobs' in troubled industrial regions (Leroy 2002). They do not usually do so, however; instead, they tend to favour in-plant forms of participation to save firms. Service sector unions might do the same through living wage campaigns to reduce wage-based price competition among government contractors, and through sector-specific initiatives (Reynolds 2002). In health care, for example, this entails passing laws such as minimum staffing standards that improve the quality of both treatment and jobs (Mills 2001). Unfortunately, much of the partnership in the service sector is beset by a form of 'mutual gains' between one set of workers and an employer, whose strategy for competitiveness brings partnership unions into conflict with other interested groups such as consumer advocates, and other unions (CNA 2002). American union strategy development faces an additional, more fundamental problem: outside the union strongholds discussed above, partnership is generally not converted into long-term, rule-bound behaviour, and succumbs either to conflicts of interest within the union camp (Preuss and Frost 2003), or to 'defections' by employers brought on by unsuccessful business strategies (Frost 2001).

British unions have been historically steeped in the ways of adversarial labour relations. Coming from a political and economic environment generally hostile to their inclusion in both managerial and political decision-making processes, they have—like their counterparts in the United States—been wary to embrace the opportunities and challenges associated with partnership strategies. While there is some evidence that this may be changing (Arrowsmith 2002), it is still questionable whether a growing openness toward partnership will actually meet the Trades Union Congress (TUC's) 'acid test' of partnership by yielding improvements in job security, transparency, involvement, and the quality of working life (Martínez Lucio and Stuart 2002). Not the least, this is the result of the fact that British unions have been facing a dearth of opportunities to link partnership with other strategies, largely because the move towards partnership as a proactive approach has not originated with them but with their counterparts in government and large corporations.

Nevertheless, since New Labour's ascendancy to power in the late 1990s, and despite reservations (and even outright opposition in some union quarters), some unions have signed on to such 'social partnership agreements' in large firms. The core components include flexibility for the company (task, time, pay, and staffing levels), union rights to information and consultation, and assurances of job security for existing union members coupled with training programs (Heery, Kelly, and Waddington 2003). Participating unions favour such agreements because they tailor the provision of training to the individual employee through 'on-the-job' programmes with wage subsidies. Moreover, these agreements sometimes give unions a role in local and national consultative bodies. In one case, at a newly opened Tesco store in a depressed section of Leeds, the shopworkers' union, USDAW, was involved from the beginning in a variety of workplace development programmes. These included such activities as monitoring both the quality of the training, assuring that skills were transferable and useful on external labour markets, and the working conditions at the store as well as implementing provisions for the payment of 'rate-for-the-job' to trainees. The union also negotiated the hiring of 160 unemployed people from the neighbourhood (Andersen and Mailand 2002). In addition to creating jobs for previously unemployed, non-union persons, this agreement presented an opportunity to attract new members and build bridges to an excluded community neighbourhood without threatening the existing membership with potential job loss. By comparison, an account of the partnership at the employment agency Manpower suggests that British attempts for 'high road' strategies outside the core of union members can conflict with the interests of the union's traditional constituency (Heery et al. 2004).

Besides the changes in the British political environment, which have affected labour, the current interest in developing corporate governance systems has also made an impact on union approaches by fostering steps towards the inclusion of union representation in company decision-making processes. Although the foundations of labour–management partnerships are often based on company initiatives to develop such systems, evidence provided by some studies shows that both the effectiveness and the duration of such agreements are strongly influenced by the product and service quality rules they engender. When these force firms to upscale their operations, managers must convince shareholders of the long-term benefits to be accrued from sustained cooperation with the union. In addition, cooperation hinges on the strategy perspective developed by management and directors as well as on the continuing availability of a strong, cooperative union (Deakin et al. 2002). At the same time, this environmental support would seem to reciprocally contribute to augmenting union power.

Still, scepticism abounds regarding the kinds of partnerships developing and the postulated link between partnership and union revitalization. First, research has concluded that there is only sparse evidence connecting partnership to the outcomes we might associate with a revitalized labour movement, such as enhanced wages, job security, or union membership levels. Using matched pairs of cases taken from individual enterprises, Kelly (2004) shows that companies with labour–management partnership agreements do not exhibit better outcomes for workers than those without partnerships. This would seem to derive from the limited, company-based dimensions of these pacts, thus lending credence to the criteria we have advanced for linking partnership to union revitalization. Second, individual firm-level partnerships have been shown to be an inadequate instrument for harnessing management prerogatives over employment and restructuring strategies. Martínez Lucio and Stuart (2002), for example, use survey data and case studies from several sectors to find that partnerships were riddled by unilateral behaviour on the management side (such as outsourcing without consulting the union) and a managerial culture of 'limited transparency' (see also Stuart and Martínez Lucio 2002). Third, although they desire more involvement and less adversarial relations with management, unionists are usually excluded from decisions over investment, training, and staff planning. From a union perspective, partnerships therefore usually have little to offer in the way of fitting a union agenda. Guest and Peccei's (2001) survey of unionists and managers finds that partnerships tend to emphasize the contribution of employees to the enterprise more than employee welfare and vigorous representation.

Taking these critical appraisals into account, the question is which union strategy approaches could overcome the enumerated deficits. How can unions in Britain turn the tide and implement social partnership agreements more attuned to their interests? Beyond the self-evident need for them to become active agents in shaping the meaning of 'social partnership' (Ackers and Payne 1998), British unions face the task of integrating this instrument into their primarily adversarial approach to strategy. Whether done by means of parallel organization structures or sequentially (Heery 2002), the effective use of social partnership to bolster union revitalization will depend greatly on its coherency with other union policies. As Munro and Rainbird (2000) have pointed out, unions must be in control of the overall impact of partnerships on their strategy. In the case of joint workforce development programmes promoted by public services union UNISON, they show that this kind of 'single issue' form of partnership can be insulated from arenas of conflict and at the same time be linked to member recruitment, work skills training, broadening the bargaining agenda, and training for union activists.

The further evolution of such strategies as well as their accompanying debate will also be impacted by structural and legal requirements mandated by the European Union. Indeed, the 1994 directive on European Works Councils, the recent EU Directive on Information and Consultation of Employees, and the spreading acceptance of the EU

Social Dialogue (European Commission 2002) present British unions with new instruments—and challenges—for developing social partnership approaches which go beyond the local or national realm. Strengthening cross-border cooperation may enable British unions to link ongoing union organizational efforts at the workplace to the broader issue of the provision of social goods. The TUC has expressed keen interest in this policy at least since the early 1990s (Teague 1989).

GERMANY, ITALY, AND SPAIN: SOCIAL PARTNERSHIP AS AN OVERARCHING PHENOMENON

Germany

In contrast to the liberal market economies of the Anglo-Saxon countries, where until recently the designations 'social partners' and 'social partnership' appeared to be 'bizarre' (Hyman 2001*b*: 39), both concepts are established terms of labour relations vocabulary in Germany. In the Weimar Republic, but even more so since 1949, they have been used so extensively that to many they have become synonymous with the German model of labour relations. Although especially promoted by the conservative Christian Democrats in the early post-war years of West Germany (Schmidt 1985), emphasizing harmony and integration, the concept of social partnership also has social democratic roots. Here, class conflict has become institutionalized with an ensuing 'deadlock between strongly organized parties' leading to 'pragmatic accommodation...in the interests of mutual survival' (Hyman 2001*a*: 41), or to 'conflict partnership' as Müller-Jentsch (1999) has labelled it.

Nevertheless, there is not much recent debate in Germany over the ramifications of these potentially conflicting conceptions, nor can it be said that the inclusion of other civil society actors in the future development of social partnership in Germany has received much attention. Indeed, the issue of the impact of social partnership as currently understood on union revitalization has as yet hardly been broached (Behrens, Fichter, and Frege 2003).[4]

Within the dense institutional political and economic network which has grown out of the post-Second World War 'dual system' of works councils and regional–sectoral pattern bargaining, social partnership is a widespread approach, not a matter of single (company) cases (Turner 1998: 18–19). Even under changing conditions in which new issues re-format the negotiating field, existing multi-level relations enable pattern agreements, such as training arrangements or new collective bargaining provisions, to develop. Social partnership in Germany is both part of, and an extension of, collective bargaining; it has been institutionalized on a national scale (very much in contrast to the Anglo-Saxon experience) and is practiced throughout the field of employment regulation and labour relations, whether tripartite policy-making in the apprenticeship system, bipartite sectoral bargaining between unions and employers' associations, or company-level codetermination including works councils (and sometimes union representatives) and management. As such, it has a political as well as an economic dimension; the former represented at various times by a number of tripartite and multi-partite 'Alliances for Jobs' at the national and regional level (Neumann 2000), while in the latter case, social partnership is generally equated with the arena of company or plant agreements (Mauer and Seifert 2001).

At the political level, the primary focus of such partnerships has been to address the general unemployment problem, while in the company arena, the goal has been to enhance the competitiveness of the targeted companies. The internal union criticisms of participation in the national Alliance for Jobs (1998–2002) and the meagre accomplishments of this tripartite partnership during Chancellor Schroeder's first term, and its subsequent discontinuation are telling in the current economic and political situation. Indeed, there is no evidence that this form of social partnership has contributed to union revitalization. Nor have unions explicitly pursued this kind of partnership in the interest of this goal. The regional, multi-sectoral 'territorial pacts', for example, have been viewed by union representatives as being a 'positive' exercise solely because key actors from the region, like banks and employment offices, had participated. Unionists praise the accomplishments of such pacts in providing benefits for workers (Gerlach and Ziegler 2000: 433), but the contributing role of the unions to such developments is neither directly visible nor has it been strategically exploited by them. Equally, unions generally have only a secondary role in company-level social partnerships,[5] the primary actors being the legally mandated company works council and management. At the same time, company agreements may infringe on the comprehensive framework of the sectoral contract (cf. Rehder 2002 with Brecht and Höland 2001: 501); avoiding such pitfalls, which would undermine the application of collective bargaining agreements in the workplace, requires union involvement.

Behrens, Fichter, and Frege (2003) have pointed out several different kinds of initiatives based on labour–management cooperation that adapt collective bargaining to address the needs of a differentiated and changing workforce. In contrast to tripartite Alliance politics, these efforts have the potential to assist union revitalization efforts. For example, by improving the job market and making unions part of the solution to the unemployment problem, they support membership recruitment strategies. For the IG Metall, one such issue of negotiation has been to create individualized benefit packages tied to options for time off or for training. This has not only produced a regional contract on life-long learning for which the union can claim due credit (Huber and Hofmann 2001), it has enabled the union to gain an organizational foothold in heretofore non-unionized sectors such as information technology. As an instrument of revitalization, the contract has an institutional basis traceable to an agreement reached by the now defunct national Alliance for Jobs (Heidemann 2001), and it presents an opportunity to be integrated with the union's recruitment efforts in this region.

A second topic of collective bargaining has been the creation of new jobs and the re-integration of the unemployed into the labour market. Again, the IG Metall may be singled out in connection with the notable Volkswagen project '5000 $\times$ 5000'[6] (Heidenreich 2001; Pries 2002); similarly, the mining, chemicals, and energy union (IG BCE) has negotiated a yearly increase in apprenticeships in the chemical industry during the past round of negotiations (IG Chemie 2003). By stepping up efforts to use collective bargaining to help alleviate the unemployment problem, unions could strengthen the legitimacy of their demands and attract new members. As yet, however, there is no significant evidence of such a development.

A third way in which collective bargaining and employer–union partnerships may contribute to union revitalization is through the negotiation of new job evaluation schemes for determining wage classifications. Although there is no formal discrimination of women within a particular wage category, 'women-preferred' jobs are regularly assigned to lower wage groups. At issue is the elimination of discrimination resulting from gender-biased classifications. In a country notorious for the structural exclusion of women from the labour market, these practices could broaden the appeal of trade unionism beyond the currently male-dominated and blue-collar core of union membership. The readiness of unions to actively embrace the idea of 'gender mainstreaming' will contribute to overcoming gender bias and to making union membership more appealing to women (Tondorf 2001).

A fourth area of union collective bargaining activities based on partnership relations with employers revolves around the creation of sectoral pension funds to supplement both company pensions and the state pension system. Metallrente, the joint pension fund of the employers' association Gesamtmetall and IG Metall, established in 2001, is a good example of an innovative partnership that offers long-term economic advantages to all employees in the bargaining unit. Instead of retrenchment and a purely defensive policy towards government cutbacks in the state pension system, the social partners added their own complementary pillar, a sectoral pension fund. With further cuts in the state system likely, this initiative is especially attractive to younger employees, and could help IG Metall recruit new members.

A fifth area of potential union revitalization may grow out of the current restructuring and regulation of the temporary employment field. After several months of bargaining during the first half of 2003, the unions announced that agreement had been reached on a number of national framework contracts covering temporary employment. Union opposition to the relaxation of restrictions on temporary workers was quite strong until recently, when they lost the battle over government deregulation. At this point, they moved quickly to establish collectively bargained minimum standards. These framework contracts regulate all of the major issues of temporary employment in the interests of the temporary as well as regular employees. While it is still too early to predict how effective these agreements will actually be and how well they will function in practice, they have a potential to improve working conditions in this field and to integrate temporary workers into the representational jurisdiction of the unions, which could enhance the union's bargaining power and support membership recruitment efforts.

These five reforms of collective bargaining show how German unions have used the partnership framework in an innovative way. It is on this plane, the core of union mobilizing capacities and interest representation, that some German unions have begun to develop social partnership as a policy agenda for making a strategic contribution to union revitalization. Yet, most traditional alliance politics in the workplace, have, for the most part, been disconnected both from a broad social agenda and the main thrust of union strategy. And at the regional and national level, unions have been unable to effectively rebuff the neo-liberal agenda proposals of employers as government support for their policy proposals has been dwindling.

Italy

In Italy, recent social partnership developments pose a major challenge to the way that comparative scholars view the impact of institutions and the character of a national trade union movement on the quality of social partnership. The ability to make national tripartite pacts, the development of strong union-driven statutory workplace representation, and the coverage of collective bargaining agreements throughout the economy are testament to the strong institutional position from which unions pursue social partnership in Italy. Italy's labour relations' practices thus appear to be closer to those of Germany than those of the United States or the United Kingdom, even if it does not fit into the category of a 'coordinated market economy' (Hall and Soskice 2001).

For decades, the politicized and antagonistic nature of trade unionism, as well as the highly fragmented character of the labour market, had posed problems for developing a union-backed strategy of social partnership. Baccaro, Carrieri, and Damiano point out that the Italian unions were not able to overcome a 'paradoxical coexistence' of local cooperation and innovation and national level paralysis regarding political strategies until the 1990s. At that time, all three confederal unions, the CGIL, the CISL, and the UIL, were facing organizational decline and the rise of new employee associations, when institutionalized social partnership became the primary mode of union revitalization (2003: 121). Following the scandals which discredited the entrenched political parties, the three confederations cooperated to use a window of opportunity to enhance their political participation and to push for economic and political reforms in the interest of their constituencies (Haddock 2002). At the same time, they pursued a strategy of membership involvement in union decision-making which allowed them to participate in tough decisions that were bound to adversely affect some part of their constituency. Consensual support for political and economic reforms, which moderated wage growth and temporarily suspended plant-level pay bargaining, was secured by mobilizing an otherwise passive majority through the extension of democratic rights of participation (Baccaro 2001, 2002). As such, the institutional embeddedness pursued by the unions during the 1990s supported a strategy of membership mobilization. This would indicate that the Italian unions had not only successfully used institutionalized social partnership to secure their recognition and participation in the political process but also proven capable of linking the instrument of social partnership to their immediate organizational needs. Although social partnership may have distracted Italian unions from organizing new groups of workers, the overall picture (which may be fading in the meantime) of an integrated strategy of macro-level negotiations and micro-level mobilization remains an impressive example of political action, union democracy, maintenance of membership levels, and overall capacity building. According to our criteria, this is a prime example of integrating social partnership into a comprehensive approach to union revitalization in Europe's second-most strike prone country.

Since the 2001 election of the right-wing 'House of Freedom' coalition government, however, under the leadership of Silvio Berlusconi, the benefits of national-level tripartism for the unions have become more limited. There have been few opportunities to contribute to the ongoing reform project, and, as Lo Faro (2002) has shown, the government has used the European discourse of 'social partnership' to cover its unwillingness to involve unions in policy formation. Moreover, the comprehensive approach no longer functions as a unified policy of all three confederations. The CGIL has refused to participate in several joint pacts agreed upon by the other two confederations, including a restructuring plan at Fiat and the national tripartite Pact for Italy in 2002. It is still too early to determine whether the cooperative policies of the CISL and the UIL allow them to influence national policy-making, or whether their embeddedness obliges the leadership to pursue tripartism, despite the divisions in the labour camp and the demands of the government. Recent decisions by the government to raise the threshold of its readiness to reach unanimous agreement with the social partners—a shift from 'social concertation' to 'social dialogue'—and a proposal for restructuring the collective bargaining system in the direction of greater decentralization, have rekindled common strands of criticism among the confederations. The success of two general strikes in 2002 to protest about labour market reforms, however, suggests that the years of social partnership have not harmed the labour movement's ability to strike, even when the labour movement is divided, as in the case of the CGIL's mobilization against the Pact for Italy (Paparella and Rinolfi 2002).

While the proposal for decentralizing collective bargaining has been widely discussed, no significant refocusing to the local level has been initiated. Italian unions are strong in this regard, since union density and involvement in the factory committees remains quite high. Participation in factory committee elections has been at around 75 per cent, and at the most recent election, 90 per cent of the votes at over 4,000 workplaces went to the major union confederations (Locke and Baccaro 1999: 254). Although control of such a decentralization process and its use to strengthen direct membership participation could be to the advantage of revitalization efforts, unions fear that it would also leave them vulnerable to bargaining patterns that would allow more competition based on labour cost savings. Their exclusion from such local concertation efforts as the Milan Employment Pact (Regalia 2002), which represents a case of 'social partnership' without unions, is a further example of decentralization which has made them wary.

Finally, there is the issue of working with employers and central authorities for common public policy goals. The concertation successes of the 1990s[7] enabled the Italian unions to stem the tide of major membership decline faced in the other four countries, while participating in unpopular (but arguably necessary) decisions to reform the welfare state and the labour market; in response they won an expanded legal framework for collective bargaining and found a vehicle to communicate with and involve members. Hence, although subsequently diminished, the role of Italian unions in policy-making as partners with employers and the state did enhance their bargaining power and their political influence for a time. Whether the Italian unions will be open for partnerships with other non-state organizations remains an unanswered question at the moment.

Spain

Although the institutions of labour relations—widely applicable collective bargaining agreements, tripartite pacts, and statutory workplace committees—in post-Franco Spain have not had a long time to develop, they appear to be stable and conducive to social partnership. The activity of unions under Franco was circumscribed and their opposition to the authoritarian government precluded any democratically founded partnerships. In the decade following Franco's death (1975), the new government sought to prevent social unrest and to legitimize its democratization course via social pacts with employers and the unions. Although this cooperative approach aided the UGT (General Workers' Confederation) in its rivalry with the Workers' Commissions (CC.OO), and produced tangible gains in its early phase, its acceptance among the unions began to wane by the 1980s, when economic growth made wage restraint unfeasible for unionists in elected factory councils (Ruiz 2001). State interest in cooperation with the unions declined along with union membership, and a new wave of confrontation ensued which only resided after a change of government in the mid-1990s. Following the signing of agreements on social security and pensions in 1996, the way was opened for the successful negotiation of long-awaited labour market reform (Andersen and Mailand 2002: 31) based in part on a series of pacts with labour and employers. The unions attached special importance to one of these, which strengthened the rights of Spain's temporary workforce, the largest in Europe, because they had been accused of representing the 'insiders' in a sharply segmented labour market (Fraile 1999).

Given the problem of segmentation in Spain, it is not surprising that unions have been keen on focusing attention on training and lifelong learning. National agreements in the late 1990s along with the development of a tripartite funding mechanism, have created institutional structures that allocate significant resources to workplace training and lifelong learning. In the meantime, however, the positive reception of these high-level national agreements within the unions has dissipated. Activities in this field have shifted to regional and local tripartite arenas, but the result has been regional funding disparities and unclear divisions of responsibilities. In addition, there has been a growing feeling among unionists that 'they are talked to, but not listened to' (Mailand and Andersen 2001: 8). Nevertheless, by promoting lifelong learning, Spain's unions have been able to develop an agenda connected to the concerns of those outside the group of 'core' permanent employees.

The case of the Employment Pact is generally cited as a notable exception to this union criticism of recent tripartite developments. Using EU Structural Funds, a territorial employment pact was created in 1998 in Vallés Occidental, an industrialized Catalonian county near Barcelona, which at the time had a comparatively high level of unemployment. Unions supported this pact because of the employment creation prospects it offered, because of the possibility to 'empower the processes of con-certation and social dialogue in order to affect both public policies and the wider dynamic of industrial relations', and, in addition, because of the financial resources available through participation (Lope, Gilbert, and de Villacian 2002: 27–29).

One reason why the Vallés Occidental Pact has been given a generally favourable review in the literature (cf. Mailand and Andersen 2001: 12) is that the pact has linked the territorial with the company-level and has integrated collective bargaining structures into its overall framework. It has provided a solution to the challenges fac-ing collective bargaining in Spain, including the fragmented and decentralized char-acter of labour market regulation. It is a good example of how unions have pursued the 'widening of bargaining agendas around such issues as variable pay, functional and geographic mobility, working time, and the establishment of permanent employment' (Hamann and Martínez Lucio 2003: 67). Observers differ over the issue as to whether the still fragmented nature of the system is a possible advantage for the unions (Hamann 1998), or whether it makes the integration of micro- and macro-level strategies more difficult (Artiles Martin and Moner 2003). Nevertheless, within the existing framework, accords on training have been reached and successfully implemented which identify unions with improvements in job market opportunities. Such 'partnerships at a distance' between unions and employers are beneficial to both the sectoral social dialogue (by adding a further layer of consultation) as well as to workers in SMEs in need of training access (Rigby 2003). As such, the unions are decidedly opposed to recent proposals to decentralize the institutions of continuous training because they regard such a step as destructive for the current inter-connec-tion between these institutions and collective bargaining (Artiles Martin 2002). With bargaining still not well articulated at lower levels and employers tending to be unwilling to implement agreements at higher levels, unions are concerned about the actual impact of such partnerships at the workplace and in terms of their own revitalization efforts. In order to meet employer initiatives on the development of new forms of both workplace and human resource organization, unions are showing signs of considering employee involvement and development in more strategic terms (Martínez Lucio and Blyton 1995). In this sense, they may be willing to bargain over longer-term restructuring agreements which allow for greater organizational and time flexibility in exchange for employment security. This would be a step towards constructing a new understanding of partnership in the Spanish workplace that could translate self-proclaimed bargaining successes and relatively widespread bar-gaining coverage into stronger workplace influence.

Caught between their institutionalized role in labour relations and a fragmented civil society and labour market, the unions are struggling to redefine their identity and devise new strategies in a contradictory environment both through mobilization and partnerships outside of the realm of collective bargaining such as the regional ones and those on training. Because of a general weakness of supportive organizations, however, these coalitions are transitory and do not develop into more long-term strategic alliances (Hamann and Martínez Lucio 2003: 65).

CONCLUSION

Can partnerships with employers help revitalize unions? Our answer is a heavily qualified affirmative, given the limitations of partnerships as a union strategy that we observe in a wide range of national contexts. We have argued that unions have to be able to integrate partnership activities into the full spectrum of the union's activities, that they need to link partnership to a broad agenda for social goods, and that they need institutional anchors. The national cases have shown, however, that there are often tensions among these factors. For example, the same strong German institutions that have furthered and solidified union power may also be stifling momentum towards union revitalization. Furthermore, unions are rarely able to realize all three of these factors simultaneously; at the same time, the cases have shown us that without all three, partnership is problematic for unions. Territorial employment pacts, for example, work in all of the countries to broaden what unions do and are tied to widely shared policy goals, but are rarely integrated with collective bargaining and sometimes—as in the case of the Milan Employment Pact—create problems for applying collective agreements.

Because a focus on partnerships with employers should not obscure the need for unions to find new agendas and organize new groups of workers, we have pointed to partnerships that contribute to broadening support for unionization. This is possible in all of the countries. Examples include German partnerships to use collective bargaining to conclude agreements addressing new issues; Italian partnerships to reform the welfare state and involve workers in the policy process; American and Spanish partnerships to improve workforce development (or 'lifelong learning') institutions; and British partnerships to improve contingent work.

As with other union revitalization phenomena, however, there is little evidence showing how widespread these kinds of partnerships are, and they all raise questions about their limitations. The case of the Seattle building trades, for example, illustrates a partnership linked to coalition-building with organizations located in working-class, minority neighbourhoods. It remains to be seen, however, whether the payoff from partnership at the local level can be sustained in the broader geo-political context. This case, as with most others, shows that revitalization is incremental, not wholesale, and limited to places that appear small in comparison to the national units of analysis this study is built around. Isolated instances cannot be expected to turn the overall tide of receding union density, they must be replicated and infused into the broader socio-political arena. By comparison, in countries where unions benefit from institutionalized frameworks, national social partnership currently suffers increasingly from a neo-liberal political turn and from the failure of unions to respond proactively. Thus, we find that integrating social partnership into a broad revitalization strategy is often frustrated by a combination of external challenges from government and employer strategies, and internal organizational problems of the unions.

In sum, despite the proliferation of literature about labour–management partnerships and the widespread belief that they ensure better outcomes for workers when unions are strong, there is still little understanding of how they can help unions revive themselves. In this chapter, we have developed a framework for considering the costs and benefits of social partnership for unions, an important project, given the strategy's importance for so many European and American unions. We find that partnerships built on broadly appealing policy agendas, an institutionalized role for unions, and strong union capacities produce detectable increases in bargaining power, membership density, or political power. Unfortunately, the vast majority of partnerships lack those qualities and tend to feed into the process of union decline.

Notes

1. Cooperation has, in our usage, a much broader definition than partnership. Cooperation occurs in nearly every workplace and bargaining relationship, even where it is not formalized as a partnership or shaped by a union capable of wielding countervailing power.
2. While making no claim to being comprehensive, the following section will enable the reader to pick up our arguments in their relationship to selected bodies of English-language literature on social partnership and labour–management partnership in the various countries, as well as the applicable concepts in the union revitalization literature. This approach does not do justice to the existing German, Spanish, and Italian literature. However, in addition to the obvious argument of limited space, it is also not the intention of this chapter to provide such an extensive treatment.
3. For evidence on the widespread use of PLAs, see the anti-PLA website operated by the Associated Builders and Contractors (Anonymous 2003). The agreement exists in the urban strongholds of the labour movement such as Boston, Chicago, and Detroit; in upcoming union cities like Las Vegas and Los Angeles; and even on federal government construction projects in the hinterlands of Idaho and eastern Washington.
4. While the term has appeared often in the titles of publications in recent years, most authors do not attempt to define its usage.
5. VW is a notable exception to this because the company is not a member of the employers' association and therefore it negotiates all contracts directly with the IG Metall. The union has an intensive working arrangement with the various works councils at the company.
6. In late 1999, VW proposed hiring 5,000 unemployed workers at a fixed monthly pay rate of DM 5,000 (ca. € 2,556) to produce a new model. Under this scheme, working time would not be fixed but employees would be obliged to work as long as necessary (up to the statutory maximum working week of 48 hours) to reach a certain production target without any overtime or other extra pay. Moreover, Saturdays were to become a regular working day. Two years later the company concluded a set of agreements with the IG Metall for new pay and working time provisions below the level set by the main VW company agreement, but equivalent to the level of the sectoral collective agreement for metalworking. Furthermore, the agreements include innovative provisions on continuing training, work organization and co-determination rights (Schulten 2001).
7. Under the subsequent government, the unions negotiated a series of national pacts. The first two pacts (1992 and 1993) replaced the wage indexation system (a popular program which had created problems both for employers and unions (Locke and Thelen 1995) with a new system of collective bargaining operating simultaneously at the local and national levels. Subsequent pacts dealt with other controversial issues such as pension reform (1995) and contingent workers (1996), in both cases, making the labour market more flexible

while providing protections for workers and some control to unions. The 1996 agreement also encouraged territorial partnerships involving a large number of stakeholders (banks, universities, cooperatives, nonprofits, etc.) to supplement collective bargaining and promote economic development in Southern Italy. The 'Christmas Pact' of 1998 further expanded the range of issues in which the government consulted employers associations and unions, and devolved certain functions to the social partners for bipartite regulation.

References

Ackers, P. and Payne, J. (1998). 'British Trade Unions and Social Partnership: Rhetoric, Reality, and Strategy'. *International Journal of Human Resource Management*, 9/3: 529–50.

Andersen, S. and Mailand, M. (2002). *The Role of Employers and Trade Unions in Multipartite Social Partnerships*. Copenhagen: The Copenhagen Centre.

Arrowsmith, J. (2002). *United Kingdom. Partnership 'Alive and Well'*. EIRO, available at www.eiro.eurofound.ie/2002/05/Feature/UK0205103F.html edn.

Artiles Martin, A. (2002). *2001 Annual Review for Spain*, EIRO, available at www.eiro.eurofound.ie/about/2002/01/feature/ES0201152F.html edn.

Artiles Martin, A. and Moner, R. A. (2003). 'Between Decentralisation and Centralisation of Collective Bargaining'. *Industrielle Beziehungen*, 10/1: 64–96.

Baccaro, L. (2001). ' "Aggregative" and "Deliberative" Decision-making Procedures: A Comparison of Two Southern European Factories'. *Politics and Society*, 29/2: 243–71.

——(2002). 'The Construction of "Democratic" Corporatism in Italy'. *Politics and Society*, 30/2: 327–57.

——Carrieri, M., and Damiano, C. (2003). 'The Resurgence of the Italian Confederal Unions: Will It Last?'. *European Journal of Industrial Relations*, 9/1: 43–59.

——Hamann, K., and Turner, L. (2003). 'The Politics of Labour Movement Revitalization: The Need for a Revitalized Perspective'. *European Journal of Industrial Relations*, 9/1: 119–33.

Banks, A. and Metzgar, J. (1989). 'Participating in Management: Union Organizing on a New Terrain'. *Labor Research Review*, 14: 1–56.

Behrens, M., Fichter, M., and Frege, C. M. (2003). 'Unions in Germany: Regaining the Initiative?' *European Journal of Industrial Relations*, 9/1: 25–42.

Brecht, H. and Höland, A. (2001). 'Gewerkschaften und politische Bündnisse'. *WSI-Mitteilungen*, 54/8: 501–7.

Christopherson, S. and Storper, M. (1987). 'The Effects of Flexible Specialization on the Labor Market and Industrial Politics'. *Industrial and Labor Relations Review*, 42: 331–47.

CNA (2002). *Kaiserwatch*, www.calnurses.org.

Deakin, S., Hobbs, R., Konzelmann, S., and Wilkinson, F. (2002). 'Partnership, Ownership and Control: The Impact of Corporate Governance on Employment Relations'. *Employee Relations*, 24/3: 335–52.

Eaton, A. and Kriesky, J. (2001). 'Union Organizing Under Neutrality and Card Check Agreements'. *Industrial and Labor Relations Review*, 55/1: 42–59.

Erlich, M. (1986). *With our Hands: The Story of Carpenters in Massachusetts*. Philadelphia, PA: Temple University Press.

European Commission (2002). *Industrial Relations in Europe 2002*. Luxembourg: Office for Official Publications of the European Communities.

Fraile, L. (1999). 'Tightrope: Spanish Unions and Labor Market Segmentation', in A. Martin and G. Ross, (eds.), *The Brave New World of European Labor*. New York: Berghahn Books.

Frost, A. (2001). 'Creating and Sustaining Local Union Capabilities: The Role of the National Union'. *Relationnes Industrielles*, 56/2: 307–35.

Gerlach, F. and Ziegler, A. (2000). 'Territoriale Beschaeftigungspakte in Deutschland—Neue Wege der Beschaeftigungsfoerderung?' *WSI-Mitteilungen*, 53/7: 430–7.

Gray, G., Myers, D., and Myers, P. (1999). 'Cooperative Provisions in Labor Agreements: a New Paradigm?'. *Monthly Labor Review*, 122/1: 29–45.

Guest, D. E. and Peccei, R. (2001). 'Partnership at Work: Mutuality and the Balance of Advantage'. *British Journal of Industrial Relations*, 39/2: 207–36.

Haddock, B. (2002). 'Italy in the 1990s: Policy Concertation Resurgent', in S. Berger and H. Compston (eds.), *Policy Concertation and Social Partnership in Western Europe. Lessons for the 21st Century*. New York: Berghahn.

Hall, P. A. and Soskice, D. (2001). *Varieties of Capitalism: The Institutional Foundations of Comparative Advantage*. Oxford: Oxford University Press.

Hamann, K. (1998). 'Spanish Unions: Institutional Legacy and Responsiveness to Economic and Industrial Change'. *Industrial and Labor Relations Review*, 51/3: 424–44.

—— and Martínez Lucio, M. (2003). 'Strategies of Union Revitalization in Spain: Negotiating Change and Fragmentation'. *European Journal of Industrial Relations*, 9/1: 61–78.

Heery, E. (2002). 'Partnership versus Organizing: Alternative Futures for British Trade Unionism'. *Industrial Relations Journal*, 33/1: 20–35.

—— Kelly, J., and Waddington, J. (2003). 'Union Revitalization in Britain'. *European Journal of Industrial Relations*, 9/1: 79–97.

—— Conley H., Delbridge, R., and Stewart, P. (2004). 'Seeking Partnership for the Contingent Workforce', in M. Martínez Lucio and M. Stuart (eds.), *Assessing Partnership: The Prospects for and Challenges of Modernizing Employment Relations*. London: Routledge.

Heidemann, W. (2001). 'Bausteine für lebenslanges Lernen: Tarifvertrag zur Weiterbildung'. *Die Mitbestimmung*, 47/10: 58–9.

Heidenreich, M. (2001). 'Die Zukunftsfähigkeit der industriellen Beziehungen. Das Beispiel des VW-Tarifmodells'. *Gegenwartskunde. Zeitschrift für Gesellschaft, Wirtschaft, Politik und Bildung*, 50/3: 353–62.

Herod, A. (2001). *Labor Geographies*. New York: Guilford Press.

Huber, B. and Hofmann, J. (2001). 'Der Tarifvertrag zur Qualifizierung in der Metall- und Elektroindustrie Baden-Württembergs'. *WSI-Mitteilungen*, 54/8: 464–6.

Hyman, R. (2001*a*). 'Some Problems of Partnership and Dilemmas of Dialogue', in C. Kjaergaard and S. Westphalen (eds.), *From Collective Bargaining to Social Partnerships: New Roles of the Social Partners in Europe*. Copenhagen: The Copenhagen Centre.

—— (2001*b*). *Understanding European Trade Unionism: Between Market, Class, and Society*. London: Sage.

IG Chemie (2003). 8 May 2003-last update, *Chemie-Tarifpaket 2003. 2,6 Prozent mehr Entgelt, VIII/30*, available at www.igbce.de/IGBCE/CDA/Artikelseite/0,2888,artikelId%3D6250,00.html [18 June 2003].

Juravich, T. (1998). 'Employee Involvement, Work Reorganization, and the New Labor Movement: Toward a Radical Integration'. *New Labor Forum*, Spring/Summer Issue: 84–91.

Katz, H. C. (1985). *Shifting Gears: Changing Labor Relations in the U.S. Automotive Industry*. Cambridge, MA: MIT Press.

—— (1993). 'The Decentralization of Collective Bargaining: A Literature Review and Comparative Analysis'. *Industrial and Labor Relations Review*, 47/1: 3–22.

Kelly, J. (1998). *Rethinking Industrial Relations*. London: Routledge.

—— (2004). 'Social Partnership Agreements in Britain: Labor Cooperation and Compliance'. *Industrial Relations*, 43/1: 267–92.

Kjaergaard, C. (2001). 'From Collective Bargaining to Social Partnerships', in C. Kjaergaard and S. Westphalen (eds.), *From Collective Bargaining to Social Partnerships: New Roles of the Social Partners in Europe*. Copenhagen: The Copenhagen Centre.

Klare, K. (1988). 'The Labor–Management Cooperation Debate: A Workplace Democracy Perspective'. *Harvard Civil Rights–Civil Liberties Law Review*, 23: 39–83.

Kochan, T. A., Katz, H. C., and McKersie, R. (1986). *The Transformation of American Industrial Relations*. New York: Basic Books.

Leroy, G. (2002). 'Smart Growth for Cities: It's a Union Thing'. *WorkingUSA*, 6/1: 56–76.

Linder, M. (1999). *Wars of Attrition*. Iowa City: Fanpìhuà Press.

Lo Faro, A. (2002). 'Fairness at Work? The Italian White Paper on Labour Market Reform'. *Industrial Law Journal*, 31/2: 190–98.

Locke, R. (1992). 'The Demise of the National Union in Italy: Lessons for Comparative Industrial Relations Theory'. *Industrial and Labor Relations Review*, 45/2: 229–49.

——and Baccaro, L. (1999). 'The Resurgence of Italian Unions?', in A. Martin and G. Ross (eds.), *The Brave New World of European Labor*. New York: Berghahn Books, 217–68.

——and Thelen, K. (1995). 'Apples and Oranges Revisited: Contextualized Comparisons and the Study of Comparative Labor Politics'. *Politics and Society*, 23/3: 337–67.

Lope, A., Gilbert, F., and de Villacian, D. (2002). *The Local Regulation of the New Forms of Employment and Work. The Case of Catalonia*. Milan: LOCLEVCONC—Project on Local Level Concertation.

Mailand, M. and Andersen, S. K. (2001). *Spain. Social Partnerships in Europe. The Role of the Employers and Trade Unions*. Copenhagen: The Copenhagen Centre.

Martínez Lucio, M. and Blyton, P. (1995). 'Constructing the Post-Fordist State? The Politics of Labour Market Flexibility in Spain'. *West European Politics*, 18/2: 340–60.

——and Stuart, M. (2002). 'Assessing Partnership: the Prospects for, and Challenges of Modernisation'. *Employee Relations*, 24/3: 252–61.

Mauer, A. and Seifert, H. (2001). 'Betriebliche Beschäftigungs- und Wettbewerbsbündnisse—Strategie für Krisenbetriebe oder neue regelungspolitische Normalität?'. *WSI-Mitteilungen*, 54/8: 490–500.

Mills, N. (2001). 'New Strategies for Union Survival and Revival'. *Journal of Labor Research*, 22/3: 599–613.

Müller-Jentsch, W. (1999). *Konfliktpartnerschaft. Akteure und Institutionen der industriellen Beziehungen*. Schriftenreihe Industrielle Beziehungen 1, 3rd edn., München-Mering: Rainer Hampp Verlag.

Munro, A. and Rainbird, H. (2000). 'The New Unionism and the New Bargaining Agenda: UNISON–Employer Partnerships on Workplace Learning in Britain'. *British Journal of Industrial Relations*, 38/2: 223–40.

Neumann, G. (2000). 'Bündnisse für Arbeit in Deutschland—Ein Überblick'. *WSI-Mitteilungen*, 53/7: 419–29.

Northrup, H. (1997). 'Construction Programs to Regain Jobs: Background and Overview'. *Journal of Labor Research*, 18/1: 1–15.

Paparella, D. and Rinolfi, V. (2002). *CGIL Organises General Strike*. EIRO Online, 14 March 2002. www.eiro.eurofound.ie/2003/03/InBrief/IT0303101N.html edn.

Parker, M. and Slaughter, J. (1994). *Working Smart: A Union Guide to Participation Programs and Reengineering*. Detroit: Labor Notes.

——(1997). 'Advancing Unionism on the New Terrain', in B. Nissen, (ed.), *Unions and Workplace Reorganization*. Detroit: Wayne State University Press.

Preuss, G. and Frost, A. (2003). 'The Rise and Decline of Labor–Management Cooperation'. *California Management Review*, 45/2: 85–106.

Pries, L. (2002). '5000 × 5000: Ende gewerkschaftlicher Tarifpolitik oder innovativer betrieblich-tariflicher Sozialpakt?'. *Industrielle Beziehungen*, 9/2: 222–35.

Regalia, I. (2002). *Introduction and Summary of Main Findings*. Milan: LOCLEVCONC Project on Local Level Concertation.

Rehder, B. (2002). *The Interaction of Pacts for Employment and Competitiveness and the Collective Bargaining System in Germany*. Cologne: Max Planck Institut fur Gesellschaftsforschung, Unpublished Manuscript.

Reynolds, D. B. (2002). *Taking the High Road: Communities Organize for Economic Change*. Armonk, NY: ME Sharpe.

Rigby, M. (2003). 'Spanish Trade Unions and the Provision of Continuous Training: Partnership at a Distance'. *Human Resources Abstracts*, 38/1: 5–136.

Ruiz, J. A. (2001). 'Without Unions, but Socialist: The Spanish Socialist Party and its Divorce from its Union Confederation (1982–96)'. *Politics and Society*, 29/2: 273–96.

Schmidt, W. (1985). *Sozialer Frieden und Sozialpartnerschaft. Kapital und Arbeit in der Gesellschaftspolitik der westdeutschen Christdemokraten 1945 bis 1953*. Frankfurt (Main): Lang.

Schroeder, W. and Weinert, R. (1999). 'Managing Decentralization: The Strategy of Institutional Differentiation in German Industrial Relations'. *German Politics and Society*, 17/4: 52–73.

Schulten, T. (2001). *Agreements Signed on Volkswagen's 5000 × 5000 Project*, www.eiro. eurofound.ie/about/2001/09/feature/DE0109201F.html edn.

Streeck, W. (1984). *Industrial Relations in West Germany: A Case Study of the Car Industry*. London: Heinemann.

Stuart, M. and Martínez Lucio, M. (2002). 'Social Partnership and the Mutual Gains Organization: Remaking Involvement and Trust at the British Workplace'. *Economic and Industrial Democracy*, 23/2:177–200.

Teague, P. (1989). 'The British TUC and the European Community'. *Millennium: Journal of International Studies*, 18/1: 29–45.

Thelen, K. (2001). 'Varieties of Labor Politics in the Developed Democracies', in P. A. Hall and D. Soskice (eds.), *Varieties of Capitalism*. Cambridge: Cambridge University Press.

Tondorf, K. (2001). 'Gender Mainstreaming in der Tarifpolitik'. *WSI-Mitteilungen*, 54: 434–41.

Turner, L. (1991). *Democracy at Work*. Ithaca, NY: ILR Press.

—— (1998). *Fighting for Partnership*. Ithaca, NY: ILR Press.

WAI (2000). *High Road Partnership Report*. Washington, DC: AFL-CIO.

—— (2002). *Helping Low-Wage Workers Succeed Through Innovative Union Partnerships*. Washington, DC: AFL-CIO.

Walton, R., Cutcher-Gershenfeld, J., and McKersie, R. (1994). *Strategic Negotiations: A Theory of Change in Labor-Management Relations*. Ithaca, NY: ILR Press.

Wells, D. M. (1987). *Empty Promises: Quality of Working Life Programs and the Labor Movement*. New York: Monthly Review Press.

6

Unions as Political Actors:
A Recipe for Revitalization?

KERSTIN HAMANN AND JOHN KELLY

INTRODUCTION

Political action has been one of the most prominent forms of activity undertaken by unions and union movements in our country cases. This is mainly because of the central role of the state in devising economic, social, and industrial relations policies in response to global economic pressures (see Weiss 2003; Behrens, Hamann, and Hurd, Chapter 2, this volume). Although governments are constrained by national political and economic institutions, including welfare regimes (Hall and Soskice 2001; Swank 2002), their policy choices are not entirely predetermined by these factors (Weiss 2003). As governments retain some degree of choice, they become valuable targets for unions in their quest to acquire and deploy political power. Changes in both national and international economies have, in many ways, undercut the organizational base for unions, and diminished both their propensity to act through strikes or other sanctions and, consequently, their economic power.

Parallel to their decrease in economic power, unions also lost political allies in government just when protection from the state was most needed to compensate for their weaknesses in the economic arena. The period since the late 1980s has witnessed a considerable increase in state intervention in the economy as many governments have sought to reform labour markets and welfare systems in order to facilitate national competitiveness in a context of increasingly global competition. This occurred alongside a move towards market regulation of the economy—a move that was spearheaded and managed by national governments, which became active planners and implementers of this process (Lodovici 2000). These reforms have extended either directly or indirectly to the sphere of industrial relations. Many industrial relations issues have been regulated, for instance through the enactment of EU directives (such as work time). Governments have also implemented cuts in welfare provisions, such as unemployment benefits, in an attempt to control public spending as well as labour market reforms to increase flexibility and heighten the competitiveness of national economies. In addition governments set the 'legal framework within which unions must operate' and favourable 'Legal reform will enable unions to become more effective...' (Levi 2003: 46). Many of these national policy innovations have been unfavourable to labour.

In analysing union political action, we address two questions: How have unions become involved in the political process in response to these developments? And to what extent has their political action contributed to revitalization? In each case we pay particular attention to differences and similarities across countries at a point in time and to changes and continuities within a country over time, especially since the early 1980s.

We analyse these questions drawing on the theoretical framework developed in Chapter 3 of this volume. That is, union responses to the current 'union crisis' are shaped by the following factors: economic and political institutions, the strategies of employers and the state, union identity, and union leadership. Our analysis primarily focuses on the major unions and confederations at the national level. We are aware that both the supranational and the subnational level are of increasing importance for union activity, and that unions within countries vary widely in their use of political action. Yet, for the purposes of cross-national comparison, we concentrate on the national level, which still constitutes the primary arena for many unions, and on major unions or confederations, which tend to be the most influential actors in national politics. Finally, we focus on the most important forms of political action in relation to revitalization for each country to capture major trends that are useful for comparative purposes.

CONCEPTUALIZING THE FORMS AND OUTCOMES OF POLITICAL ACTION

Political action is designed to influence the state's policy-making process and involves union involvement at many different levels of government. As noted in Chapter 2, three spheres of activity fall within the political domain: elections, legislation, and the implementation of policies.[1] Unions' electoral activity may involve candidate selection, participation in electoral campaigns, and voter mobilization. Within the electoral sphere unions may participate as independent organizations or as bodies that are institutionally or financially linked to a political party. In regard to the legislature, unions typically become involved in either initiating measures of their own or supporting or blocking measures emanating from elected party representatives. Unions will clearly be interested in procedural legislation that affects their rights to organize, represent workers, or take collective action. They are also likely to be concerned with legislation that directly or indirectly affects the welfare of their members, such as legislation on pensions, unemployment benefits, or working time. Finally, unions may also engage in political activity to ensure that legislation is effectively implemented, for example, by regulatory agencies covering minimum wages or health and safety. In seeking to influence the legislature and the administration unions can play a variety of different roles: they can operate as a negotiating partner in a social pact with government; they may operate as a lobbying group; they may function as a social movement, using collective action such as general strikes to pressure politicians (see Frege, Heery, and Turner, Chapter 8, this volume); finally unions can act as litigants, using the courts to challenge the legality of government measures or actions.

While analytically distinct, these forms of political action can be used in conjunction—for example, strikes might be used simultaneously with lobbying. Similarly, there is no clear link between the issues that motivate union activity and a particular form of political action. For instance, beneficial social policies can be pursued through electoral activity (anticipating specific policies once the preferred party is elected), lobbying, strikes, social pacts, or legal avenues (for instance, where the implementation of EU directives is concerned). These different forms of political action are also distinguished by the degree to which they depend on strategic interaction with governments or parties, that is, they will be more effective in the presence of a receptive or friendly party/government rather than a hostile one. For example, the extent to which unions can rely on their ties to political parties depends on the extent to which the party is willing to incorporate labour demands; social pacts can only be signed when governments are willing. We disaggregate political action into different forms because in a comparative context we want to find out why unions use different types of political action, and how successful these are in their respective political, economic, and social contexts. This allows us to link political action to union revitalization.

FORMS OF POLITICAL ACTION IN FIVE COUNTRIES

United Kingdom

The first major change in recent British politics has been the election of the Labour Party to government in May 1997 under the leadership of Tony Blair. It secured a parliamentary majority of 179 (and a similar majority, of 167, in the 2001 election), which meant that its legislative programme would almost certainly be passed even in the face of sizeable opposition from within its own ranks. The second key development has been a growing antagonism between the industrial and political wings of the British labour movement.

Despite this recent antagonism, however, the link to the Labour Party remains the primary form of union political activity. Twenty-two unions with a membership of 5.1 million are affiliated to the Labour Party and seek to influence policy through the regular channels of the party's decision-making process, in particular the annual conference.[2] During the long period of Conservative rule and union exclusion from state policy-making (1979–97), the Labour Party underwent a process of radical restructuring in four key areas (Minkin 1992). First, the autonomy of the party leadership was enhanced at the expense of both the party conference and organized labour. Policy formation was shifted into a leader and minister-dominated executive committee, the Joint Policy Forum, and a new pre-conference discussion body, the National Policy Forum, in which unions were allocated just thirty out of 180 seats (Fielding 2003: 128–37). Second, the union share of votes at the party conference was reduced from approximately 90 per cent in 1993 to 50 per cent by 1998. Third, the party diversified its funding sources to reduce its dependency on union income: by 1995 it obtained just 45 per cent of its annual income from the unions, down from 77 per cent in 1984 (McIlroy 1998). Finally, a process of policy convergence by

Labour towards a broadly neo-liberal economic policy meant that the Conservative anti-union laws would be preserved (Hay 1999: 105–33). Union compliance with the restructuring that created New Labour was secured in part through party pledges on two issues central to the union agenda: a law that would compel employers to recognize unions where a majority of the workforce voted in favour and a statutory national minimum wage. Both measures were enacted in 1999.

Since the beginning of Blair's government, relations with the unions have undergone a significant shift. Initial union enthusiasm soon gave way to frustration with the slowness and content of legislative change, tempered by expectations of greater union influence in Labour's second term. Since the mid-1990s unions have found it increasingly difficult either to place items on the legislative agenda or to restrain the recent New Labour agenda of privatization and public service reform (McIlroy 2000). While the government is eager to have new public hospitals and schools financed and managed by private firms, unions are equally keen to avoid private capital and the possible fragmentation of national bargaining and deterioration of pay and conditions. The result has been a strain on the union–party relationship. Leadership elections in the major unions since 2001 have invariably been won by candidates highly critical of New Labour, such as Woodley in the Transport Workers (TGWU). Several major unions, such as GMB and RMT, have cut their funding to the Labour Party; four unions have conducted inquiries into the union–party link (train drivers, firefighters, GMB, and UNISON); and two have even balloted members on disaffiliation from Labour (television workers (BECTU) and white-collar transport workers (TSSA)).

However, the discontent should be kept in perspective: every union conference vote on affiliation in 2002–3 has overwhelmingly endorsed the status quo (LRD 2003; Ludlam and Taylor 2003). Moreover the unions have continued to provide substantial electoral support for the Labour Party. In the 2001 election, for example, turnout among union members was 5 percentage points higher than among non-members, and the incidence of Labour voting was 8 percentage points higher among trade unionists (Ludlam and Taylor 2003: tables 1 and 2). Working through regional structures of the Trade Union Labour Party Liaison Committee, unions mobilized even more activists in more districts in the 2001 election than in 1997, targeting 146 constituencies in 2001 as compared to ninety-three constituencies in 1997 (Ludlam and Taylor 2003: 16).

Lobbying of government ministers and members of parliament does not rank as a major strategy of British unions despite the fact that lobbying itself—especially of select committees—has become an increasingly vital part of the policy-making process in recent years (Norton 1999; John 2002: 17–23). Trade unions still only account for one percent of the clients of professional lobbyists (John 2002: 13) and the Trades Union Congress (TUC) appointed its first parliamentary lobbyist only in 1996 (Heery 1998: 343). Many union–government links after 1997 were rather *ad hoc* and since 2001 the TUC has, therefore, sought to increase their frequency and formality (TUC 2002: 164). Individual unions, such as the printworkers GPMU, have taken similar steps to increase their input into governmental and EU policy-making (*Newsletter* 2003). However, union lobbying occurs in very unpropitious circumstances because the government has a large parliamentary majority and strong party discipline means that many MPs are reluctant to vote against the party line. Consequently, union lobbying of individual MPs on major issues has proved relatively ineffectual. For example, unions lobbied extensively to reform the union recognition law so as to curb employer campaigning and include small workplaces within its remit: both these and other union demands were rejected by the government (DTI 2003). By contrast, the TUC has enjoyed more success within the institutions of the European Union, lobbying around the content of Directives, most recently on information and consultation for example (TUC 2002).

British unions have made extensive use of the European Court of Justice (ECJ), successfully gaining rights denied them by both Conservative and Labour governments. In 2001, for example, the ECJ ruled that under the Working Time Directive, workers employed on short-term contracts had the right to receive 4 weeks of paid holidays per year, overturning the Labour government's limitation of the right to those who had worked at least 13 weeks for their employer. A survey of all ECJ cases between 1958 and 1998 found that no less than 25 per cent of 'Social Provision cases' emanated from Britain, a figure that was disproportionately high in relation to the size of the country within the European Union (Sweet and Brunell 2000). In the face of ECJ rulings the government has had no choice other than to amend the law. Legal action has, therefore, proved effective in forcing government compliance with the letter and spirit of European Directives. Social pacts have not featured as a revitalization strategy in Britain. Although Labour has engaged in far more consultation with unions than its Conservative predecessors, it has confined the union role to consultative status on single-issue working parties and advisory groups such as the Low Pay Commission and the Public Services Forum (TUC 2003*a, b*).

In summary, British unions have enjoyed modest success through political action, more so in the 1990s than in recent years. Although the union recognition law has assisted a limited recovery of membership (see Heery and Adler, Chapter 4, this volume), unions and the TUC have not succeeded in positioning themselves as major political actors with whom governments must interact and negotiate.

United States

Political action by US unions has historically taken three main forms: links with the Democratic Party, voter mobilization, and lobbying of federal and state government. Throughout the 1980s and into the early 1990s this approach appeared to be paying off: the Democrats retained control of the lower house (the House of Representatives) through the Reagan (1980–88) and Bush presidencies (1988–92); they won control of the upper house (Senate) in 1988 and secured the presidency in 1992. Finally, in 1993, unions secured their long-running demand for a government inquiry into labour law in the form of the relatively pro-labour Dunlop Commission. The union certification law, first established in 1932 to assist union membership, had increasingly turned into a major constraint on growth and from a union perspective was in serious need of reform (see Hurd, Milkman, and Turner 2003; Heery and Adler, Chapter 4, this volume).

During the 1990s unions attempted to strengthen still further their ties to the Democratic Party. For example, after the 1995 election of John Sweeney as American Federation of Labor-Congress of Industrial Organizations (AFL-CIO) President, the Federation voted to spend $35 million in the 1996 congressional elections (in addition to the $65 million that would come from individual unions through Political Action Committees, PACs) (Dark 2001: 184–5). Union expenditure in the 2000 election appears to have been even higher (Freeman 2002: 1).

Union electoral activity does make a significant difference to voter turnout and to the Democratic vote. Freeman (2002) found that in the 2000 Presidential election union member turnout was four percentage points higher than among non-members, even when other variables were controlled for and the Democratic vote was eight percentage points higher. Radcliff (2001) also found a positive, though smaller, union effect on turnout over a longer time period. Following the Republican victories in 1994, when they took control of both Houses of Congress from the Democrats, increased union finance and voter mobilization appeared to have delivered some success: in 1996 Clinton was re-elected for a second term and the Democrats gained nine seats in the lower House, though were still in a minority. By 2002, however, the outcomes looked very different: in part because of significantly increased corporate expenditure, Republicans won the Presidency in 2000 and consolidated their hold on both Houses (Dark 2001: 149). It is true, the 2000 Presidential result was very close and a victory for the Democratic candidate Al Gore in just one more large state, such as Florida, would have given him the Presidency. But this proposition is seriously misleading, because it downplays the continued Republican majorities in Congress.

Both these electoral outcomes and the free trade policies of the Clinton presidency, unpopular with many unions, exacerbated latent, but powerful, tendencies towards union organizational autonomy and pragmatism (Ludlam, Bodah, and Coates 2001; Shoch 2001). The Teamsters' union successfully negotiated with the federal government in 2000–1 to protect jobs in Alaska, despite protests from environmental groups. In New York a number of radical organizing unions such as Service Employees International Union (SEIU), HERE, and UNITE backed the Republican candidate for governor, believing they could negotiate better agreements with him than with his Democratic rival. The same unions have also contributed a small but growing percentage of their political funds to Republican candidates; SEIU, for example, gave around 3 per cent of its political expenditure to Republican candidates in the early 1990s, but that figure has increased to 9 per cent since 2000 (Phillips-Fein 2003). These divisions among unions were compounded by the resignation of the Carpenters' union from the AFL-CIO in 2002, ostensibly in protest at the Federation's failure to promote organizing with sufficient vigour.

Lobbying has been a prominent form of political action in the United States that is sometimes virtually indistinguishable from electoral support. The number of labour-oriented electoral funding bodies—PACs—increased from 201 in 1974 to 325 in 1998. The Federal Election Commission listed the Teamsters Union, the Labourers Union, and the Electrical Workers Union among the top six PAC contributors to Federal Campaigns in 1995–96 (Hrebenar, Burbank, and Benedict 1999: 255–6). This is an example of electoral support as well as lobbying because the PAC contributors are not just aiming for electoral victory but also hope for access and influence through their campaign contributions. This 'sponsorship' overlaps with other lobbying activities including contacts with elected representatives and bureaucrats. For example at the height of the ultimately unsuccessful campaign to reform US healthcare in summer 1994, fifty-three union organizers worked full time on lobbying representatives and senators (Dark 2001: 168). During the mid-1990s' debates on free trade, the AFL-CIO bolstered its lobbying with threats to cut funds to individual Democrats, a threat rendered credible by their increased dependency on union finance (Shoch 2001: 297–300). This intensive lobbying and campaign spending has often paid off. According to the annual survey of the AFL-CIO's Committee on Political Education, the percentage of union-favoured bills that succeed is far higher under a Democratic than a Republican president (Freeman and Medoff 1984: 197; Dark 2001: 165–6). This finding indicates that the success of union lobbying is highly context-dependent, which resonates with the more general finding that the impact of interest group and PAC lobbying on congressional voting is variable (Baumgartner and Leech 1998: 134). Finally, we should note that neither social pacts nor general strikes have played a role in the revitalization strategies of the US unions.

Political action is a substantial component of the repertoire of US trade union action, consuming sizable amounts of money and time. Yet, in recent years the returns for this union effort have been increasingly meagre. Control of the Presidency, House, and Senate—central to US union political effectiveness—remains firmly in the hands of the Republican Party despite unprecedented levels of unions' electoral expenditure. In the absence of radical legal changes at federal level that might have come through political action, unions' organizing efforts have failed to halt the decline of membership and density (see Heery and Adler, Chapter 4, this volume).

Germany

The crisis of German unions is expressed in falling membership, increasing fragmentation of the employers' organizations, weakening ties to the governing Social Democratic Party (SPD) under the leadership of Chancellor Gerhard Schröder, and the failure of social pacts. Much as in Spain in 1982, unions had hoped that their position would be strengthened when Schröder was elected in 1998 after 16 years of conservative rule. Yet, 6 years after the return of the left, these hopes have been all but disappointed despite the initial positive response of the government and favourable legislation, for instance in the reform of the works councils. Rather than gaining strength, unions have witnessed an overall decline of their economic and political power in recent years.

Despite historically close ties between German unions and the SPD, the unions have largely maintained the autonomy from political parties they had established in the post-war period. Unions are prohibited from funding parties directly and are officially non-partisan. This tradition is reflected in the fact that while many senior officials of unions are in fact SPD members, others are high-ranking members of other parties including the Christian Democrats (CDU). Nevertheless, recent years have witnessed contradictory trends. On the one hand, the overlap in personnel and more generally, voters, between the SPD and the unions has declined: There are fewer union officials among SPD parliamentarians than 20 years ago; no union president gained a seat in the Bundestag after the 2002 election; and the president of ver.Di, the country's largest union, is not an SPD member. Yet, after the 1998 elections, which resulted in an SPD–Green coalition government, the number of union members in the lower house of parliament increased by twenty-five (277 out of a total of 669) and 241 out of the 298 SPD deputies were union members (DGB *Einblick* 07/99). In 2002, union members voted disproportionately for the SPD (51.2 per cent compared to 38.5 per cent of all voters), but in comparison with 1998, the share of union members voting for the SPD fell by 4.5 per cent (from 60.9 to 53.5 per cent), while the CDU/CSU gained 4.3 per cent of the union members' vote (DGB *Einblick* 17/02). These trends demonstrate that the ties between unions and the SPD are weakening but remain strong on the level of membership overlap. The same is true for links between unions and the conservative CDU, which marginalized the representation of workers' interests within its organization.

On the other hand, the prolonged period of CDU rule (1983–98) strained the traditional non-partisan policy of the DGB (German Trade Unions' Federation), the German unions' umbrella organization. In the 1998 election, and again in 2002, the confederation moved considerably closer to the SPD by openly campaigning for the party, a move that provoked a backlash from CDU union members (Silvia 1999: 97–8). Yet, the voice of the unions within the SPD has been weakened since the re-election of the SPD–Green coalition in 2002. Government proposals stemming from the Hartz Commission to reduce unemployment benefits and raise the mandatory retiring age to 67 met with intense hostility and protests from the unions but the measures were, nevertheless, passed by the lower house (Bundestag) in October 2003.

Unions also resort to lobbying, a practice that is long established in the German parliament, particularly on the level of the committees and in parliamentary hearings. Trade unions are particularly well represented in hearings of the Committee of Labour and Social Affairs. The impact of trade union lobbying is balanced, though, by the fact that other interest groups, including employers and outside 'experts', are also actively engaged in lobbying and invited to hearings. Occasionally, lobbying activities extend to corporatist-type meetings in the Chancellor's office (e.g. in the 1987 steel industry crisis or the coal industry crisis of the same year) (see von Beyme 1998: 54–65). In 2001, the DGB successfully negotiated legal extensions to the coverage of works councils in exchange for concessions over pension reforms. In the first round of elections under the new Act the number of individual works councillors increased by 11 per cent, the first increase for some years, although the number of organizations with works councils remained unchanged (EIRO 2002*a*; Schafer 2003: 13).

German unions have also become engaged in attempts at social concertation in recent years, a tradition that dates back to the early post-war period. In 1998, they participated in the Alliance for Jobs, a tripartite forum designed to create dialogue between the social partners about Germany's exceptionally high level of unemployment. Few initiatives emerged from the forum and it was not extended to other issues such as pensions. It did not approximate the Concerted Action of the 1960s and 1970s either in effectiveness or scope (Behrens, Fichter, and Frege 2003) and its relevance as a union revitalization strategy was always somewhat questionable. This judgment has been vindicated by the government's abandonment of the Alliance in spring 2002 and its promotion of unemployment benefit and pension reforms in autumn 2003 that had their origins in the Hartz Commission (see above). Even though the unions had been participants in the commission and had supported some of the initial reforms, they staunchly opposed the more recent policies promoted by the government.

Unions' use of the ECJ is infrequent, even though recently the police union considered suing the government in an attempt to force it to comply with the EU directives on working time regulation. Much like medical doctors, members of the police force want the time they spend on call to count as regular working time (*Saarbrücker Zeitung*, 19 February 2003). However, there is no evidence of any strategic use of legal action at the European level by unions comparable to the British case, in part because many of the EU social policy Directives have sought to implement measures such as controls on working time that already exist in Germany.

German unions have shown very little success in revitalization through strike action. One recent example was the IG Metall strike over working time in Eastern Germany, which was called off in June 2003 without an agreement, and which portrayed the union leadership as out of touch with key sections of its membership. Although the union has a new top leadership, the power struggle that preceded this change further deepened the impression that German unions are without direction. While leadership changes and decisions can potentially boost the relevance of political action for union revival, in the German case the most visible examples of union leadership have underscored the crisis of German unionism rather than generated revitalization.

Spain

Traditionally, one of the prominent forms of political action of Spanish trade unions was their relationship to leftist political parties. For the decade after the inception of democratic rule in Spain until the late 1980s, Spanish unions used their close ties to leftist political parties to gain access to the policy-making arena. This was particularly true for the UGT (General Workers' Union) and the Socialist Party (PSOE). That relationship deteriorated, however, when the PSOE government under Felipe González took office in 1982 and pursued economic and social policies at odds with union preferences. Formal and informal contacts between union and party leaderships were few and generally non-cooperative until the mid-1990s. The communist-oriented union CC.OO. (Workers' Commissions) had begun to increase its autonomy from the Communist Party (PCE) in the early 1980s, but the relationship between the union and the party did not become as hostile as between the Socialist Party and the UGT. Consequently, by the 1990s unions were left without strong ties to leftist parties and without the effective access to the legislature previously provided by the PSOE.

Since the mid-1990s, unions have used their new autonomy from leftist political parties to pursue more pragmatic relationships with all major parties, including the PSOE, indicating a timid rapprochement, and the governing conservative Popular Party (PP). The current ties to political parties are thus more informal and looser than in the early 1980s, but they are also broader in that they involve both the right, the left, and regional parties. Though differing on many policy issues with the unions, the PP government under Aznar has been willing to include unions in negotiations of issues pertinent to their interests and has established a pragmatic working relationship with the two main confederations. Initially, the main reason for this position was the PP's need to overcome its Francoist heritage and establish itself as a legitimate democratic force. In addition, its status as a minority government (1996–2000) meant that it sought support for its policies outside of parliament (Hamann 2001*a*).

Unions' support for parties at election time has changed substantially in the past twenty years. Union and party programmes and ideology became more distinctive particularly throughout the 1980s, which resulted in policy controversies and culminated in the decision of the UGT not to endorse the PSOE at all in the 1989 election. By the 2000 election, though, unions were officially non-partisan, but emphasized their programmatic proximity to leftist parties. The unions supported the coalition agreement between the socialist PSOE and the communist-led United Left (IU) prior to the 2000 election, for instance, without however explicitly asking union affiliates to vote for the leftist coalition (*El País*, 2 April 2000: 17). Union support for leftist parties was limited to rhetoric and programmatic endorsement and did not extend to financing, canvassing, or other mobilizing activities.

Social pacts formed a crucial component of Spanish union strategy until the mid-1980s but the growing conflict between unions and the PSOE government resulted in their demise until the mid-1990s. Since 1996 social pacts have primarily covered two of the issues central to the European resurgence of tripartite agreements: pensions and labour market reform (Goetschy 2000). Unions agreed in 1997 to accept new types of permanent contracts that facilitate the dismissal of workers, an issue on which they had long refused to concede. In return, restrictions on the use and types of temporary contracts were introduced in an attempt to reduce the high rate of workers on such contracts (about 30 per cent of the employed workforce). At the same time, the wage bargaining system has been subject to negotiation. Wage restraint, the third major issue in European social pacts, was conspicuously absent from the agenda until December 2001, when unions issued a recommendation that wages should be in line with predicted inflation rates while factoring in productivity. Moreover, unions also participate in the Social and Economic Council, an advisory tripartite body mandated by the constitution and established in 1992. Even though the Council has no policy-making prerogative, it presents a forum for tripartite discussion and policy recommendations.

Another pivotal feature of Spanish unions' political action is the use of strikes. Despite falling strike rates since the 1980s, Spain has, nonetheless, retained the highest level of strikes of our country cases: Spain lost 182 working days per 1,000 employees in all industries and services due to strikes between 1996 and 2000, compared to

Germany with two; the United Kingdom 21, the United States of America 61, and Italy 76 (Monger 2003). In addition, unions have organized national general strikes. Both major union confederations called general strikes in 1988, 1992, 1994, and 2002 to protest against governments' social and economic policies and labour market reforms, though with varying success. The 2002 strike is generally considered successful—in the months following the strike and numerous additional mobilizations and demonstrations the government repealed virtually all measures proposed in its unemployment benefits reform package. The strikes also illustrate the importance of union leaders' strategic choices. For instance, in negotiations with the government over a pension reform early in 2001, the UGT leadership decided that the government's proposal was unacceptable and refused to sign the agreement, while the CC.OO. accepted the agreement. Although the UGT leadership favoured a general strike against the reform plan, CC.OO. leaders opposed the idea, and the strike was not organized.

Parliamentary lobbying is not well developed in Spain, where the standing order of parliament mandates party discipline, and parliamentary party groups are very hierarchically structured, which renders lobbying individual deputies an ineffective strategy. Instead, unions retain permanent working relations with parliamentary party groups of both the left and the right. With the increased autonomy of the unions since the late 1980s, consultation and lobbying across parliamentary party groups has become the rule. Consequently, unions have regular contact with the parliamentary groups of all major parties (Tijeras 2000).

The heightened involvement of Spanish unions in political exchanges with the government—largely absent from the late 1980s to the mid-1990s—has certainly helped to boost the unions' revitalization efforts. For one, unions have again been included in social pacts, which grants them a voice and some influence in deciding on the contents of labour market and social policy reforms. That, and the strategic use of the general strike, re-established the unions as legitimate and important social and political actors. This participation in social pacts has been facilitated by the unions' distance from leftist parties and a pragmatic relationship with all major parties. Political action has, thus, played a major part in the revitalization of unions in Spain (Hamann and Martínez Lucio 2003).

Italy

Ties between unions and parties in Italy changed dramatically between 1992 and 1994, when the party system disintegrated (Baccaro, Carrieri, and Damiano 2003). The disappearance of the Socialist and Christian Democratic parties and the move towards the centre of the Communist Party (PCI) led each of the three main union confederations—CGIL, CISL, and UIL—to a policy of increased political independence. For example, all three confederations have 'incompatibility' rules that prevent union leaders from running for office (at least while they are union members). Traditionally, the left union confederation—the CGIL—acted as a 'transmission belt' for the influence of the communist party. Yet, today the CGIL's relationship with the Democratic Party of the Left (DS, successor to the PCI) and the other opposition parties is a far cry from the 'transmission belt' model. If anything, the direction of influence has reversed in recent years. A sizeable faction within the DS argues that the party should move away from soft 'third way' positions, embraced by the present leadership, and get closer to the positions of the CGIL and of the anti-global capitalism movement. An alternative faction within the DS advocates the need for reform of existing social and labour market protections, to make them better attuned to globalized markets. For this latter group, the unions (and especially the CGIL) are just one of the left's constituencies and support of the CGIL's position may alienate the electoral support of other groups in society. The leaders of the CGIL are quite explicitly supportive and even individually affiliated to the three major post-Communist parties.

The CISL has officially embraced a position of 'autonomy' from political parties. De facto, its leaders are divided between support for the Margherita (a centre–left Catholic party) and support for various centre–right parties. Although the top leadership of the UIL is formally affiliated to the Democratic Party of the Left, its intermediate leadership, however, seems to be divided. While no data are available on the vote of union members in the last political elections in 2001, traditional blue-collar areas have predominantly (but by no means overwhelmingly) supported the centre–left candidates (Franzosi 1995: 207–8). In Italy, union endorsement for political parties tends to be more subtle and plays out mostly on the local level where unions provide substantial support in campaigns for parties and candidates. The confederations as such tend to refrain from campaigning for a specific party. In other words, relations between unions and parties in Italy have become much looser and more fluid in recent years. Despite these changes in the party system, though, parliament has retained a crucial role in the policy-making process, and has thus remained a core target of interest groups'— including unions—lobbying activity (della Sala 1999).

Relations between government and unions also underwent a dramatic shift in the early 1990s. In the midst of a combined economic and political crisis the three union confederations signed what was to be the first of several social pacts. The 1993 agreement was both radical and wide-ranging, finally abolishing pay indexation (the *scala mobile*) and replacing it with a looser system in which pay rises would be regulated by inflation and productivity (Hyman 2001: 160). Subsequent pacts covered more specific issues such as pensions (1995), employment creation (1996 and 1998), and working time (1997) (Negrelli 2000: 95–101). Negotiations were often difficult and occasionally broke down, leading unions to call general strikes, as in 1994 on the issue of pension reform (Regini and Regalia 2000: 377).

The resurgence of the new social pacts can be primarily explained by the weakness of the national governments after the disintegration of the party system in the early 1990s. The three trade union confederations emerged as one of the few social forces with any widespread legitimacy, a position enhanced by their new-found unity. This unity contributed to their combined strength, and they were too powerful to be ignored, even by governments of the Right (Regini and Regalia 2000: 379). Economic weakness also prompted successive Italian governments, including the current right-wing Berlusconi administration, to engage the unions in national-level social bargaining as the support of the social partners promised to be a successful strategy in the move towards monetary union. Many of the reforms agreed through social pacts have not been especially welcome to unions, for example, the 2003 reforms to the dismissal laws were opposed by the CGIL, but union leaderships have tended to the view that it was preferable to be involved in negotiations rather than exercise opposition from outside (Hyman 2001: 164). Moreover, they also took the view that involvement in such talks would strengthen the union movement by enhancing its legitimacy and underlining its essential role in contemporary politics.

As in Spain, the Italian confederations have used the general strike as a means of protesting against government policy and of persuading the government to enter or resume negotiations. In December 2001 the Berlusconi government announced plans to eliminate the right of reinstatement for workers found to have been unfairly dismissed. When talks with the government broke down unions called a general strike for 16 April 2002. The resumption of negotiations eventually led to an agreement in July—the Pact for Italy—but also to a split among the confederations as the CGIL continued its opposition with another general strike in October that year. The inter-union split seemed however to have been short-lived: by April 2003 all three confederations were again involved in negotiations with the government over pension reforms and jointly organized a general strike in October 2003 (EIRO 2003*a*, *b*). In summary therefore, Italian unions have consolidated their position as key political actors through involvement in social pacts and through the strategic use of the general strike.

FORMS AND OUTCOMES OF POLITICAL ACTION

The five countries exhibit distinctive differences in the dominant forms of political action. Spain and Italy stand out for their use of negotiations with the government over labour market and welfare reforms, which have resulted in—and reflect—a considerable degree of political power. In both countries these achievements are fairly recent: Social pacts re-emerged in Spain only in 1996 and the Italian confederations only achieved their current political status after 1993. German unions have used electoral support for the SPD and negotiations with the government to secure a significant reform of the works council law in 2001; their campaigning helped the SPD obtain re-election in 2002 in a closely fought contest. Similarly, unions in the United Kingdom used negotiations with the Labour Party and government to obtain a new union recognition law. Electoral support has been one of the main forms of political action in the United Kingdom, much like in the United States, where unions have also heavily relied on lobbying. In other words, the forms of political action vary considerably.

However, if we organize the countries by the impact of political action on revitalization, the picture is rather different. It seems that unions in the Mediterranean countries have been most successful in extending and using their political power. Both right and left-wing governments in these countries have repeatedly included union leaders in negotiations over their proposed reforms and sought to reach agreement with them. It is true that the agenda covered by national pacts has largely been initiated by governments anxious to restrain public debt and enhance private sector competitiveness, as part of the EU criteria for monetary union, codified in 1997 (Pochet 2002). But even though unions have rarely secured all of their demands, they have frequently obtained sufficient concessions to sign agreements, and have sometimes done so through use of the general strike as well as participation in pacts. Meantime both union movements have also recorded some degree of revitalization on the membership dimension. Spanish union density has been slowly rising since the 1990s to almost 14 per cent after having fallen in the previous decade. Italian membership (excluding the large and growing number of union pensioners), began to recover from 1998 (see Heery and Adler, Chapter 4, this volume). What is less clear is precisely how, if at all, the exercise of political power has had an impact on membership growth.

The second group of countries comprises the United Kingdom and the United States as well as Germany. We find both similarities and differences in these three countries. In Germany and the United Kingdom, unions were successful in using their political influence and relations to leftist parties to secure some significant legal rights (union recognition in the United Kingdom and works councils in Germany) during the early phase of a leftist party in government. In both countries this initial success was short-lived and union influence over government subsequently declined. In the absence of social pacts and general strikes, and with union influence over the Labour Party and government heavily constrained, British unions remain politically weak. Yet, in the United Kingdom, union membership began to recover in 1998 while the slide in density came to a halt the same year. In Germany, by contrast, unions are in a rapidly deteriorating situation with incremental employer withdrawal from the collective bargaining system, falling union membership and density—stable throughout the 1980s at around 34 per cent but plummeting during the past 10 years—failing strikes, and protracted leadership problems in the IG Metall. The SPD government's pursuit of welfare reforms, despite union opposition, suggests that the SPD does not consider the unions as a necessary or valuable ally for policy and electoral purposes. The political power of German unions may not have reached the nadir of their American counterparts, but recent events and trends suggest it may be moving in the direction of the United States rather than of Italy and Spain. Unions in the United States have had to face the limits of their political influence: their political weakness reflects the dominance of the Republican Party, the absence of institutionalized channels of influence such as social pacts, and the limitations of lobbying. Despite occasional legislative victories, unions failed to make progress on one of their key demands, for reform of the union certification system, and union membership and density have continued their long-standing and steady decline. How can these patterns of action and outcomes be explained?

EXPLAINING THE FORMS AND OUTCOMES OF POLITICAL ACTION

To account for the variety in the forms and outcomes of political action in the five countries, we focus on our core variables: political and economic institutions (by economic institutions we refer to industrial relations institutions specifically as well as to the more general 'Varieties of Capitalism'), the choices of political leaders, union identities, and union leadership. Our principal argument is that different types of both economic and political institutions favour some forms of political action over others. Within these parameters the actions pursued by union leaders are, in part, a reflection of union traditions, as embodied in union identities, but are also shaped by the actions and choices of the political leaders with whom they interact. We can distinguish three patterns or clusters: a recovery of political power in Spain and Italy, a more limited and partial recovery in the United Kingdom, and continued crisis in the United States and in Germany.

Political Power in Spain and Italy

The Spanish and Italian configuration of social pacts and occasional general strikes reflects three key factors. First, the industrial relations institutions of these countries are conducive to negotiations between governments and unions: union confederations—though competing with each other for affiliates and representation at the shop floor—are themselves highly centralized and wield considerable authority over their affiliates; the structure of collective bargaining is also highly coordinated and bargaining coverage is approximately 80 per cent. Moreover, the state has traditionally played a strong role in industrial relations, and is thus somewhat of a default partner in negotiating a variety of issues. Governments can have some confidence that agreements with unions that affect terms and conditions of employment can be implemented across most of the labour force. Both countries fall into the 'Mediterranean' category of the Varieties of Capitalism literature. While the literature is, in general, rather vague in specifying the characteristics of this category—other than noticing a prominent role of the state—it is difficult to infer what the literature would predict for the fate of unions in these countries. Yet, as we will discuss further in the conclusion, our sample does not confirm the literature's general assessment that unions are most likely to regain or retain a strong position in the Coordinated Market Economies (CMEs), which includes Germany. Instead, the two Mediterranean countries appear to have fared substantially better than our CME case.

Political institutions have also played a role in the re-emergence of pacts. In both Spain and Italy the pacts of the 1990s were signed by union confederations whose ties to political parties had significantly weakened: in the Spanish case because of growing conflict between the Socialist government and the socialist confederation and in the Italian case because of the disintegration of the major political parties from 1993. Arguably, the greater political autonomy exercised by the confederations made it easier for them to negotiate with governments of the right as well as the left: hence the re-emergence of pacts in Spain following the conservative election victory in 1996 and the continuation of pacts in Italy subsequent to the conservative victory in 2001. We are not suggesting that unions' independence from leftist parties is a necessary and sufficient condition for social pacts; after all, pacts have been negotiated in countries such as Finland, where union movements have retained closer party links than those in Spain or Italy (Hindley 1997), but it certainly facilitated the unions' propensity to engage in concertation with conservative governments. The unions' use of the general strike also reflects the structure of political opportunities afforded by the respective political institutions to the union movements. The general strike is legal in Spain and Italy but is unlawful in the United Kingdom, United States, and Germany.

The electoral systems of Spain and Italy embody a degree of proportionality so that electoral outcomes are not especially susceptible to small swings in voter turnout in specific targeted districts compared to the first-past-the-post systems of the United Kingdom and the United States. Consequently, unions have little incentive to engage in targeted voter mobilization. Lobbying individual legislators is considerably more developed in the Italian system than in Spain. In the latter, candidates are elected on a multi-member district 'closed list system' (i.e. a list determined by the respective parties rather than the voters) and the connection between individual legislators and their electoral base is relatively weak (Hamann 2001*b*). In Italy, poor party discipline, the existence of factionalism within parties, coalition governments, and the opportunity for private bills provide pressure groups with more opportunities to influence legislators than in the Spanish case, where strict party discipline and hierarchically ordered parliamentary party groups give individual legislators a relatively minor role in influencing bills or agendas (della Sala 1999).

Second, the choices made by government leaders were also critical. Where governments (of the left or right) were weak and needed to seek allies outside of parliament, unions were more likely to be included in social pacts and to exercise some influence. Social pacts re-emerged in Spain under the 1996 Aznar government, a minority government that came to office after 14 years of Socialist rule. The seven Italian governments that ruled from January 1994 until the election of Berlusconi in June 2001 did so in the wake of the corruption scandals of the early 1990s, and therefore sought allies from outside parliament in order to increase their legitimacy. However, it would be wrong to assume that social pacts, or union inclusion more broadly, necessarily flow from government weakness. Where government and party leaders believe that union inclusion in the policy-making process would be electorally or politically damaging, then union influence over government may remain low, as in the United States under Clinton or in Germany under Schröder after 2000.

This leads us to our third explanatory variable, union leaders' strategic choices. Even though some forms of political action suggest themselves more clearly in some institutional, political, or identity-related contexts than others, union leaders nonetheless retain some leeway in which forms of political action they choose to pursue. For example, leaders of the two main confederations in Spain occasionally disagree on the use of general strikes or negotiations with the government and relations between confederations in Italy have undergone cycles of cooperation and disagreement. Similarly, union leaders can decide how many concessions they want to make in negotiations or when to walk out of negotiations, or whether they prefer to bargain with the government on a set agenda rather than opposing the agenda from outside.

The independent effect of union identity on the choice of forms of political action and union revitalization is difficult to assess. Union identities are themselves subject to change as new strategies, issues, or leaderships evolve. Yet, it is probably safe to say that Spanish unions shifted their identity from being ideologically based during the period of democratic transition to a more functional understanding of their role as a social movement or interest group in the late 1980s (see Hamann 1997: 131). This, in turn, facilitated their cooperation across ideological divides and also made it possible to enter pacts with a conservative government.

Limited Political Recovery in the United Kingdom

Party links and electoral activity comprise the most salient forms of political action for UK unions and they have helped achieve some degree of revitalization. Political institutions provide a key part of the explanation for this mode of political action. The British Labour Party's dependency on union finance and openness to union influence both declined throughout the 1990s, but unions were still able to secure a Labour commitment to reform industrial relations law. The party is also dependent on union activists for electoral campaigning although in view of its large majority over a divided opposition in the 1997 and 2001 elections, this can hardly be counted as a critical dependency. Labour's autonomy from the unions is further strengthened by the United Kingdom's first-past-the-post electoral system, resulting in a two-party dominant system, which means that unions and voters disaffected with Labour have no obvious, electorally credible alternative.

Political and economic institutions also help explain the absence of social pacts and the limited scale and effectiveness of union lobbying. The absence of centralized bargaining and of a powerful union confederation lowers the incentives for the state to engage unions in centralized negotiations. Conversely, the Labour Party in parliament has a highly centralized structure of control that is quite inhospitable to union lobbying. Government appointments are controlled by the prime minister and so union lobbying efforts often collide with pressures on members of parliament emanating from the party leadership. This type of conflict is especially acute where unions are seeking to encourage votes against government policy.

Some of these institutional factors however are themselves the product of strategic choices by party leaders. Tony Blair and his supporters, who have come to dominate the Labour Party since 1994, believed that strong trade unions, exercising substantial power inside the Labour Party, were a major electoral liability. As a result, they were determined to marginalize union influence both inside the party and over government: hence their very limited reforms of labour law, their extensive restructuring of the Labour Party, and their antipathy to social pacts.

Union leaders have also made strategic choices, particularly within conference debates on the union–Labour link. Interestingly, most of the new national union leaders highly critical of the Labour government have argued strongly for continued affiliation. It appears they prefer the familiar channels of decision-making—passing resolutions through Labour and TUC conferences—to the uncertainties of operating as an independent political force, despite the fact that these conferences are now far less significant than they once were. This orientation towards Labour may also reflect part of the identity of a section of the union movement. Documents on the Labour link produced by national leaderships of the train drivers and firefighters' unions, for example, both refer to the long-standing, historic connections between the union and party wings of the 'labour movement'.

If British unions have secured only a limited recovery of political power they have fared somewhat better on the dimension of union membership, where an upsurge of union organizing has halted long-term membership decline (see Heery and Adler, Chapter 4, this volume). This outcome should also be understood as a function of political action by unions. The renewed emphasis on organizing did pre-date the union recognition law, which was enacted in 1999 and took effect from June 2000. But research has shown that employers became more willing to concede recognition to unions, even before 2000, because they knew the law was imminent (Heery and Adler, Chapter 4, this volume). So it was the combination of political action and organizing which arguably made the difference to union membership.

Political Weakness in the United States and Germany

The American union movement is heavily oriented towards electoral activity and lobbying in Congress, an orientation that is best explained by political institutions, in particular the character of the electoral and party system. In the American first-past-the-post system the overall election result is often highly sensitive to small fluctuations in voter turnout in key constituencies. Small gains in turnout among pro-Democrat voters can, therefore, make a significant difference to election results, and consequently American unions focus their electoral activity and resources, particularly union personnel, in key districts. By contrast, the outcomes in proportional or mixed electoral systems in Spain, Italy, and Germany, are far less susceptible to such targeted campaigning. Political institutions also account for the prevalence of lobbying in the US legislature. Lobbying individual legislators makes sense where they represent individual districts or constituencies, as in the US electoral system; where representatives are amenable to influence because party discipline is weak and because the fate of the executive does not hinge on majority support in the legislature; and where unions have few alternative channels of political influence such as strong party ties (as exist in the United Kingdom) or social pacts (as in Italy and Spain).

The structure of the industrial relations system and the strategies of employers also account for the lack of social pacts: highly decentralized bargaining, normally at company level, and highly decentralized unions with dwindling membership provide hardly any incentive either for employers or government to engage in centralized negotiations. In addition, the welfare reforms that have preoccupied many European governments and led some of them into social pacts with unions are less salient in the United States because of the significantly lower levels of public welfare expenditure. For example, the ratio of average unemployment benefit to wages (the replacement ratio) in 1991 was 40 per cent lower in the United States than the Organization for Economic Cooperation and Development (OECD) average (Blau and Kahn 2002: 94).

A third important factor in US labour's political weakness is the policies of the Democratic Party. Unions failed to commit the Democratic Party leadership to wholesale reform of the labour relations certification system and by 1992 had succeeded only in obtaining a procedural commitment, to establish a Commission of Inquiry. This implies that even a Democratic administration is not necessarily a guarantee for strong support for reviving unions through legislative action.

Finally, union leaders themselves have chosen to retain their commitment to the Democrats, despite major policy disagreements. Indeed, measured by finance, union support for the Democrats was actually strengthened rather than weakened under the radical new AFL-CIO leadership of John Sweeney and his supporters.

The German case is more intriguing because the unions' political power is in a state of flux. The institutional conditions for a social pact appear to be present—centralized negotiations, high bargaining coverage, and a social democratic government—and a pact was attempted in the late 1990s. But the Alliance for Jobs did not involve concrete reforms agreed by the parties and came to nothing. However, some of Germany's economic institutions are undergoing incremental change. The German industrial relations system is under pressure, not just from the union side with rapidly dwindling union density and leadership disputes, but also from the employers' side, where an increasing number are opting out of collective employer representation and consequently, collective bargaining agreements.

In the German case, the seemingly favourable institutional conditions for a social pact were outweighed by the sharp policy divergence between unions and the government. For example, while the metalworkers' union leadership was striking to cut working hours and create jobs, the SPD leadership had already embarked on its programme of radical labour market and welfare reforms—Agenda 2010—without union support and indeed in the face of union opposition. There continue to be some areas of consensus, though, for instance on the need to push employers to provide sufficient apprenticeship positions. This illustrates that while political and economic institutions are important, they cannot decisively predict the choices government and union leaders make. The German union movement has few options to reorient or boost fundamentally its involvement in politics. It lacks even the limited financial influence over the SPD enjoyed by its UK and US counterparts; it faces a government with no apparent interest in or need for Spanish or Italian-style social pacts; and parliamentary lobbying is open to interests other than organized labour, meaning that unions' lobbying efforts are often matched or exceeded by those of business and independent experts (von Beyme 1998). Union leaders' choices have also been important, but in the German case, have in some cases contributed to an acceleration of the crisis rather than recovery of lost ground. The prolonged leadership discussion in the IG Metall in 2003 and a failed strike in the same year contributed to the popular image of the unions as being removed from political and social realities, and membership losses were accelerated in the period after the strike (EIRO 2003c). These occurrences, in turn, facilitated the choice of the government to push ahead with economic and social welfare reforms against union opposition. All of these developments may well lead to the need for German unions, not just to revisit their strategies for political action, but also for a more fundamental reconsideration of their role in the economic system and society, and ultimately, their identity.

CONCLUSIONS

Comparing the forms and successes of various forms of political action, we can summarize that in Italy and Spain a combination of social pacts and worker mobilization through strike action has consolidated the unions' political influence (compared with the late 1980s and early 1990s) and has been associated with a recovery of union membership. American unions have continued to lose membership, as well as bargaining power and political influence, though for different reasons. Unions substantially increased their electoral activity and lobbying as they moved closer to the Democrats but these measures proved insufficient to overcome the even more powerful business lobbies and to dilute the continuing militant anti-unionism of US employers. The modest degree of political action by German unions helped secure two SPD electoral victories, but it has not so far translated into a recovery of union membership, bargaining and works council coverage, or political influence. British unions experienced a weakening in their ties to the Labour Party and were unable to secure any kind of social pact with the government, but nonetheless were still able to lobby successfully for legal changes that facilitated an upsurge in organizing and a modest recovery in membership, halting a near 20-year period of membership decline. They have also embraced new opportunity structures with some success, in particular at the EU level through lobbying and the ECJ, again illustrating that union leaders do retain some level of strategic choice, even though it might be more limited in some countries than in others.

These cross-national patterns are shaped by several factors: political and economic institutions, the choices of party and government leaders, union identities, and the choices of union leaders. Changes in political activity over time, especially in party–union ties, in electioneering and in social pacts, can be accounted for by some, though not all, of the same factors. The strategic choices of union leaders are critical as they respond to growing economic pressures, from monetary union in Europe and from trade liberalization in the United States. The choices made by union leaders, in turn, largely reflect the channels of influence they perceive as available to them (the opportunity structure). Political action might well be a fundamental task to (re)install union rights, but it is also a strategy whose fortune is highly dependent on the actions of governments and employers. The influence of union identities is perhaps the most difficult to assess, in part because identity itself is dynamic and shaped by the institutions and choices that union leaders make. This is particularly true in situations where old union strategies and policies appear insufficient to respond to new contexts and challenges, as appears to be the case in the last decade or so.

One further difficulty in evaluating these forms of political action is that the causal connections between union activities and immediate outcomes are not clear-cut. For example, the reduction of unemployment, a key union objective, has been successfully pursued during the periods of the social pacts in Spain. However, since the pacts occurred against a background of economic growth and job creation, it is possible that unemployment would have fallen even without union support for government policies. In addition, unions have also pursued other strategies, which makes it difficult to isolate the impact of political action. The interconnections between different union strategies become clear when we look at the links between successful national-level bargaining and union structures at the inter-confederal level. The union movements of Spain and Italy are divided on political lines, a fact that has been often been exploited by governments, including the current Italian government. Therefore, one of the requirements for effective political action through negotiations and general strike action is a restructuring of inter-confederal relations (see Behrens, Hurd, and Waddington, Chapter 7, this volume). Where the confederations have reached agreement around a set of bargaining demands and on tactics, a successful outcome has been more likely, as in Spain 2002.

Similarly, the unions might be successful in obtaining immediate outcomes, such as getting their preferred party elected, but that does not necessarily translate into favourable policies that would actually strengthen the union movement, for instance through favourable legislation or membership increase. Both the forms of political action and their success are contingent on the responses of other political actors, most notably governments, but also employers, and are therefore difficult to predict. In sum, political action has been a pivotal strategy for all five union movements; yet, the results have been very different across the countries.

ACKNOWLEDGEMENTS

Our thanks to all the participants at the Labour Movement Revitalization Conference, LSE, September 2002 and especially to Lucio Baccaro, Martin Behrens, Ed Heery, Richard Hyman, and Lowell Turner.

Notes

1. Unions also engage in other forms of activity around broader political issues, such as anti-racism or anti-terrorism that are not necessarily linked to work-related issues narrowly defined, but these are covered in the chapter by Frege, Heery, and Turner on coalition-building.
2. British unions traditionally affiliate to the Labour Party on a membership figure significantly lower than their actual membership. In 2002, for example, the twenty-two labour unions affiliated 2.74 of their 5.2 million members (TULO 2003).

References

Baccaro, L., Carrieri, M., and Damiano, C. (2003). 'The Resurgence of the Italian Confederal Unions: Will it Last?'. *European Journal of Industrial Relations*, 9/1: 43–59.

114   *Kerstin Hamann and John Kelly*

Baumgartner, F. R. and Leech, B. L. (1998). *Basic Interests: The Importance of Groups in Politics and in Political Science*. Princeton, NJ: Princeton University Press.

Behrens, M., Fichter, M., and Frege, C. M. (2003). 'Unions in Germany: Regaining the Initiative?'. *European Journal of Industrial Relations*, 9/1: 25–42.

Blau, F. D. and Kahn, L. M. (2002). *At Home and Abroad: U.S. Labor Market Performance in International Perspective*. New York: Russell Sage Foundation.

della Sala, V. (1999). 'Parliament and Pressure Groups in Italy', in P. Norton (ed.), *Parliaments and Pressure Groups in Western Europe*. London: Frank Cass, 67–87.

DGB Einblick (07/99). 'In der Union eine Randgruppe: Gewerkschaftsmitglieder im Bundestag'. Available online at http://www.einblick.dgb.de/archiv/9907/gf990703.htm.

—— (17/02). 'Gewerkschafter: Gewinne für die Union'. http://www.einblick.dgb.de/archiv/0217/gf021702.htm.

Dark, T. E. (2001). *The Unions and the Democrats: An Enduring Alliance*. Ithaca, NY: ILR Press.

DTI (2003). *Review of the Employment Relations Act (1999)*. London: Department of Trade and Industry.

EIRO. (2002*a*). 'Provisional Results of 2002 Works Council Elections'. www.eurofound.ie/2002/12/feature/de0212204f.html

—— (2003*a*). '2002 Annual Review for Italy'. www.eurofound.ie/2003/01/feature/it0301205f.html

—— (2003*b*). 'Unions And Government Discuss Pensions Reform'. www.eurofound.ie/2003/05/inbrief/it0305102n.html

—— (2003*c*). 'IG Metall Elects New Leadership'. www.eurofound.ie/2003/09/inbrief/de0309202n.html

El País. 'Los Sindicatos Garantizan a Almunia y Frutos so Total Apoyo a De Gobierno PSOE-IU'. 2000, Madrid.

Fielding, S. (2003). *The Labour Party: Continuity and Change in the Making of 'New' Labour*. London: Palgrave.

Franzosi, R. (1995). *The Puzzle of Strikes: Class and State Strategies in Postwar Italy*. Cambridge: Cambridge University Press.

Freeman, R. B. (2002). *What Do Unions Do . . . to Voting?* Cambridge, MA: Harvard University, unpublished MS.

—— and Medoff, J. L. (1984). *What Do Unions Do?* New York: Basic Books.

Goetschy, J. (2000). 'The European Union and National Social Pacts: Employment and Social Protection Put to the Test of Joint Regulation', in G. Fajertag and P. Pochet (eds.), *Social Pacts in Europe—New Dynamics*, 2nd edn. Brussels: European Trade Union Institute, 41–60.

Hall, P. A. and Soskice, D. (2001). 'An Introduction to Varieties of Capitalism', in P. A. Hall and D. Soskice (eds.), *Varieties of Capitalism: The Institutional Foundations of Comparative Advantage*. Oxford: Oxford University Press, 1–68.

Hamann, K. (1997). 'The Pacted Transition to Democracy and Labour Politics in Spain'. *South European Society and Politics*, 2/2: 110–38.

—— (2001*a*). 'The Resurgence of National-level Bargaining: Union Strategies in Spain'. *Industrial Relations Journal*, 32/2: 154–72.

—— (2001*b*). 'Spain: Changing Party-Group Relations in a New Democracy', in C. S. Thomas (ed.), *Political Parties and Interest Groups: Shaping Democratic Governance*. Boulder, CO: Lynne Rienner, 175–91.

—— and Martínez Lucio, M. (2003). 'Strategies of Labour Union Revitalization in Spain'. *European Journal of Industrial Relations*, 9/1: 61–78.

Hay, C. (1999). *The Political Economy of New Labour*. Manchester: Manchester University Press.

Heery, E. (1998). 'The Relaunch of the Trades Union Congress'. *British Journal of Industrial Relations*, 36/3: 339–60.

Hrebenar, R. J., Burbank, M. J., and Benedict, R. C. (1999). *Political Parties, Interest Groups, and Political Campaigns*. Boulder, CO: Westview.

Hurd, R. W., Milkman, R., and Turner, L. (2003). 'Reviving the American Labour Movement: Institutions and Mobilization'. *European Journal of Industrial Relations*, 9/1: 91–118.

Hyman, R. (2001). *Understanding European Trade Unionism: Between Market, Class and Society*. London: Sage.

John, S. (2002). *The Persuaders: When Lobbyists Matter*. Houndmills: Palgrave Macmillan.

Levi, M. (2003). 'Organizing Power: The Prospects for an American Labor Movement'. *Perspectives on Politics*, 1/1: 45–68.

Lodovici, M. S. (2000). 'The Dynamics of Labour Market Reform in European Countries', in G. Esping-Andersen and M. Regini (eds.), *Why Deregulate Labour Markets?* Oxford: Oxford University Press, 30–65.

LRD (2003). 'Unions Hold Back from Party Split'. *Labour Research*, 92/7: 7.

Ludlam, S. and Taylor, A. J. (2003). 'The Political Representation of the "Labour Interest": Is the British "Labour Alliance" Finished?'. *British Journal of Industrial Relations*, 40/4: 727–49.

——Bodah, M., and Coates, D. (2001). 'Trajectories of Solidarity: Changing Union–Party Linkages in the UK and the USA'. *British Journal of Politics and International Relations*, 4/2: 222–44.

McIlroy, J. (1998). 'The Enduring Alliance? Trade Unions and the Making of New Labour, 1994–1997'. *British Journal of Industrial Relations*, 36/4: 537–64.

——(2000). 'The New Politics of Pressure—the Trades Union Congress and New Labour in Government'. *Industrial Relations Journal*, 31/1: 2–16.

Minkin, L. (1992). *The Contentious Alliance: Trade Unions and the Labour Party*. Edinburgh: Edinburgh University Press.

Monger, J. (2003). 'International Comparisons of Labour Disputes in 2000'. *Labour Market Trends*, 111/1: 19–27.

Negrelli, S. (2000). 'Social Pacts in Italy: Similar Strategies and Structures; Different Models and National Stories', in G. Fajertag and P. Pochet (eds.), *Social Pacts in Europe—New Dynamics*, 2nd edn. Brussels: European Trade Union Institute, 85–112.

Newsletter of the Trade Union Group of MPs, London, Spring 2003.

Norton, P. (1999). 'The United Kingdom: Parliament under Pressure', in P. Norton (ed.), *Parliaments and Pressure Groups in Western Europe*. London: Frank Cass, 19–42.

Phillips-Fein, K. (2003). 'Does That Elephant Bite? Union Alliances with the GOP'. *New Labor Forum*, 12/1: 7–16.

Pochet, P. (2002). 'Introduction', in P. Pochet (ed.), *Wage Policy in the Eurozone*. Brussels: European Trade Union Institute, 15–35.

Radcliff, B. (2001). 'Organized Labor and Electoral Participation in American National Elections'. *Journal of Labor Research*, 22/2: 405–14.

Regini, M. and Regalia, I. (2000). 'The Prospects for Italian Trade Unions in a Phase of Concertation', in J. Waddington and R. Hoffmann (eds.), *Trade Unions in Europe: Facing Challenges and Searching for Solutions*. Brussels: European Trade Union Institute, 365–92.

Schafer, C. (2003). 'The WSI Surveys of Works and Staff Councils—An Overview'. *WSI Mitteilungen*, 56: 3–13.

Shoch, J. (2001). 'Organized Labor Versus Globalization: NAFTA, Fast Track, and PNTR With China', in L. Turner, H. C. Katz, and R. W. Hurd (eds.), *Rekindling the Movement: Labor's Quest For Relevance in the 21st Century*. Ithaca, NY: ILR Press, 275–313.

Silvia, S. J. (1999). 'Every Which Way but Loose: German Industrial Relations Since 1980', in A. Martin and G. Ross (eds.), *The Brave New World of European Labor: European Trade Unions at the Millennium*, New York: Berghahn Books, 75–124.

Swank, D. (2002). *Global Capital, Political Institutions, and Policy Change in Developed Welfare States*. Cambridge: Cambridge University Press.

Sweet, A. S. and Brunell, T. L. (2000). 'The European Court, National Judges, and Legal Integration; A Researcher's Guide to the Data Set on Preliminary References in EC Law, 1958–98'. *European Law Journal*, 6/2: 117–27.

Tijeras, R. (2000). *Lobbies: Cómo Funcionan los Grupos de Presión Españoles*. Madrid: Temas de Hoy.

TUC (2002). *General Council Report 2002*. London: Trades Union Congress.

—— (2003*a*). *TUC Welcomes Establishment of Public Services Forum*. London: Trades Union Congress, Press Release.

—— (2003*b*). *Directory 2003*. London: Trades Union Congress.

TULO (2003). *Trade Unions and Labour Party Directory 2002*. London: National Trade Union and Labour Party Liaison Organisation.

von Beyme, K. (1998). *The Legislator: German Parliament as a Centre of Political Decision-making*. Aldershot: Ashgate.

Weiss, L. (2003). 'Introduction: Bringing Domestic Institutions Back In', in L. Weiss (ed.), *States in the Global Economy: Bringing Domestic Institutions Back In*. Cambridge: Cambridge University Press, 1–33.

7

How Does Restructuring Contribute to Union Revitalization?

MARTIN BEHRENS, RICHARD HURD, AND
JEREMY WADDINGTON

INTRODUCTION

As we look cross-nationally at labour movement revitalization, we see a complex process of change that varies depending on the socio-political/economic context. Although we observe a diverse set of union strategies and outcomes, we find that structural adjustment is a common element of revitalization efforts. The mere presence of restructuring does not, of course, assure positive results. In this chapter we define various forms of restructuring, outline factors that shape and promote restructuring, and discuss the likelihood that restructuring leads to union revitalization by using examples from our cross-country comparison.

Concrete cases of unions' structural change take a variety of forms that fall into three predominant categories. The first is 'external structure' (Clegg 1976: 40) or 'external shape' (Hyman 1975: 3), which comprises the boundaries of a labour movement. As such, external shape embraces the principles that underpin the pattern of union organization, decisions on which workers, occupations, and industries to include or exclude, as well as border or demarcation lines between unions. In some cases there are notable modifications in the relationship between different levels of the labour movement. Specifically, this might involve redefinition of the role of the peak level *vis-à-vis* individual national unions. External restructuring may result from altered arrangements among unions at the same level, in most notable cases leading to mergers. A union may also unilaterally engage in external restructuring by redefining its own borders. This might involve creating a subsidiary, in essence, to enter a new industry, occupation, or geographic jurisdiction in order to extend 'job territory' (Undy et al. 1981: 60).

The other two categories of union restructuring are internal to the specific organization. One internal component is union governance, the analysis of which centres on union democracy, representation, and participation (Undy et al. 1981: 37; Weil 1997: 204). It is, thus, concerned with internal union politics and relations between different groups within a union. The governance process may be altered to increase the authority exercised by a national union over its locals as part of a programme to shift priorities. The other internal category is union administration, which focuses on union management and the allocation of resources. This aspect of restructuring within a labour organization might relate to specialization of certain functions, reallocation of resources, or the reform of management systems (Clark and Gray 1991: 196; Weil 1997: 217–20). While the distinctions between the two internal aspects of structure are not clear-cut, they capture different elements of the revitalization of union organizational life.

Whatever the form, restructuring neither automatically contributes to labour movement revitalization, nor necessarily increases a union's power. In order to appreciate the potential for meaningful restructuring and the obstacles to progress via this route, it is necessary to map both the factors that influence success and the motivations for structural change. Once a framework has been established, we will review the experience with restructuring in the five countries and will highlight those efforts with some potential to promote revitalization. At the end of the chapter we will evaluate that experience in the context of the dimensions of revitalization introduced in Chapter 2.

FACTORS THAT DRIVE RESTRUCTURING

As entrenched institutions, labour movements face major hurdles as they embrace new priorities and attempt to restructure to facilitate pursuit of these priorities. The more radical the change, the more substantial the obstacles are likely to be (Nord and Tucker 1986). As with other institutions, the most serious obstacles to union revitalization stem from internal resistance to change (Kotter 1995). Similar to other organizations, trade unions are subject to strong inertial pressures, which often allow for only a conservative transformation of their goals, structure and tactics (Selznick 1957; March and Simon 1993; Voss and Sherman 2000). There is inevitably a high degree of internal resistance faced by almost any kind of comprehensive restructuring. This may come from members comfortable with the status quo and concerned about being disenfranchised, from leaders worried about losing their political base, or from staff unsure where they will fit in the new organization (Fletcher and Hurd 2001). But what does it take to overcome this resistance? In Figure 7.1 we present a model that captures common elements of successful transformation in unions. This model is not intended as a definitive treatment of structural change, but rather as a simplification that will help highlight key aspects of the change process.

There are two mutually supportive causal chains that are associated with successful union restructuring. In the countries we have studied, resistance to restructuring is neutralized where there is a sufficient level of environmental pressure to start the process. As shown in the upper section of Figure 7.1, such pressures can raise the level of urgency within the union. Environmental pressure alone may not be sufficient, however. Awareness can be facilitated by union leaders and staff who educate members about the existence and impact of the external pressures in order to win support for organizational change (Armenakis et al. 1993; Fletcher and Hurd 2001: 207).

Environmental pressures, even when widely understood, will not directly produce comprehensive restructuring on their own, however. In addition unions need a

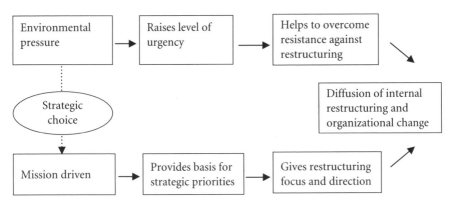

Figure 7.1. *Organizational change in unions*

clearly articulated conception of their future, which might be formally codified as a mission (or vision) that provides a basis for strategic priorities. This is depicted in the lower part of Figure 7.1. If restructuring is not driven by mission, or at least by clearly articulated goals, initiatives almost inevitably will stop short of transformation because there is no focus and direction (Allaire and Firsirotu 1985). This is not to say that without a mission there would not be restructuring at all, but rather that such cases would result in a limited 'structural fix' (Grabelsky and Hurd 1994; Behrens 2002).

But how are we to distinguish between structural change that is cosmetic, amounting to little more than a short-term expedient glossing over fundamental weaknesses, and restructuring that has the potential to contribute substantially to labour movement revitalization? It is our collective qualitative judgement that the character of restructuring is linked to the motivations that initiate the change process. To help unravel the complexity of motivations for structural change, we adopt a framework that borrows heavily from the literature on union mergers.

Table 7.1 summarizes different motivations that shape the three aspects of restructuring delineated above: internal changes in union government, internal administrative modification, and external restructuring. We posit that three alternative motivations can underpin union restructuring: *aggressive, defensive*, and *transformative*. The merger literature describes cases where a larger partner seeks to assimilate other unions with the primary intent of increasing the size of the individual union (Chitayat 1979: 129; Undy et al. 1981: 167). Among the intentions that might underpin such *aggressive* restructuring are the consolidation and strengthening of the political control of union leaders, and the extension of the boundaries of the individual union. If restructuring is merely *aggressive*, however, it is unlikely to translate into net membership growth for the labour movement as a whole, nor to any notable enhancement of union bargaining power or political influence. Union leaders might implement *aggressive* internal restructuring to increase their personal control of a

Table 7.1. *Motivation to restructure*

	Internal		External
	Governance/ Democracy	Administrative	
Aggressive	• Increase leader(s) control of decision-making • Silence critics of leader(s)	• Increase leader(s) control over budget and staff • Augment administrative authority of leader(s)	• Growth through acquisition • Increase external influences of leader(s)
Defensive	• Silence critics of leader(s) • Respond to members' desires to preserve status quo • Insulate leader(s) from external shocks	• Downsizing to balance budget • Resource shift for survival	• Consolidation to stem decline, reduce rivalry • Merger/ affiliation for survival
Transformative	• Enhance members' participation and democracy • Engage diverse constituents in change process	• Align union's structure with mission/ priorities • Reallocate resources to promote growth	• Capture economies of scale • Increase union's political and economic power

union's governance system and administrative apparatus (Chitayat 1979: 131). Alternatively, they might adopt a narrow interpretation of corporate models and attempt to increase personal power through *aggressive* external restructuring: for example, affiliating independent unions and adding units (Chaison 1996: 8), or possibly by reaching 'sweetheart' agreements with employers, thus adding members and dues revenue without providing representational services.

In sum, if restructuring is merely *aggressive*, it is unlikely to translate into net membership growth for the labour movement as a whole, nor to any notable enhancement of union bargaining power or political influence.

The most commonly mentioned motivation in the merger literature is survival (Waddington and Hoffman 2000: 73–4). Similarly, we label as *defensive* those restructuring initiatives that are reactions to declining fortunes and that attempt to stabilize the union. Although this may involve appropriate adaptation to economic change, if the restructuring is merely *defensive* it does not offer great potential to increase union power per se. *Defensive* restructuring may focus on internal procedures, attending to the short term interests of members and leaders in effect by retrenching and erecting barriers that attempt to limit the impact of external challenges and threats to the union's established culture and practice. External *defensive* restructuring is not as insular, however, as it involves efforts to form alliances with other organizations that might help forestall decline. The *aggressive* and *defensive* forms of restructuring capture the vast majority of union mergers. A study of union mergers in five countries by Chaison concluded that 'in each country, mergers were unable to resolve the fundamental problems that created them' (Chaison 1996: 165).

We turn to the organizational change literature for help in identifying restructuring with the potential to contribute to labour movement revitalization. The consistent message is that the more radical the change, the more essential it is to approach the effort strategically based on careful assessment and thorough preparation (Allaire and Firsirotu 1985). To capture the strategic essence of this type of change, we label as *transformative* those restructuring efforts tied to substantive organizational change that promise to augment union power along at least one of the four dimensions identified in Chapter 2. In other words, we argue that transformative restructuring is likely to support union revitalization.

Although such restructuring may include aggressive or defensive elements, these are pursued within the framework of the union's strategic plan. In essence the portion of Table 7.1 devoted to *transformative* restructuring relates back to the type of organizational change depicted in Figure 7.1. *Transformative* motivations are different in substance from those associated with merely *aggressive* or merely *defensive* restructuring. Internal changes of union government and union administration are pursued not to protect the vested interests of leaders and current members, but rather to engage all of the union's constituents and prospective constituents in the change process. The goal is to reform the union's governance and administrative machinery in order to address new strategic priorities. Similarly, whether it involves redefinition of the role of the confederation, mergers of individual national unions, or the creation of new union ventures, external *transformative* restructuring is motivated by a desire to augment the union's strategic effectiveness.

Because *transformative* restructuring potentially can contribute to labour movement revitalization, the next section emphasizes those *transformative* initiatives that are being pursued by union organizations in the five countries. We do not attempt to review all restructuring nor even to delineate all cases of structural change. Rather, we summarize the most prominent forms of restructuring and pay special attention to those with the potential to contribute to revitalization.

STRUCTURAL ADJUSTMENT AND UNION REVITALIZATION

Union restructuring can be implemented at any level of the labour movement, ranging from local unions to cross-national organizations. In order to review coherently the relevant range of structural change, it is necessary to clarify the terminology we will use. At the peak of union organization within each nation state are confederations to which national unions may affiliate. For our purposes, therefore, the American

Federation of Labor-Congress of Industrial Organizations (AFL-CIO) is a confederation, although it is often referred to as a federation within the United States, as is the British *Trades Union Congress* (TUC) and the German *Deutscher Gewerkschaftsbund* (DGB). The Italian *Federazione di Categoria* (Industrial Federations) and the Spanish *Federaciones Sindicales de Industria* (Industrial Federations), the principal affiliates of the confederations in the two countries, are treated here as similar to the national unions of Britain, Germany and the United States. At the pan-European level we have cross-national organizations that are increasingly important in the context of economic integration associated with the European Union. There is the European Trade Union Confederation (ETUC) whose affiliated organizations include the European Industry Federations (EIFs), which are comprised of individual national trade unions from EU member countries.[1]

We will first look at restructuring within the five countries at the level of confederations, then look at structural change in national unions, and conclude with a review of developments at the pan-European level. Although we will highlight where possible transformative restructuring, we note in advance that much of the structural change within the five countries is defensive in character. Furthermore, even those structural initiatives with the potential to be transformative often have failed to realize this potential. This is particularly the case where membership decline and associated financial weakness, have prompted unions to react more defensively. Nonetheless, there are clear examples with the potential to aid labour movement revitalization in each of the five countries. Furthermore, the institutional change that has accompanied the European Union since 1990 has created an environment more conducive to substantive innovation. In consequence, pan-European trade union institutions exhibit a marked structural vitality.

Peak Level: Confederations

The trajectory of recent developments in our five countries is affected by differences in the function and structure of confederations and by the influence they exercise over affiliated unions. In particular, Italian and Spanish confederations have a more wide-ranging bargaining function than their American, British, and German counterparts. To facilitate the undertaking of this wider bargaining function, Italian and Spanish confederations have greater authority over affiliated unions. By comparison American, British, and German national unions vigorously protect their autonomy from confederal interference. Furthermore, in Italy and Spain several confederations compete on the basis of different political allegiances,[2] whereas elsewhere confederal structure is unitary.[3] Italian and Spanish confederations collect union income and disperse it to affiliated organizations, whereas the reverse is the case in Britain, Germany, and the United States. This distinction further compounds the differences in the relationships between confederations and affiliated organizations.

Irrespective of these differences, a consistent theme among the confederations of the five countries is the extension and reform of external shape. To expand the external boundaries in Britain, Germany, and the United States, confederations have encouraged new affiliations, particularly of unions that organize in the expanding sectors of the economy. Since 1995 the TUC has accepted fourteen additional unions into affiliation,[4] while both the United American Nurses and the California School Employees recently affiliated to the AFL-CIO. Similarly, the DGB encouraged the involvement of the *Deutsche Angestellten Gewerkschaft* (DAG) in the *Vereinte Dienstleistungsgewerkschaft* (ver.di) merger in 2001, thereby bringing the DAG within the scope of the DGB for the first time since 1945. In Italy and Spain the relative strength of the confederations allows them to have greater influence on the pattern of expansion. Since 1998, for example, the three major Italian confederations have each established unions specifically to organize and represent 'parasubordinates' or labour only sub-contractors (Fullin 2002; Baccaro, Carrieri, and Damiano 2003: 45).

The promotion of mergers is at the core of policy initiatives to reform external shape. Again, however, differences in the political position of the confederations influence the character of these initiatives. The AFL-CIO, DGB, and TUC have no direct authority over the merger process. In consequence, while the merger process has reduced the number of affiliated unions, these confederations have had little influence over which unions are involved in specific mergers. For example, between 1990 and 2001 each experienced a decline in the number of affiliates largely as a result of mergers: AFL-CIO, from eighty-nine to sixty-six; DGB, from seventeen to eight; and TUC, from seventy-six to seventy-three.[5] Because of the limited role of the confederation, there is no consistent principle of organization that influences merger choices, with the consequence that the merger process has not 'simplified' trade union structure. In contrast, in Italy and Spain the confederations have been able to guide mergers between affiliated organizations. In Spain, this influence has been brought to bear to promote sectoral organization at the expense of regional structures (Hamann and Martínez Lucio 2003).

One issue concerning external shape specific to Italy and Spain is the closer working or merging of confederations. Throughout the 1970s and until the mid-1980s the Italian confederations maintained a formal alliance administered through the *Federazione Unitaria* with representation from the three confederations. During this period the prospect of a confederal merger was raised, although the different political affiliations of the confederations constituted an insurmountable barrier (Kreile 1988; Locke and Baccaro 1996). The dissolution of many of the traditional party-confederation affiliations following *Tangentopoli* (corruption scandals) in 1992 facilitated the development of the unity of action between the confederations and a formal proposal to merge in 2000. Political differences re-emerged after 1998, however, once again putting the merger proposal on hold. Similarly, in Spain the *unidad de accion* (unity of action) between *Union General de Trabajadores* (UGT) and *Comisiones Obreras* (CC.OO.) until 2001 represented a weakening of traditional political animosities. While the emergence of confederal mergers on the union agenda in Italy and Spain represents a marked shift in attitudes, with the occasional breakdown of these alliances in both countries it is clear that considerable barriers have yet to be overcome before they are realized and external shape is transformed.

Most of the confederations in the five countries have introduced limited changes to systems of government. In particular, systems of reserved seats for women, white-collar, young, and ethnic minority workers are now commonplace (Braithwaite and Bryne n.d.; Garcia, Hacourt, and Lega n.d.). For the most part, representation within confederations remains dependent upon the membership size of the affiliated union, a system that has been in place for much of the twentieth century. It is only in Italy that transformative changes to systems of union government have been introduced, although even these changes had their origin in defensive counter-measures.

Three developments promoted the shift in the systems of Italian confederal government. First, after the mid-1970s many skilled workers left unions affiliated with the confederations after the reforms to the *scala mobile*, which narrowed wage differentials based on skill (Regini and Regalia 2000). Second, a large number of *sindicati autonomi* (autonomous unions) were established to represent the interest of white-collar workers, who regarded the confederations as focusing too strongly on the interests of manual workers. Third, *Comitati di Base* (COBAS, rank-and-file committees) were established, primarily in the public and service sectors, in opposition to the policies and practices of the three confederations. In combination, these developments constituted a crisis for confederal union organization in Italy (Kreile 1988; Bordogna 1989). In response, the confederations instigated a series of reforms including the practice of submitting all major collective agreements to a binding vote of the membership. Coupled with legal reforms on plant-level representation structures (*rappresentanze sindicati unitarie*), this reform 're-legitimized' confederal organization and was associated with increases in membership, particularly in the service sector (Ponzellini and Provenzano 2001).

The range of administrative reforms undertaken by confederations in the five countries follows similar trajectories. Increased use of the web and sophisticated electronic hardware and software is widespread (Greene, Hogan, and Grieco 2003: Kahmann 2003; Martínez Lucio 2003), as are efforts to improve the quality of service offered by confederations. The latter point is of particular significance in Italy and Spain as it represents a formal acknowledgement that members must be engaged in union activity and politics. More specifically, the TUC has jettisoned much of its formal standing committee structure and introduced a series of task groups, which are dedicated to particular campaigns and are dissolved when the campaign objectives have been achieved. Consistent with this accentuation of the TUC's role in campaigning, a Communications Department was established to publicize campaigns initiated by the TUC (Heery 1998). In this context the TUC has successfully launched high-profile campaigns on organizing and partnership and has been able to cascade the objectives of these campaigns down to affiliated unions. The founding of the Organizing Academy to recruit and train organizers was a particularly important step.

Similarly, the election of John Sweeney to the presidency of the AFL-CIO in 1995 led to wide-ranging internal reorganization of staff, departments, and field operations. Especially important was the creation of an organizing department and major expansion of the Organizing Institute. Efforts to encourage the adoption of organizing as a priority have also intensified. More recently, the AFL-CIO has downgraded the position of the 'unwieldy' fifty-four-member Executive Council and established a seventeen-member Executive Committee in order to streamline confederal policy-making and to sharpen the focus of the AFL-CIO on political and organizing objectives (Greenhouse 2003). There is no doubt that these and similar initiatives have contributed to an impression of institutional vitality and may have enhanced administrative efficiency.

However, resistance to confederal initiatives remains entrenched in both Britain and the United States. Furthermore, union density in the two countries continues to decline. Efforts to lead revitalization from the centre, thus, remain problematic in the absence of direct confederal authority over affiliated unions. In Spain, where confederal authority is more wide-ranging, campaigning teams have been deployed by the confederations to raise membership levels, particularly during works council elections (Hamann and Martínez Lucio 2003). It remains in question whether such an approach leads to long-term membership gains. When coupled to the professionalization of service delivery, this approach may also be associated with increased centralization and the lowering of members' engagement in union activity (Sverke and Sjoberg 1997; Hamann and Martínez Lucio 2003).

At the level of confederations, then, we have two promising types of structural change. In Italy and Spain where confederations maintain closer control over their affiliates, confederal restructuring has the capacity to drive revitalization. Reductions in inter-confederal rivalries have transformative potential particularly in the political arena where labour has become a more credible force as a result of heightened unity (see Hamann and Kelly, Chapter 6, this volume). In the United Kingdom and the United States, with more decentralized traditions, the TUC and AFL-CIO have used structural change to increase the influence of the centre. The creation of the Organizing Academy, expansion of the Organizing Institute and the shift of resources to support organizing have helped the two confederations become pattern-setters. They are actively spreading knowledge, practical skills, and vision throughout the labour movement. This restructuring has clear transformative potential in countries with declining union density.

Revitalization and National Union Structure

In each of the five countries under discussion, mergers and other forms of closer coordination are commonplace as a means to reform external shape among national unions. The driving force for most mergers, though, is membership decline and associated financial weakness (Chaison 1986; Waddington, Kahmann, and Hoffmann 2003). The contraction of employment in specific industries is particularly effective in promoting mergers when it occurs in the context of industrial unionism. Trade unions in the agriculture, mining, textile, and timber industries, for example, have been acquired by larger unions in many countries with the result that independent union organization in these industries no longer exists. Furthermore, potential economies of scale are too often dissipated in post-merger rationalization and early retirement schemes, which are often introduced to reduce the number of full-time staff in the combined organization. Thus, most mergers fit the category of defensive restructuring.

Some mergers completed by larger unions, however, have the stated intent of extending organization to sectors of the economy where the parent union had no initial presence. To be successful such policies require both strategic selection of merger partners and considerable post-merger investment in recruitment and organizing. The Service Employees International Union's (SEIU) merger with 1199 (National Health and Human Service Employees) in 1998 enabled the acquiring union to increase membership in the health sector by 25 per cent to 500,000 (Fan 1998: 26). This augmented earlier mergers and clearly established SEIU as the dominant health care union in the United States, a position that was subsequently solidified by shifting substantial resources to organizing to secure a more wide-ranging presence. Similarly, the large newly established German service sector union, ver.di, resulted from a merger of five unions and displaced IG Metall as the largest union in Germany.

In Britain, Germany, and the United States, confederations exert no direct influence on national union structure. Decisions on mergers and other steps to alter external shape rest almost exclusively within the national unions involved. In consequence, the external shape of the union movements in these countries exhibits no uniform pattern of development. In Britain and the United States, larger unions are tending to extend their membership bases both by mergers and through recruitment efforts. Although traditional jurisdictions sometimes influence national union decisions regarding external boundaries, there is a consistent trend for memberships to become more heterogeneous. With the new membership base extending both vertically and horizontally, an increasing number of organizations are adopting the characteristics of general unions, with only limited industrial and occupational restrictions to recruitment. Although there are exceptions, in Germany, Italy, and Spain multi-industry unions tend to result from mergers as industrial unions combine. In Germany, for example, *Industriegewerkschaft Metall* (Metal Workers' Union) acquired the *Gewerkschaft Textil-Bekliedung* (Textile and Clothing Union) and the *Gewerkschaft Holz und Kuntstoff* (Wood and Plastics Union) to extend its recruitment base beyond its traditional base in engineering.

Increasing membership heterogeneity is also associated with new forms of union government. Similar to confederal restructuring, many unions have supplemented regional and industrial forms of representation with structures for women, white-collar, young, and ethnic minority workers. Such measures reflect changes in membership composition and are intended to raise participation levels among such groups, to encourage horizontal interlinkages between different vertically organized groups of members, and to facilitate the development of union policies to incorporate items of direct concern to these groups. In short, as membership becomes more heterogeneous, systems of union government become more sophisticated. Arguably, union government also becomes more expensive in such circumstances, thus mitigating the impact of any economies of scale that might arise from merger involvement (Waddington, Kahmann, and Hoffmann 2003).

It is also far from clear-cut that these measures have achieved their intended results. Take the case of women, for example. A variety of reserved seats systems, women's sections and the appointment of Women's Officers, have raised the profile of women trade unionists, although they tend to operate only at the senior levels within the union hierarchy rather than at local or regional levels. These systems have yet to result in the proportional representation of women in the decision-making structure of most unions at the national level (Braithwaite and Byrne n.d.; Garcia et al. n.d.), although women's sections have allowed more women to participate in union affairs. Furthermore, they have acted as additional articulating mechanisms that assist in linking the local and regional levels with national activities. They have, not however, elevated the status of issues of specific concern to women during bargaining (Cyba and Papouschek 1996; Colling and Dickens 1998). Nor have they prevented large numbers of women from leaving unions and citing the inadequacy of union organization as being their prime reason (Waddington and Kerr 1999). Many of these new approaches to union government have, thus, not yet transformed systems of union democracy.

Two developments have greater potential for change: the systems of union government adopted by UNISON in Britain and ver.di in Germany. Both of these unions were founded by merger, and representatives of the participating unions set out to establish 'new' unions.[6] Underpinning the approach adopted by UNISON and ver.di is the principle of proportionality, whereby the composition of each committee within the union must reflect the composition of the membership. In other words, if 60 per cent of a group of members are women, then 60 per cent of the committee that represents the group should also be women. Allied to the adoption of the principle of proportionality in UNISON are novel approaches to fair representation and self-organization. The UNISON rulebook defines fair representation as,

The broad balance and representation of members of the electorate, taking into account such factors as the balance between part-time and full-time workers, manual and non-manual workers, different occupations, skills, qualifications, responsibilities, race, sexuality and disability. (UNISON 1993: 65)

Self-organization is also promoted among women members, black members, members with disabilities, and gay and lesbian members. In combination, these approaches by UNISON have reshaped the traditional model of trade union democracy (McBride 2001). Women, black and gay and lesbian members are engaged in decision-making processes on a wider scale than hitherto and have developed new skills appropriate to this engagement (Humphrey 2002). Furthermore, alliances between different self-organized groups are now likely and present opportunities to extend the influence already secured (Colgan and Ledwith 2000). While the situation in ver.di is less developed because the merger was more recent, the point is that these approaches constitute a significant development beyond traditional approaches to equality.

There have also been marked shifts in the approaches of national unions to administration, with an increased emphasis placed on efficiency, new management techniques, and budgetary control. German and Spanish unions have paid particular attention to the provision of increasingly sophisticated legal services, reflecting the juridified industrial relations systems of the two countries (Schmidt and Trinczek 1993; Hamann and Martínez Lucio 2003). In addition, several German unions such as the construction workers union IG BAU, the IG Metall, and the chemical and mineworkers unions IG BCE have initiated comprehensive programmes for organizational development which seek to optimize the division of labour within the union to formalize routines, and to distribute efficiently both responsibilities and resources. In several cases, these programmes involved outside consultants (Behrens, Fichter, and Frege 2001: 15–16).

Increased use of opinion polls and market research to obtain the views of members and non-members, coupled to the targeting of specific groups of potential members, is now more widespread. In Germany, for example, the IG Metall initiated a so-called 'debate on the future' (*Zukunftsdebatte*) which included 'polling weeks' used to determine the views of the 120,000 workers who took part in surveys, interviews, and group discussions. In addition, the union commissioned nine comprehensive literature reviews on subjects related to the debate (EIRO 2002). In some instances devolved budgetary control has been introduced in conjunction with the centralized setting of targets and monitoring of individual performance, which has facilitated the retention of centralized control within an overall tendency of shifting more resources to the local level (Waddington, Kahmann, and Hoffmann 2003). This tendency is most marked where bargaining is decentralized.

There are very few examples where the introduction of administrative change has transformed union organization. Even where organizing budgets have been markedly increased, the absence of a clear connection between a union's membership strategy and broader transformative restructuring has often undermined the impact of the additional funds. Two notable exceptions in the United States to this general framework are the SEIU and the United Brotherhood of Carpenters (UBC). The SEIU now allocates 50 per cent of its national budget to organizing and requires locals to follow suit wherever possible. These initiatives, however, are also connected to partial revisions of union government. To move the process along, the SEIU is engineering mergers of locals it deems too small to pursue an effective organizing agenda independently. Although this intrusion into local union affairs has been questioned in some quarters within the union, support among elected leaders for the organizing priority has helped control opposition. Top-down structural change has been matched by an aggressive grassroots organizing approach, as the SEIU has continued its steady growth while other unions have struggled (Hurd, Milkman, and Turner 2003: 102, 111). The change effort is mission-driven under the union's New Strength and Unity Programme and clearly has transformative potential.

The UBC's top-down restructuring has been successful in the particular sense of recruiting additional members, but has stirred controversy. Shortly after assuming the union's presidency in 1995, Doug McCarron cut national office staff by half, eliminated departments, and rented out nine and one-half floors of the ten storey national headquarters to generate revenues. These changes helped fund a shift of 50 per cent of the union's resources into organizing. Subsequently, McCarron reorganized the union's regional and local structure, eliminating many locals and shifting control of resources to regional councils dominated by his political allies (Cleeland 2002). These aggressive changes have allowed the UBC to expand its organizing programme dramatically. Membership increased from about 500,000 in 1996 to

538,000 in 2002 (Gifford 1997: 50, 2003: 42). Although there are transformative elements to the UBC restructuring in terms of labour movement revitalization, there have been destructive components as well. On 29 March 2001 the UBC seceded from the AFL-CIO, ostensibly because the Sweeney administration compromised its commitment to organizing (Cleeland 2002).

The most promising restructuring at the national union level is tied to internal modifications. Although formed by mergers, the transformative aspects of the operation of UNISON in the United Kingdom and ver.di in Germany are the governance systems created by the new organizations with provisions to increase the role of women, minorities and young union members. In the United States, both the SEIU and UBC have restructured administration and governance to elevate dramatically the importance of organizing initiatives.

Pan-European Level

The development of the ETUC and the EIFs is closely linked to the successive enlargements of the European Union and to the process of European integration. From the perspective of external shape, both the ETUC and the EIFs have thus repeatedly extended their coverage to embrace successive enlargements. This happened with the affiliation of the communist-oriented confederations, and most recently the accession of confederations from Central and Eastern Europe. With the affiliation of the *Confederation Generale du Travail* (CGT) in 1999, the coverage of the ETUC was almost complete in Western Europe. Only some small confederations of civil servants and professional and managerial workers are now outside. Over 60 million trade union members from more than thirty countries are affiliated to the ETUC through confederations and national unions.

While this pattern of development has markedly extended the external shape of the ETUC, it has merely allowed the coverage of the ETUC to match that of the European Union. In other words, to retain influence in the European Union the ETUC was obliged to extend coverage. Internal democracy remains embedded in an 'intergovernmental' system based on nationality and membership size. Recent reviews of this system, under the chair of Johan Stecklenburg (1990) and John Monks respectively, have not recommended fundamental changes to the operation of this system. The 4-yearly congress[7] remains the supreme decision-making body, while an Executive and a relatively small secretariat are responsible for administering the organization between congresses.

Concurrent with the Stecklenburg review was a series of important developments within the European Union. The most prominent among these were preparations for the single market, an Intergovernmental Conference on treaty reform, negotiations on a framework to institutionalize the role of the social partners, and preparations for economic and monetary union. In combination these developments prompted two structural reforms of the ETUC of transformative potential.

The first of these concerned the assignment of wider bargaining powers to the ETUC by affiliated confederations at the ETUC Congress in 1991. The extent of the bargaining powers granted to the ETUC were not as wide-ranging as initially envisaged by those that proposed the motion, due largely to opposition from Nordic confederations (Dolvik 1999: 132–40). The granting of any authority to the ETUC to enable it to bargain independently, however, represented a fundamental transformation to its political influence. The subsequent engagement of the ETUC in negotiations on a range of issues including European works councils, parental leave, part-time workers, and fixed-term contracts of employment, together with its involvement in broader matters of social dialogue, illustrate the impact of the initial decision to grant it bargaining rights. Although the direction of ETUC policy is contested (Waddington 2000), movement towards a European industrial relations area required an ETUC with the authority to bargain, a development of transformative potential.

A second reform of the ETUC adopted in 1991 arose from a recommendation of the Stecklenburg Report. The constitution of the ETUC initially allowed only national level confederations to affiliate directly. In 1991 this was amended to enable EIFs to affiliate directly to the ETUC, and to grant seats to representatives of the EIFs on the Executive of the ETUC. In practice, this decision meant that national unions were linked to the ETUC through two routes; geographically via a national confederation and sectorally via the EIFs. The adoption of this measure, thus, represented the abandonment of country of origin as the sole basis to organization.

The amendment also has the long-term potential to be transformative in the context of bargaining power. Throughout Europe a range of cross-border bargaining initiatives were developed after about 1995, most of which were sector-specific and fostered by unions affiliated to particular EIFs (Gollbach and Schulten 2000; Prince 1995). Furthermore, in 1999 the ETUC Congress resolved to strive for 'the paramount goal' of a coordinated collective bargaining policy 'developed at sectoral or cross-sectoral level' with 'primary responsibility for coordination in the field of collective bargaining at European level' allocated to the EIFs (ETUC 1999: 67). There are many difficulties to overcome before European sectoral bargaining becomes a reality, not the least of which is the absence of employers' organizations prepared to enter into bargaining arrangements. Designating the principal role in this function to the EIFs, however, represents the potential to diminish further the influence of the national confederations and to transform the ETUC into a European confederation of EIFs, each of which conducts bargaining.

The institutional vitality of trade union organizations at the pan-European level is thus associated with the developing polity of the European Union. The development of a bargaining function by the ETUC and marked shifts in the position of the EIFs represent changes of transformative potential. Other reforms of the EIFs are more defensive in character. The reduction in the number of EIFs after 1996 as a result of mergers, for example, results primarily from membership decline and financial weaknesses.[8] Furthermore, there is little or no correspondence between these mergers and the structural reform of national unions, thus minimizing any benefits that might arise from economies of scale. The limited resources available to the EIFs also limit the transformative capacity of all of these developments. National level union organizations are the primary source of these resources. Membership decline, and associated financial difficulties at the national level effectively restricts the allocation of additional resources to the pan-European level.

In sum, restructuring at the pan-European level has great transformative potential. The wider role established by the ETUC within the European Union has substantially increased labour's political influence. Furthermore, the direct affiliation of the EIFs with the ETUC has opened the window of opportunity for European level bargaining and wider sectoral integration.

THE CONTRIBUTION OF STRUCTURAL CHANGE TO UNION REVITALIZATION

Restructuring has been integral to revitalization initiatives in all five of the countries we have studied and at the pan-European level. National unions have pursued mergers and introduced internal reforms in governance and administration with the clear intent to achieve transformative results. Confederations have restructured to demonstrate new priorities and to lead renewal efforts. The ETUC working with EIFs has been actively involved in shaping labour's role in the emerging integration of the European economy. Our review shows that there are indeed incidents of structural change that meet the standard of 'transformative' restructuring, or at least have transformative potential. During a time of upheaval in labour relations systems, only transformative restructuring with its embedded strategic perspective can contribute to labour movement revitalization. Because union external shapes were established when different social, political, and economic circumstances prevailed, it is necessary to reform trade union structures to eliminate outdated demarcations. Furthermore, internal reform of systems of union government and administration provides the opportunity to by-pass conservative vested interests and introduce new systems appropriate for the changed environment. While possibly an insufficient basis for union revitalization in its own right, transformative restructuring will almost certainly play a key role in labour movement renewal. But have the restructuring efforts as described been successful? Has the transformative intent translated into actual revitalization? In order to interpret further the impact of restructuring it is useful to return to the four dimensions of labour movement revitalization introduced in Chapter 2.

Within the *membership dimension* restructuring at both the confederation and national union levels has the capacity to shift resources to organizing, and also to achieve economies of scale which may free resources for intensified recruitment campaigns. Thus, mergers are frequently justified to enlarge membership numbers and to overcome competition in organizing members between unions with overlapping jurisdictions. However, although strategically driven mergers and targeted creation of subsidiaries may facilitate national union organization in new arenas, or may intensify organizing in markets where the union is already established, this type of result seldom accompanies the widespread effort to consolidate unions in the countries we have studied (see Heery and Adler, Chapter 4, this volume). In addition, restructuring can be used to enhance organizing strategies. The TUC and the AFL-CIO have taken the lead in establishing organizing as a priority in the United Kingdom and the United States, shifting resources and creating new units to achieve this result. Individual unions in the United States, especially SEIU and UBC have gone even further by reorienting the respective unions to recruitment activity.

Restructuring also can affect the *economic dimension* of revitalization, in three ways. First, by improving administration, unions gain resources and organizational flexibility. Second, restructuring may enable unions to establish more effective ways to process information on the outcomes of bargaining and other union activities, and use the information to mobilize members and resources more effectively. Third, by changing external structure unions can reform the bargaining framework and level to 'fit' changing labour markets and company organizational structure. Unfortunately, the evidence we have reviewed does not indicate great progress along the economic dimension. Increased coordination among confederations in Spain and Italy has, however, contributed at least modestly to increased leverage. Perhaps the greatest potential exists at the pan-European level where the EIFs offer the opportunity to deal more effectively with multinational corporations.

Structural change can have an effect on the *political dimension* of revitalization in two respects. First, by changing their external structure unions can pool their resources *vis-à-vis* political power holders and gain leverage in the field of political lobbying or corporatist arrangements. In this regard, increased collaboration in Italy and Spain has improved the political influence of confederations. Similarly, increased support for the ETUC that accompanied direct affiliation by the EIFs enhanced political influence within the European Union. Second, improvements in the field of union government provide labour's political allies with an opportunity to benefit from their legitimacy. In spite of some evidence of positive change in this aspect of internal operation, there is little evidence of associated increase in political influence.

The potential power of structural change is strongest in the *institutional dimension*, which was defined as a composite of unions' institutional shape, identities and dynamics. Although structural change clearly alters the shape of union institutions, this alone is not sufficient to assure progress towards revitalization. In contrast to the 'old institutionalists', many of whom were inspired by Robert Michels and the iron law of oligarchy (1989), the potential power of restructuring is viewed here as infusing a commitment to dynamic change into the union. In other words, if structural change helps labour overcome strategic rigidity and accept innovation, then there is clearly progress in this dimension. The restructuring that has occurred in the United States and the United Kingdom to promote organizing, or in some German unions to promote more democratic and efficient organizations, has certainly contributed to institutional vitality. Similarly, the confederal reforms in Italy and Spain have strengthened coordination and injected new life into those labour movements. Also, the increased visibility and role of the ETUC has helped to infuse dynamic change into that organization.

In spite of these encouraging signs at various levels of the labour movements in and across these countries, we must conclude that structural change in itself does not hold great potential to drive revitalization. Restructuring, clearly, has enhanced institutional vitality at all levels in a variety of ways. However, this is not enough. Without more substantial progress in the membership, economic, and political dimensions, this institutional progress will have little substantive impact. Moreover, it is only in conjunction with other strategic approaches that restructuring becomes important. In fact, it is in the context of new organizing, political and bargaining strategies, and the emergence of new international initiatives that structural change takes on the crucial role of institutionalizing labour movement revitalization.

Notes

1. In practice, European Industry Federations may be independent organizations, that attract members from within the European Union and a broader Europe, or they may be regional organizations of International Trade Secretariats. As this distinction does not have significance in the context of union revitalization, its implications are not examined in detail here.
2. In Spain, there are also confederations based on specific regions. These confederations are excluded from this analysis.
3. We classify Germany as a unitary system, although it should be noted that there are some small pockets of inter-union rivalry where the DGB's affiliates are facing competition from independent unions or union federations. The Christian Trade Union Federation of Germany (*Christlicher Gewerkschaftsbund*, CGB), as the most important of those competing federations, represents about 300,000 employees in several industries. In addition, some rival unions such as the pilots' union Cockpit or the Independent Association of Flight Attendants (*Unabhangige Flugbegleiter* Organization, UFO) were created in opposition to the DGB and its affiliates.
4. Affiliations to the TUC since 1995 include Professional Footballers' Association, Community and Youth Workers' Association, Community and District Nursing Association, UNIFI, Independent Union of Halifax Staff, Society of Chiropodists and Podiatrists, British Dietetic Association, Association of Flight Attendants-Heathrow Local, Association of Teachers and Lecturers, Alliance and Leicester Group Union of Staff, Association of Educational Psychologists, Nationwide Group Staff Union, Woolwich Independent Staff Union, and the Britannic Field Staff Association.
5. As noted above the TUC was also active in attracting new affiliates in the same period. The extent of the decline among the population of affiliated unions of 1990 is thus understated by these figures.
6. UNISON was formed in 1993 by the merger of the Confederation of Health Service Employees, National and Local Government Officers' Association, and the National Union of Public Employees. Ver.di was formed by merger in 2001 from Deutsche Angestellten Gewerkschaft, Deutsche Postgewerkschaft, Gewerkschaft Handel, Banken und Versicherungen, Industriegewerkschaft Medien and Gewerkschaft Öffentliche Dienste, Transport und Verkehr. Both unions organize service workers: UNISON in just the public services, whereas ver.di organizes across all services. Furthermore, the two unions are the largest unions in their respective countries (for details, see Waddington et al. 2003).
7. Before 1991 the ETUC congress was held every third year and every fourth year thereafter.
8. Several mergers involving EIFs took place from the mid-1990s. Among these mergers were the formation of the European Mine, Chemical and Energy Workers' Federation from the

European Federation of Chemical Workers' Unions and the Miners' European Federation, and the acquisition of the European Federation of Agricultural Workers' Unions by the European Committee of Food, Catering, and Allied Workers' Unions. In addition, the international trade secretariats of the International Federation of Commercial, Clerical, Professional, and Technical Employees, Communications International and the International Graphical, Media and Entertainment Federation merged to form Union Network International (UNI). This merger was also carried through at European level where the respective European regional organization merged to form UNI-Europa.

References

Allaire, Y. and Firsirotu, M. (1985). 'How to Implement Radical Strategies in Large Organizations'. *Sloan Management Review*, Spring, 26: 19–33.

Armenakis, A., Harris, S., and Mossholder, K. (1993). 'Creating Readiness for Organizational Change'. *Human Relations*, 46/6: 681–701.

Baccaro, L., Carrieri, M., and Damiano, C. (2003). 'The Resurgence of Italian Confederal Unions: Will It Last?'. *European Journal of Industrial Relations*, 9/1: 43–60.

Behrens, M. (2002). *Learning from the Enemy? Internal Union Restructuring and the Imitation of Management Strategies*. Ithaca, NY: Cornell University Ph.D. Dissertation.

—— Fichter, M., and Frege, C. (2001). *Unions in Germany: Searching to Regain the Initiative*. Düsseldorf: WSI-Diskussionspapier Nr. 97.

Bordogna, L. (1989). 'The COBAS Fragmentation of Trade Union Representation and Conflict'. *Italian Politics*, 3: 50–64.

Braithwaite, M. and Byrne, C. (n.d.). *Women in Decision-making in Trade Unions*. Brussels: European Trade Union Confederation.

Chaison, G. (1986). *When Unions Merge*. Lexington, MA: Lexington Books.

—— (1996). *Union Mergers in Hard Times*. Ithaca, NY: Cornell University Press.

Chitayat, G. (1979). *Trade Union Mergers and Labor Conglomerates*. New York: Praeger Publishers.

Clark, P. and Gray, L. (1991). 'Union Administration', in G. Strauss, D. Gallagher, and J. Fiorito (eds.), *The State of the Unions*. Madison, WI: Industrial Relations Research Association, 175–200.

Cleeland, N. (2002). 'Organize or Die'. *Los Angeles Times Magazine*, 10 March.

Clegg, H. (1976). *Trade Unionism under Collective Bargaining*. Oxford: Blackwell.

Colgan, F. and Ledwith, S. (2000). 'Diversity, Identities and Strategies of Women Trade Union Activists'. *Gender, Work and Organization*, 7/4: 242–57.

Colling, T. and Dickens, L. (1998). 'Selling the Case for Gender Equality: Deregulation and Equality Bargaining'. *British Journal of Industrial Relations*, 36/3: 389–412.

Cyba, E. and Papouschek, U. (1996). 'Women's Interests in the Workplace: Between Delegation and Self-representation'. *Transfer*, 2/1: 61–81.

Dolvik, J.-E. (1999). *An Emerging Island?*. Brussels: European Trade Union Institute.

ETUC. (1999). *Resolutions from 9th Congress*. Brussels: European Trade Union Confederation.

EIRO. (2002). IG Metall Debates Manifesto For The Future. www.eiro.eurofound.ie/2002/06/Feature/DE0206205F.html.

Fan, M. (1998). 'Unions Join in Powerful Alliance'. *New York Daily News*, 8 January.

Fletcher Jr., B. and Hurd, R. (2001). 'Overcoming Obstacles to Transformation: Challenges on the Way of New Unionism', in L. Turner, H. C. Katz, and R. W. Hurd (eds.), *Rekindling the*

Movement: Labor's Quest for Relevance in the Twenty-First Century. Ithaca NY: ILR Press, 182–208.

Fullin, G. (2002). 'The Unions for Atypical Workers in Italy'. *Transfer*, 8/3: 531–5.

Garcia, A., Hacourt, B., and Lega, H. (n.d.). *The Second Sex of European Trade Unionism*. Brussels: European Trade Union Confederation.

Gifford, C. (1997). *Directory of U.S. Labor Organizations: 1997 edition*. Washington, DC: Bureau of National Affairs.

——(2003). *Directory of U.S. Labor Organizations: 2003 edition*. Washington, DC: Bureau of National Affairs.

Gollbach, J. and Schulten, T. (2000). 'Cross-Border Collective Bargaining Networks in Europe'. *European Journal of Industrial Relations*, 6/2: 161–79.

Grabelsky, J. and Hurd, R. (1994). 'Reinventing an Organizing Union: Strategies for Change', in *Proceedings of the Forty Sixth Annual Meeting*, (Boston, January 3–5), pp. 95–104. Madison, WI: Industrial Relations Research Association.

Greene, A.-M., Hogan, J., and Grieco, M. (2003). 'E-Collectivism and Distributed Discourse: New Opportunities for Trade Union Democracy'. *Industrial Relations Journal*, 34/4: 282–9.

Greenhouse, S. (2003). 'Worried about Labor's Waning Strength, Union Presidents form Advisory Committee'. *New York Times*, 9: 22 March.

Hamann, K. and Martínez Lucio, M. (2003). 'Strategies of Union Revitalization in Spain: Negotiating Change and Fragmentation'. *European Journal of Industrial Relations*, 9/1: 61–78.

Heery, E. (1998). 'The Relaunch of the Trades Union Congress', *British Journal of Industrial Relations*, 36/3: 339–60.

Humphrey, J. (2002). *Towards a Politics of the Rainbow: Self-organization in the Trade Union Movement*. Aldershot: Ashgate.

Hurd, R., Milkman, R., and Turner, L. (2003). 'Reviving the American Labor Movement'. *European Journal of Industrial Relations*, 9/1: 99–117.

Hyman, R. (1975). *Industrial Relations: A Marxist Introduction*. Basingstoke: Macmillan.

Kahmann, M. (2003). *Trade Unions and the Growth of the Information Economy*. Brussels: European Trade Union Institute, Discussion and Working Paper.

Kotter, J. (1995). 'Leading Change: Why Transformative Efforts Fail'. *Harvard Business Review*, 73/2: 59–67.

Kreile, M. (1988). 'The Crisis of Italian Trade Unionism in the 1980s'. *West European Politics*, 11/1: 54–67.

Locke, R. and Baccaro, L. (1996). 'Learning from Past Mistakes? Recent Reforms in Italian Industrial Relations'. *Industrial Relations Journal*, 27/ 4: 289–303.

March, J. and Simon, H. (1993, first published 1958). *Organizations, 2nd edn*. Oxford: Blackwell.

Martinez Lucio, M. (2003). 'New Communications Systems and Trade Union Politics: A Case Study of Spanish Trade Unions and the Role of the Internet'. *Industrial Relations Journal*, 34/4: 334–47.

McBride, A. (2001). *Gender Democracy in Trade Unions*. Aldershot: Ashgate.

Michels, R. (1989, first published 1910). *Zur Soziologie des Parteiwesens in der modernen Demokratie, Untersuchungen uber die oligarchischen Tendenzen des Gruppenlebens*. Stuttgart: Alfred Kroner Verlag.

Nord, W. and Tucker, S. (1986). *Implementing Radical and Routine Innovation*. Lexington, MA: Lexington Books.

Ponzellini, A. and Provenzano, E. (2001). 'Italy: The Services Sector—Towards a More Inclusive and Flexible Labour Market', in J.-E. Dolvik (ed.), *At Your Service*. Brussels: Peter Lang, 305–40.

Prince, J.-P. (1995). *Interregional Trade Union Councils in Europe.* Brussels: European Trade Union Institute, DWP 95.03.01.

Regini, M. and Regalia, I. (2000). 'The Prospects for Italian Trade Unions in a Phase of Concertation', in J. Waddington and R. Hoffmann (eds.), *Trade Unions in Europe: Facing Challenges and Searching for Solutions.* Brussels: European Trade Union Institute, 365–92.

Schmidt, R. and Trinczek, R. (1993). 'Fusion und Konfusion: Gründe und Hintergr ünde für die Reorganisation des DGB', in T. Leif, A. Klein, and H.-J. Legrand (eds.), *Reform des DGB: Herausforderungen, Ausbruchspläne und Modernisierungsknozepte.* Koln: Bund Verlag, 66–88.

Selznick, P. (1957). *Leadership in Administration. A Sociological Interpretation.* New York: Harper & Row.

Stecklenburg, J. (1990). *The Stecklenburg Report. For a More Efficient ETUC.* Brussels: European Trade Union Confederation.

Sverke, M. and Sjoberg, A. (1997). 'Ideological and Instrumental Union Commitment', in M. Sverke (ed.), *The Future of Trade Unionism.* Aldershot: Ashgate, 277–94.

Undy, R., Ellis, R., McCarthy, W., and Halmos, A. (1981). *Change in Trade Unions.* London: Hutchinson and Co.

UNISON. (1993). *Rules as at Vesting Day.* London: UNISON.

Voss, K. and Sherman, R. (2000). 'Breaking the Iron Law of Oligarchy: Union Revitalization in the American Labor Movement'. *American Journal of Sociology*, 106/2: 303–49.

Waddington, J. (2000). 'Towards a Reform Agenda? European Trade Unions in Transition'. *Industrial Relations Journal*, 31/4: 317–30.

—— and Hoffmann, R. (2000) (eds.). *Trade Unions in Europe: Facing Challenges and Searching for Solutions.* Brussels: European Trade Union Institute.

—— and Kerr, A. (1999). 'Trying to Stem the Flow: Union Membership Turnover in the Public Sector'. *Industrial Relations Journal*, 30/3: 184–96.

—— Kahmann, M., and Hoffmann, J. (2003). *United We Stand: A Comparison of the Trade Union Merger Process in Britain and Germany.* London: Anglo-German Foundation.

Weil, D. (1997). *Turning the Tide: Strategic Planning for Labor Unions.* Winchester, MA: Book Tech.

8

The New Solidarity? Trade Union Coalition-Building in Five Countries

CAROLA FREGE, EDMUND HEERY, AND LOWELL TURNER

INTRODUCTION

If mature trade union movements are to undergo revitalization, it has been frequently argued, then they must recreate themselves as social movements (Turner and Hurd 2001; Voss and Sherman 2003). They must broaden their goals to encompass social progress beyond the immediate employment relationship and rediscover their capacity to mobilize workers in campaigns for workplace and wider social justice. In Waterman's (1998: 2) words, unions should 'add to the lay trinity (liberty, equality, fraternity) the values of diversity, peace and ecological care'. Integral to this prescription of 'social movement unionism' is the belief that unions should act in concert with other progressive social forces and particularly the 'new social movements', grounded in the politics of social identity, the environment, and globalization. In short, unions must form coalitions if they are to achieve revitalization (Johnston 2002; Robinson 2002).

Of course, unions have always built coalitions and in most developed societies what is known as the 'labour movement' embraces a complex of institutions, including political parties, trade unions, cooperative societies, research institutes, and community and welfare organizations (Wheeler 2002: 201–9). From anti-fascism in the 1930s to the civil rights and antiwar movements of the 1960s, moreover, unions have participated in coalitions of protest. Thus, coalition-building is not a recent innovation, devised by new 'social movement unions', but has long formed part of labour's repertoire. Nevertheless, there is a new urgency to attempts to build coalitions in the present context. This is most apparent in the United States, where unions have joined in living wage, environmental, anti-sweatshop, and anti-globalization coalitions with a broad range of partners, drawn from faith, community, student, and environmental groups (Nissen and Rosen 1999; Russo and Corbin 1999; Johnston 2001; Hurd, Milkman, and Turner 2003: 6–8). In the United Kingdom, an established tradition of unions forging coalitions to combat the restructuring of public services (Ogden 1991; Foster and Scott 1998) has been supplemented in recent years by incipient living wage and No Sweat campaigns (Wills 2002). In Germany, there has been a strengthening of union coalitions with anti-fascist and green organizations (Behrens, Fichter, and Frege 2003: 34–5). And in Italy and Spain the traditionally broad conception of trade unionism as a force for social and political change has been supplemented by alliances with environmental and immigrant organizations, respectively (Baccaro, Carrieri, and Damiano 2003: 51–2; Hamann and Martínez Lucio 2003: 64–5).

The purpose of this chapter is to present a framework for the analysis of union coalition-building and demonstrate its utility using comparative empirical material mainly from the United States, Germany, and the United Kingdom though we also comment on union action in Italy and Spain. In what follows, we seek to define union-coalitions and specify their functions, identify a variety of types of coalition and the variety of factors that encourage unions to forge coalitions. We then set out and seek to explain the variable patterns of coalition use across our five countries. The chapter concludes in speculative vein, by considering the role that coalition-building should and could play in the revitalization of national labour movements.

DEFINITION AND FUNCTIONS

The founders of the academic field of industrial relations in the United Kingdom, Sidney and Beatrice Webb (1902) classified the methods of trade unionism in terms of the mechanism used to generate employment rules, or 'job regulation'. Thus, unions can create and apply rules either unilaterally, or through joint decision-making (bargaining and consultation) with employers or through the method of 'legal regulation', which requires involvement in the political sphere. Coalition-building is a union method, though in many cases coalitions do not themselves give rise to job regulation. Rather, coalition can be viewed as a secondary union method that can be used to support any of the three primary methods identified by the Webbs. Thus, coalition may support unilateral regulation of the labour market, as when unions cooperate with community organizations to provide training and job search facilities for low-wage workers (Osterman et al. 2001: 118). It can support collective bargaining, as when the mobilization of community support in the course of a strike augments the union's bargaining power (Juravich and Bronfenbrenner 1999). And it can support legal regulation, as when unions mount living wage campaigns with other organizations to secure the upward adjustment of the statutory pay floor (Kusnet 1998).

Moreover, coalition is a method that can be, and often is, used to extend the reach of union activity beyond the sphere of job regulation, narrowly conceived, to pursue wider social and political change. As such, it can reinforce a broad conception of union purpose, seen particularly in the labour movements of continental Europe, and allow unions to engage as civic actors. Recent coalitions against the Second Gulf War in Italy, Spain, and Britain or coalitions to combat the extreme right in Britain and Germany provide examples. To quote another founder of UK industrial relations analysis, Allan Flanders (1970: 15–16), unions can act as a 'sword of justice' as well as a 'vested interest'.

Union coalitions can, therefore, be defined as involving discrete, intermittent, or continuous joint activity in pursuit of shared or common goals between trade unions and other non-labour institutions in civil society, including community, faith, identity, advocacy, welfare, and campaigning organizations. This is a broad definition but it excludes joint union action with state agencies and political parties and also excludes joint action between unions themselves and between unions, and employers. Union coalitions may draw state bodies, other unions and employers into joint activity but they are not defined by the involvement of institutions of this kind. The definition also specifies that coalition requires joint working with other institutions. Thus, the incorporation of new social movements into union organization through the establishment of women's or immigrant workers' sections or the embrace of new social movement goals, such as respect for the environment, in our view should not count as coalition-building. Actions of these kinds may strengthen the social movement traditions of unions and are frequently an outcome of their engagement with new social movements, but they are distinct from coalition itself. Finally, coalitions between unions and other groups rise and fall. It may be that the most successful coalitions run for the longer term and rest on 'bridge builders' who develop and sustain intersecting networks of labour and non-labour activists (Brecher and Costello 1990; Rose 2000) but neither permanence nor success are required by our definition.

Unions enter into coalitions for a multiplicity of purposes. Coalitions can help them win certification/recognition from employers, provide the wherewithal to sustain strikes, help unions organize minority, or other difficult-to-contact workers and provide support for legislative change. They can also allow unions to express broader ideological and political convictions, such as support for the peace movement or sustainable development that do not have immediate employment-related consequences. Whatever the objective, however, the function of coalition partners is typically to provide unions with resources that help them to achieve goals.

In many cases unions will opt not to use these resources. Reliance on traditional resources, such as the membership's willingness to act or the support of the state or employers, which are discussed in other chapters, may be sufficient for union purposes. Coalition can be a risky tactic for unions, not least because coalition-partners may prove unreliable or have only limited capacity to advance union objectives. In many cases, the default option for unions will be not to seek coalition. Nevertheless, many unions do seek coalition partners for a wide variety of reasons. Underlying this variety, we feel is union desire to access the following five resources controlled by coalition partners:

Financial and physical resources. Coalitions can yield material support for trade unions, perhaps most obviously when women's and other support groups provide cash and food to sustain strike action (Juravich and Bronfenbrenner 1999). The involvement of coalition partners in this way has become a major feature of strikes in Britain and the United States, though is less apparent in Germany where union finances continue to be strong or in Italy and Spain where strikes rarely take the form of 'trials of strength'. In Britain, the tactic dates back to the great miners' strike against pit closures in 1984–5 when there was a broad mobilization of mining communities and other interest associations and identity groups in support of the strikers (Winterton and Winterton 1989). Coalitions may also provide other valuable physical resources to trade unions including networks of activists, paid staff, and premises.

Access to new groups. Many coalition partners have a constituency, membership, or client-base and the purpose of coalition can be to allow union access to those groups. Thus, community-based organizing of new union members often relies on ethnic or faith-based partners to facilitate union access to minority workers (Bonacich 2000; Milkman and Wong 2001). Another example is provided by the British Trades Union Congress (TUC) which ran a campaign on part-time work in the mid-1990s. This involved distributing information on new employment rights to part-time workers using the Citizen's Advice Bureaux, a voluntary organization with offices around the United Kingdom, used by many low paid, non-union workers to obtain advice on employment law (Heery 1998*a*). The connection between Spanish unions and organizations of immigrant workers provides a final example. Here, dependence on the coalition partner for communication is particularly acute because illegal immigrants are prohibited from joining trade unions (Hamann and Martínez Lucio 2003: 65).

Expertise. Coalition partners may also possess specialist expertise upon which unions can draw. At the level of policy formulation, a number of German trade unions (IG BAU, IGM, Transnet) have developed policies on sustainable development for the sectors they organize in conjunction with green and environmentalist organizations. IG BAU, the construction union, which has been most active in this regard, has worked with Greenpeace to formulate a quality standard for the ecologically sound renovation of old buildings (Wieshugel 1996). At an operational level, coalition partners may supply technical advice in the fields of immigration, welfare, and other law (Needleman 1998; Milkman and Wong 2000). Thus, the campaign to unionize Mexican immigrant drywall hangers in Southern California in the 1990s drew on the legal expertise of the California Immigrant Workers' Association (Milkman 2002: 121). In Britain, the TUC's recently launched initiative on ethical trading provides another example. This campaign has involved close work with non-governmental organizations (NGOs), such as Oxfam, which possess expertise on labour conditions in developing countries, international contacts, and a history of action on labour standards.

Legitimacy. The presence of a coalition partner can confer legitimacy on a trade union and its activities. In many cases, the function of coalition is to endorse trade unionism, particularly when faith or ethnic organizations provide backing for union organizing campaigns. Unions may also gain 'reflected legitimacy' by association with organizations, like Greenpeace, which have a positive public image among identity groups that unions are anxious to influence. Moreover, association can allow unions to shake off public suspicion that they act as a (non-legitimate) 'special interest', while joint campaigning in concert with other bodies can add weight to the union cause. For a number of years the TUC, for example, has campaigned jointly on pension reform with a range of other organizations, including Age Concern, Help the Aged, Stonewall, and the Police Federation (Heery 1998*b*).

Mobilization. Coalition may facilitate the mobilization of popular support for trade unions and the policies they espouse in demonstrations, voting or consumer boycotts. Again, action of this kind has been apparent in union organizing campaigns in the United States, where faith and community organizations have rallied their supporters against the employer (Peters and Merrill 1998). It has also been seen in the antiwar and anti-globalization movements. The pivotal demonstration in Seattle against the policies of the World Trade Organization brought together 30,000 demonstrators organized by labour groups with 20,000 from environmental, religious, human rights, and other groups (Hawken 2000). In Britain the United Kingdom's main public service union, UNISON, has worked with tenants' organizations in Birmingham against the transfer of public housing from local authority control to new 'social landlords'. This campaign produced a resounding, tenants' vote against transfer in 2001, which protected public service jobs, and has provided the basis for further cooperation. In 2002 when UNISON organized national strike action in furtherance of a pay dispute, Birmingham tenants supported the action and joined the union's demonstration in the city. A final example can be seen in the living wage movement in the United States. Here, unions have joined with a broad range of other organizations to mobilize popular support and voting power for the passing of living wage ordinances by city governments, with successes being registered in cities across the States (Figart, Mutari, and Power 2002: 195–7; Hurd, Milkman, and Turner 2003: 106).

In sum, we regard coalition as a secondary method of trade unions that is used to support the primary activities of organizing and servicing members, engaging with employers and participating in the political process. It rests on the process of alliance building with other institutions and associations that operate in civil society, either for the shorter or the longer term. Coalitions can be used to advance a broad set of substantive goals, but at its heart lie union attempts to access the resources controlled by their coalition partners. The latter include physical and financial resources, networks of communications, expertise, legitimacy, and the capacity to mobilize constituencies and popular support.

TYPES OF COALITION

Not all union-backed coalitions are the same. Coalitions differ in life span, the identity of the coalition partner or partners, their goals, methods, and degrees of success. Given that coalitions rest on an exchange between unions and non-labour organizations, however, the task of classification can best begin by noting the variable pattern of interaction between coalition partners. At one extreme, the interests of the union may dominate, while at the other unions may accede priority to the interests of their coalition partner. In between, a number of intermediate positions are possible, and on this basis we believe that three main types can be identified as follows and can be found across all five countries:

Vanguard coalitions. Here, unions seek coalition on the basis of partners accepting a subordinate role, in which they offer solidarity and support for union objectives. In this situation, it may be assumed that the activities of the union embody a general progressive or class interest to which other groups and institutions should lend support. The union, in other words, constitutes a vanguard, which demands, or is deserving of, the solidarity of its coalition partners. Vanguard coalitions of this kind often form in the context of major 'trials of strength', long and bitter industrial disputes which are backed by support groups and a range of other organizations that lend assistance to strikers (Juravich and Bronfenbrenner 1999). The union may actively appeal for this support, but generally it is offered on an unconditional basis and it is rare for the views of supporting partners to influence strike strategy. The best documented example in Britain is probably the miners' strike of 1984/85, which was sustained for months by the mobilization of mining communities and other sympathetic groups (Adeney and Lloyd 1986; Winterton and Winterton 1989). At the heart of this mobilization were the women's support groups and although the union's leadership proposed a change to the National Union of Mineworkers (NUM) constitution to allow representation of these groups, this was resisted by the constituent regions of the union, which were anxious not to surrender control of strike strategy. Support was welcome but on the basis of solidarity not shared decision-making.

Common-cause coalitions. This second type of coalition is characterized by an attempt to identify separate but associated interests behind which a coalition can form. The union enters the coalition to advance its distinctive interests, while its non-labour partners do the same. The two sets of interests are complementary and as such provide a basis for cooperative, joint action. Many union-backed coalitions take this form. The UNISON campaign to block the transfer of social housing in Birmingham, described above, provides an example. In this case, the union was motivated by a desire to maintain secure jobs in the public sector and to prevent the fragmentation of its own organization as the city's large housing department was broken up into a series of non-profit making 'social landlords'. The coalition partner, the tenants' organizations, in contrast were concerned primarily about future rent rises and the possibility of housing stock being demolished and land sold to generate revenue. Both sets of interests sustained the joint campaign to win a 'no' vote and block the city's proposals to restructure the housing service. In the United Kingdom, common cause campaigns of this kind appear to dominate in what is probably the most frequent context for coalition-building: efforts by unions to win client support for attempts to halt the restructuring of public services (Terry 2000: 217). The distinct but complementary interests of workers in preserving jobs and conditions and clients in preserving service quality allow coalitions to form.

The institutional expression of common-cause coalitions is often the creation of an umbrella organization by trade unions and their coalition partners. Thus, the United Kingdom's Ethical Trading Initiative brings together unions and NGOs, together with businesses that accept the objective of raising labour standards. A North American example is the Coalition for Justice in the Maquilas, which has drawn US and Canadian unions into joint work with religious and community-based organizations to help organize workers in Mexico (Frundt 2002: 49–51). A final example comes from Italy, where the CGIL has created centres for the promotion of the rights of transsexuals in Bologna and Turin in cooperation with the Italian Transsexuals' Movement (Beccalli and Meardi 2002: 129).

Common cause coalitions can prove unstable as the distinct interests of unions and their coalition partners move out of alignment. In the United States, there has been tension within the Alliance for Sustainable Jobs and the Environment, the umbrella organization for local coalitions on environmental issues over the appropriate response to global warming, oil drilling in Alaska and automobile mileage require-ments (Moberg 1999; Rose 2000). The interest of one partner in growth and job secu-rity has proved difficult to marry to that of the other in sustainability. This is not an inevitable consequence, however, and elsewhere there is evidence of repeated interac-tion between unions and coalition partners leading to a broadening of their common interests. In Germany, the initial relationship between unions and the green move-ment in the 1970s was rather hostile, with a marked division over the issue of nuclear energy. The effect of environmental catastrophes, such as Sandoz and Tschernobyl, and the growing sensitization of the German population (including union members) to green issues, however, encouraged change in the 1980s. Today, the DGB and indi-vidual German unions engage in a broad set of coalitions with green organizations, including Greenpeace, BUND, and *Deutscher Natur Ring*. Partly this is based on the identification of a new common interest, as environmentally friendly production has been identified as a potential niche for German business, helping to secure jobs. This process of identifying a broader field of common interest through repeated contact has also been seen in the relationship between green organizations and unions in Italy (Baccaro, Carrieri, and Damiano 2003: 51–2). Common cause coalitions can, there-fore, follow a varying trajectory, consisting of breakdown and disintegration in some cases but a broadening and deepening of contact in others.

Integrative coalitions. The third type of coalition arises when unions offer uncondi-tional support to their non-labour partners. In this situation, the union effectively 'takes over' the objectives of non-labour organizations and accepts them as its own. This may arise when activists from new social movements achieve positions of influ-ence in trade unions. In the United States, United Kingdom, Italy, and Germany, unions have espoused elements of a women's agenda over the past 30 years, as feminists have become active in unions and pushed for changes in policy (Beccalli and Meardi 2002: 123; Cobble and Michal 2002: 233; Koch-Baumgarten 2002: 142–4; Ledwith and Colgan 2002: 16–17). A similar development can be traced with regard to the gay, dis-ability, and minority movements in the United States, in particular, but also in other countries (Cobble and Michal 2002: 248–50; Ledwith and Colgan 2002: 20).

Integrative coalitions are particularly apparent in Germany, where the union move-ment has responded to appeals for solidarity from environmentalists and anti-fascist campaigners and participated in joint action. This type of coalition reflects the fact that trade unions are value-rational organizations; they are driven at least in part by ideology and conviction and their activists respond to requests for support on the basis of the intrinsic merits of the appeal. Nevertheless, unions must balance support for non-labour organizations against internal constraints and need to protect their institutional interests. For this reason, unions tend to form integrative coalitions when it is relatively costless for them to do so. Thus, in Germany unions have joined with national and local anti-fascist organizations to campaign against the far right in response to the intensification of neo-Nazi activity since the mid-1990s. But they have been less active in seeking to challenge racism or political extremism among their own members. Integrating or espousing the interests of coalition partners, therefore, is most likely in fields of activity which are secondary or relatively remote from the core interests of unions. In Germany, it is either unions that can gain from or are not threatened by a green agenda which have been most ready to form coalitions. Those that are threatened, such as IGBCE the chemical, mining, and energy union, have been notably less keen to take the coalition path (Kädtler and Hertle 1997). Another example is provided by Italy, where unions at national level have worked with disability organizations to promote stronger rights for disabled workers. At local level, however, where the costs of adjustment may be met in part by non-disabled workers, engagement is less evident (Beccalli and Meardi 2002: 128). This suggests that integrative coalitions may be most easily formed at higher levels of union organization where the redistributive costs of policy are less likely to be felt (Terry 2000: 224–5).

A second way of thinking about types of coalition is in terms of the methods they use. In particular, coalitions differ in how they interact with the state, the primary target of much coalition activity. According to McIlroy (2000), trade unions can intervene in politics as 'insiders' or 'outsiders'. In the first case, they are accepted as legitimate representatives and engage in dialogue with ministers and civil servants to refine public policy, while in the second they are excluded from influence and seek to exert pressure on state agencies through industrial action or generating popular protest. This kind of distinction can be applied to labour-backed coalitions.

On the one hand, it is possible to identify 'coalitions of influence', in which unions seek coalition with other 'insider' organizations in order to make use of their expertise and legitimacy in advancing their own policy to government. The coalition-building of the TUC and DGB in recent years has largely assumed this form. It can also be seen in individual unions. The Association of First Division Civil Servants is a union of senior public servants in the United Kingdom, which has worked closely with an organization called *New Ways to Work* to advance its policy on family-friendly working and work–life balance. The union has run joint seminars for politicians and managers with its partner and commissioned research to identify the successful use of flexible working practices in senior management positions. *New Ways to Work* is an influential and expert lobbying organization and unions developing 'coalitions of influence' are likely to be drawn to partners of this kind; continuous, formal organizations that are structured and behave in a manner similar to unions themselves. In Germany, for instance, unions have largely rejected joint working with the radical, anti-globalization protest movement in favour of more limited campaigns to secure social trade clauses and codes of conduct. Thus, ver.di has affiliated to ATTAC, which is committed to the democratization of the global economy, while the DGB has joined with FIAN and Transfer to press German employers and government for a code of conduct to regulate the employment practices of German MNCs in developing countries.

On the other hand, we can identify 'coalitions of protest', which seek to mobilize union members and other constituencies to generate external pressure on government. The US living wage and anti-sweatshop campaigns take this form as do the attempts at community-based organizing used by Service Employees International Union (SEIU), Union of Needle Trades, Industrial and Textile Employees (UNITE), Hotel Employees and Restaurant Employees International Union (HERE), and other US unions (Needleman 1998; Bonacich 2000; Wells 2000). Coalition partners in this case may often be loosely structured, local organizations, while the union initiative may come from the activist base rather than the centre. The latter is not a hard-and-fast rule, however, and national union leaders may sanction 'coalitions of protest'. The Sweeney leadership of the American Federation of Labor-Congress of Industrial Organizations (AFL-CIO) has adopted this position, perhaps most notably in the Union Cities campaign (Kriesky 2001). The AFL-CIO Union Summer has also been important in creating connections between student activists and the labour movement, which have come to fruition in the anti-sweatshop movement. The costs of the umbrella organization for the movement, moreover, United Students Against Sweatshops, have been underwritten by UNITE. Even the risk-averse British TUC has sponsored 'coalitions of protest' and in the 1990s worked jointly with a broad range of anti-racist and black organizations to campaign against the extreme right in the East End of London. Choices over coalition tactics do not map one-to-one onto structural positions within the labour movement.

To summarize, coalitions can be classified on several dimensions, but we believe that it is useful to focus on two aspects. The first is the relationship between trade unions and their coalition partners, which can be based on a demand for solidarity, the identification of common interests or the adoption of the coalition partner's goals. The second dimension refers to the degree of integration of the coalition into state policy-making, where we distinguish coalitions-of-influence and coalitions-of-protest. Either type can be combined with the three forms of relationship with coalition partners.

FACTORS PROMOTING COALITION

Our analysis of the five national cases suggests that two types of pressure encourage unions to enter coalition with non-labour organizations. The first type arises mainly within unions themselves and effectively 'pushes' union strategy towards coalition. Unions are more likely to engage in coalition, when they are faced with exclusion from other kinds of resource, when their policy agenda is broadening to include non-traditional issues, when their activist base includes a significant proportion of 'bridge builders' with experience of other social movements, or when union purpose is conceived in terms of broader social change. The second type of pressure arises beyond trade unions and has to do with the supply of coalition partners and political opportunities for using coalition to effect change. The critical variables in this case therefore are the strength of civil society and the structure of the state, factors that can 'pull' trade unions towards experiment with coalition.

Diminishing Resources

Accounts of union-backed coalitions often stress the difficulties encountered in marrying different structures, cultures and goals (e.g. Needleman 1998). For this reason, unions may eschew coalition when they have ready access to other resources and traditional methods continue to yield results. The search for coalition therefore may be a function of union decline; a method adopted *in extremis*. This principle can be illustrated with three examples. Accounts of coalition in the US literature are most common in two circumstances, living wage campaigns and attempts to organize low-wage workers (Turner and Hurd 2001). It is when unions seek to represent workers with low 'organizational power' (capacity to sustain collective organization) and low 'positional power' (low skills and secondary labour market positions) that they are most likely to turn to coalition (Edwards and Heery 1989: 10–11). In other words, when unions cannot rely upon the organizational and bargaining strength of workers themselves they look for other resources, for coalition partners, to advance their goals.

In Britain, experiments with coalition developed after the election of the radical rightwing government of Margaret Thatcher. The 1980s were characterized by Crouch (1986) as a period of 'union exclusion' when unions were denied legitimacy and access to political influence by the governing party and it was in this context that experiments with coalition began. Unions tried to use vanguard and common cause coalitions in a series of largely unsuccessful attempts to block the privatization and restructuring of public services. Significantly, with Labour's return to power in 1997 there has been some slackening of this effort as unions have partly re-acquired 'insider' status. Although there is an incipient living wage campaign in Britain, the core union effort on wage regulation has been exercised within the tripartite Low Pay Commission, which recommends the level of the minimum wage to government. And while community support has been a feature of some recent organizing campaigns, unions have preferred to rely on traditional direct approaches to employers and the new statutory certification procedure to organize non-union sites. There is disenchantment with New Labour in the union movement and this has prompted continued resort to coalition, like UNISON's Birmingham housing campaign. To date though this has been a minority response.

Germany also provides evidence to support the 'resource-based' view of coalition. Although the German trade union movement is in decline, it has not faced the challenge to its legitimate status experienced by its counterparts in the liberal-market economies and public policy and the framework of employment law has remained broadly supportive. Accepted as a social partner by government and as an industry-level bargaining partner by most employers, German unions have been under least pressure to embrace coalition. When they have used the method, it has taken the form of integrative coalitions concerned with very important issues but not vital union interests. Coalition in this case has been a supplementary method, used to develop novel policy, by a union movement enjoying a high level of institutional security.

Expanding Interest Representation

German unions have turned to coalition partners as they have broadened their policy of interest representation to embrace international labour standards, anti-fascism, and environmental protection. The same pattern can be seen in Britain, where unions have worked with coalition partners to promote a new agenda of work–life balance and family-friendly legislation. It can also be seen in Italy or Spain, where coalitions have formed over environmental protection and immigration.

These coalitions may occur for two reasons. First, unions may lack expertise or other resources that are necessary for effective representation in these areas and be dependent on their partners to supply what they lack themselves. As was suggested above, coalition partners may supply unions with expertise, legitimacy, access to constituencies, and a capacity for mobilization. Second, environmental protection, international labour standards, and the integration of work and family are all issues that have been colonized by social movements and advocacy organizations. As interest representation extends beyond labour's traditional agenda, unions almost inevitably become drawn into contact with pre-existing campaigning and advocacy organizations. Thus, in Italy union campaigning on disability and sexuality at work has occurred alongside other groups that have a long-standing and dedicated interest in these issues (Beccalli and Meardi 2002: 128–9). It seems that as unions expand onto the territory occupied by other representative institutions the potential for coalition is increased.

Activism and Leadership

An important background to coalition-building identified in research is the presence of activists and leaders in trade unions with experience of other social movements. This theme has been especially prevalent in recent American literature. Thus, Voss and Sherman (2003: 65–9) have argued both that forming community coalitions is a distinctive feature of revitalized US union locals and that a frequent precondition of revitalization is the presence of activists with a non-union background (see also Voss and Sherman 2000). As with other research that identifies leadership change as a key influence on union behaviour (Heery 2003: 294–5), they identify a mix of generational and ideological factors at work. Older activists in revitalized locals brought experience of community and welfare rights campaigning from the 1970s and 1980s, while younger activists tended to have a background in campus and identity politics from the 1990s. Experience of Central American Solidarity Movements and Anti-Apartheid were particularly prevalent. Other research has pointed to a link between feminist activism and coalitions with women's organizations in a number of countries (Beccalli and Meardi 2002: 123; Cobble and Michal 2002: 241). At Britain's TUC, policy officers with a history of involvement in women's organizations have been instrumental in the launch of coalition-based campaigns on part-time work, work–life balance, and homeworking.

The presence of activists with a non-union background appears to have a dual significance. On the one hand, they can act as bridge builders, linking unions to the other movements in which they have experience. These activists bring a 'cosmopolitan' perspective to union work, acting as the nodes in multi-agency networks in a way that union leaders who are schooled solely in the traditions of the labour movement may find difficult. On the other hand, they can act as innovators introducing to unions the 'repertoires of contention' used by other movements. For Sherman and

Voss (2000), these activists have helped put the 'move back in the labor movement' by transferring the skills and practices of new social movements to trade unions. A readiness to seek coalition is precisely one such practice.

Union Identity

In a recent analysis of European trade unionism, Richard Hyman (2001) has argued that national labour movements have approximated to one of three primary identities: business unionism, where the union defines its sphere of representation as the market; class opposition where the union seeks to mobilize its membership for a challenge to the existing social and economic order; and integrationist unionism, where the union conceives of itself as a social partner that accepts the broad constitution of society (and a plurality of legitimate interests) but seeks reform in the labour interest Hyman takes pains to stress that each 'identity' is an ideal type and that real unions inevitably blend the different conceptions. Nevertheless, the framework is useful and can help guide the analysis of coalition-building.

Unions that approximate to the first type are arguably least likely to seek coalition. In the United States it is notable that experiment with coalition has been advocated by critics of business unionism and that use of the method has grown as the failings of business unionism have become more apparent (Turner and Hurd 2001; Voss and Sherman 2003). This suggests that coalition is likely to arise as market-oriented unions seek to change their identity and broaden their conception of union purpose, either in the direction of class mobilization or social integration. Which of these two directions is chosen will influence the form of coalition. Recent developments in Britain exemplify the route from business to class unionism. There is a strong syndicalist current on the union left in Britain, visible in Arthur Scargill's leadership of the NUM in the 1980s and also in the newer generation of left union leaders elected in opposition to New Labour (Waddington 2003: 339–40). The class identity of these traditional left unions typically finds expression in militancy rather than coalition-building. Where the latter occurs it tends to take the form of a 'coalition of protest' with the union in a vanguard position. Examples can be seen in the miners' strike of 1984/85, the Liverpool dock strike of the 1990s and recent calls for industrial action by the rail union, RMT, in support of the re-nationalization of the rail network and to halt the privatization of the London Underground. In all of these cases, union goals are assumed to have primacy because the union serves as a vehicle for class conflict; the appropriate role for other progressive forces is to lend support.

In Germany, in contrast common-cause and integrative coalitions feature more strongly, reflecting the country's tradition of social partnership. Coalition here reflects acceptance of plural interests and an established commitment to working with other groups. The non-militant tenor of coalition, moreover, is reflected in the preference for 'coalitions of influence', not protest, seen most clearly in German unions' refusal to endorse radical anti-globalization protests (and linking up with the more moderate ATTAC instead). In the United Kingdom, 'coalitions of influence' have been developed most strongly by the TUC under the definite influence of the

European model of social partnership (Heery 1998*b*). Unions with a broad conception of their purpose, therefore, are more likely than business unions to engage in coalition-building. Attachment to class or partnership conceptions of this broader role, however, exert an additional influence and help explain the types of coalition favoured by unions.

While coalition is associated with a broadening of union purpose, the relationship between union identity and coalition-building may not be unilinear. A weak propensity to form coalitions might be found, not just where union purpose is narrow but also where it is very broad. Where unions are institutionalized as encompassing, class-based organizations then they may eschew coalition. Of the five countries we have examined, Spain and Italy are seemingly the two with the least developed traditions of coalition-building. Other features of Spanish and Italian societies may explain this relative absence but it is likely that union identity is partly responsible. The left unions, in particular, in both countries have a tradition of broad ranging political and social activism that may serve to reduce the need for or interest in coalition with other institutions or movements (Martínez Lucio 1999).

Availability of Partners

Unions require partners if they are to form coalitions and the supply of partners is therefore an additional factor promoting coalitions. Trends here seem to face in opposing directions. On the one hand, the privatization of social life, the decay of traditional occupational communities, and the emergence of more dispersed patterns of settlement have probably served to reduce the number of potential coalition partners. Survey research in Britain (Heery et al. 2000) indicates that most union organizing activity does not involve cooperation with community bodies, probably because workers generally are not drawn from any single 'community' whose institutions can lend support. On the other hand, the strengthening of forms of identity, grounded in gender, demography, sexuality, consumption, and issue-based politics, is providing a source of fresh coalition partners. Coalitions on environmental questions can be readily concluded by German (and to a lesser degree US) unions because of the strength of the country's green movement.

The differential supply of coalition partners may also explain differences in the extent of coalition across countries. In the United States, unions have been able to ally with student organizations in the anti-sweatshop campaign, reflecting the continuing vitality of student politics (albeit supported by programmes like Union Summer). In the United Kingdom, where student radicalism has substantially declined, the No Sweat campaign has failed so far to elicit a similar response. More generally, the greater religiosity of the United States, when compared with Europe (Crouch 1999), and the historical strength of American local civil society, noted since de Tocqueville, probably furnishes a stronger basis for coalition than exists elsewhere. The multiplicity of locally based community associations in the United States provides a basis for a dispersed, localized pattern of union-based coalition. At the other extreme lie Italy and Spain. According to Eurobarometer data both countries have weak civil societies, as measured by the proportion of the population affiliated to associations though in Italy's case it is probable that this judgement applies mainly to the south of the country (Hamann, forthcoming: 4). Partly as a consequence, coalition features less prominently in the repertoire of collective action of the Italian and Spanish trade union movements.

Political Opportunity

The final factor that helps promote coalition is the structure of political opportunity: Unions will form coalitions when the structure of governing institutions encourages them to do so. Unions will be encouraged to form coalitions (and coalitions will be more successful) where states are structured to provide multiple points of access to policy. Thus, it is notable that living wage coalitions have developed most strongly in the United States, where there is scope for influence at city and state levels. In Britain, where there is a universal national minimum wage and local government has less autonomy, similar coalitions have been attempted but have not flourished. This may change, however, and the living wage movement has had most resonance in London where the first incumbent of the newly created office of mayor, Ken Livingstone, has been keen to lend backing. Livingstone has developed a contract compliance policy, which encourages public service contractors to pay living wages thereby giving fresh impetus to the campaign. In general, though, the centralized nature of the British state, coupled with an election system that tends to produce strong, majority governments, has not provided fertile ground for labour-backed coalitions. In Germany a third pattern seems to be apparent. Here, the consultative style of government, with its emphasis on involving social partners in dialogue has supported 'coalitions of influence'. On the issues of international labour standards and environmental protection, the German state has endeavoured to involve all relevant stakeholders, including trade unions and NGOs.

It seems, therefore, that the degree of centralization of state decision-making primarily influences the frequency of coalition: the more decentralized is decision-making the more incentive there is for unions to form coalitions to exert influence. Multiple opportunities encourage multiple experiments with coalition-building. The nature of state interaction with civil society, in contrast, influences the type of coalition. Where the state is inclusive of civil society actors, as in Germany, then coalitions of influence will tend to form (Kriesi et al. 1995: 215). Where the state is exclusive of such actors then coalitions of protest will emerge. Some of the most notable examples of the latter in recent years have been the protests against the Second Gulf War in Britain, Spain, and Italy where governments have supported the American aggression in the face of strong popular opposition.

NATIONAL PATTERNS

The lack of systematic evidence on union coalition-building across our five countries means that it is difficult to specify national patterns with certainty. Nevertheless, evidence that is available suggests that there are differences both in the level and form of coalition-building across the national cases, though our summary of these patterns is necessarily speculative and to be treated with due caution.

In the United States, growth of coalition-building is most apparent though arguably the method continues to have secondary status (Hurd, Milkman, and Turner 2003: 106–8). The building of newly active coalitions—most of them at the local level, organized around a wide variety of issues—has been an important and widely discussed component of the recent revitalization attempts of the US trade union movement. Arguably, these developments have attracted such attention because of the previously isolationist stance of American unions with regard to other social movements. Most national unions in the United States (led by the AFL-CIO) sat out the social movements of the 1960s, though some local unions in cities like San Francisco, Seattle, and New York, did participate in antiwar and civil rights coalitions. As those movements declined in the 1970s, labour's limited participation (which for the most part did not include cooperation with feminist or environmental groups) also declined. In response to deep recession and plant closings in the 1980s, however, new labour–community coalitions emerged in campaigns to save jobs (Brecher and Costello 1990). On that foundation, a new wave of labour-backed coalition efforts expanded through the 1990s across a range of issues. There have been coalitions with faith, community, student, and environmental groups on living wages, labour standards, sustainable development, fair trade, union organizing, and other issues in recent years (Nissen and Rosen 1999; Russo and Corbin 1999; Johnston 2001).

This ending of the isolation of American unions within US civil society reflects changes in their underpinning identity. There has been a partial movement from business to social movement unionism and associated redirection of policy to embrace a broader social and political agenda (Turner and Hurd 2001). The hostile political and industrial relations context, moreover, has prompted unions to seek coalition as other resources have been denied to them. Opportunities have been provided by the devolved structure of the US state, which has presented openings for unions and coalition partners to influence local legislatures. There have also been opportunities at supra-state level with the growing debate over labour standards within the framework of the World Trade Organization. The hostile context facing American labour has also shaped the form of coalition, which in the United States has often approximated to a 'coalition of protest', in which unions and their coalition partners have identified a common cause.

In the United Kingdom, coalition-building has seemingly been less prevalent. Where it has occurred it has often followed a similar pattern to the United States: unions have developed coalitions of protest in response to political exclusion and the restructuring of the public sector. These coalitions have a vanguard form, when forged by left unions, and common cause coalitions in other cases. The degree of exclusion experienced by UK unions has been less however, and since New Labour's election in 1997 there has been some withdrawal from coalition as unions have turned to more traditional routes of influence. The opportunities for lobbying and 'social dialogue' at European level have also been significant in this regard (see Behrens, Hurd, and

Waddington, Chapter 7, this volume). Disillusion with New Labour is currently prompting a revival of coalition and the United Kingdom has seen the emergence of living wage and anti-sweatshop campaigns, based on those in the United States. There have also been renewed attempts to forge coalitions with the users of public services in order to deflect Labour-initiated restructuring. A constraint on this kind of development, however, is the centralization of the British state and the relatively limited opportunities afforded to union-backed coalitions to make significant progress at local government level: local government is less autonomous and less vulnerable to campaigning pressure in Britain than it is in the United States. While the British pattern largely follows the American though in weaker form, there are also differences. The TUC's aspiration for social partnership on a European model and opportunities to influence state policy in the area of work–life balance (pensions, working time, family-friendly benefits) have generated coalitions of influence, alongside the more challenging coalitions of protest. In union coalition-building, as in much else, the United Kingdom stands between Europe and America.

In Germany, there is a third pattern. Coalition has been an established feature of the labour movement and has largely taken an integrative form. This pattern reflects the stronger political identity of German unions, the tradition of corporatist state–union relations and the structuring of civil society, with reliance on national intermediary associations as opposed to the locally, based associations prevalent in the United States. The key opportunity afforded German unions has been the strength of new social movements, which has provided an ample supply of potential coalition partners (Meyer 1992; Kriesi et al. 1995; Krüger 2000). Coalitions with new social movements, such as the green and peace movements, emerged in the 1970s. The green movement, in particular, developed a strong political presence and by the late 1970s had forced the, initially unreceptive, unions to acknowledge environmental concerns. During the 1980s, the dialogue became more cooperative and more recently German unions have formed coalitions with anti-fascist campaigners, the unemployed, and elements of the anti-globalization movement.

The defensive coalitions against restructuring and the privatization of public services seen in Britain and the organizing coalitions seen in the United States are not apparent in Germany. This probably reflects the greater institutional security of German unions. Also reflecting this greater security is the tendency for German unions to forge coalitions of influence, not protest. The identity of German integrationist unions and the practice of social partnership have both reduced the need for, and shaped, the form of union-backed coalition.

The final pattern is seen in both Italy and Spain. The most striking feature here is the relative absence of coalition. There have been recent instances of unions in both countries acting in concert with identity, peace, and anti-globalization campaigners. But these developments are not central to attempts to revitalize unions in either country and arguably are marginal to their primary concerns. The explanation lies in large part in the environment of both union movements. Civil society is weakly organized, particularly in Spain, and the profusion of potential coalition partners seen in the United States is absent in these cases. Moreover, while traditions of social partnership are less established in Spain and Italy than they are in Germany, unions enjoy a fairly high degree of institutional security. Election procedures at workplace level provide a test of union legitimacy and allow unions access to state resources. Given this support, there is less incentive for unions to seek alliances with other institutions in civil society; there is less need to borrow the power of other movements. The pattern also reflects the identity of unions in these two countries. There is a strong, class identity to the union movement in both cases; unions are energetic political actors, embracing a broad agenda of interest representation, and frequently incorporate issues of new social movements in their political agendas. In this they share characteristics with German trade unions. In Spain and Italy, however, a broad conception of union purpose tends to be allied to a vanguardist position, which precludes the active search for coalition partners. For example, unions in Spain have a history of action on housing and other urban development issues, but this has tended to occur under the umbrella of left political parties rather than through direct coalition with urban social movements (Martínez Lucio 1999).

To conclude, on the available evidence it is possible to identify different national patterns of coalition-building, in terms of both the level of activity and its form. National union movements differ in the extent to which they resort to coalition, their stance towards potential coalition partners and the degree to which coalitions assume a mobilizing or influencing form. These patterns, in turn reflect the different identities and contexts in which unions operate. The pressure to forge coalitions is strong where unions face hostile governments and employers, while the opportunity to use the tactic arises where civil society is strongly organized and the state is decentralized. A hostile context also encourages coalitions of protest, while the reverse is true where the state seeks to govern through dialogue with social partners. In this context coalitions of influence tend to form. The effects of union identity are twofold. Recent coalition-building is a feature of unions, like those in the United States, which have moved from a strong market orientation to a broader conception of union purpose. In Europe, in contrast, where union purpose has long been broadly defined, coalition-building is shaped by the nature of this definition. Where union identity contains a strong class element then there is both less resort to coalition and a preference for vanguard coalitions and coalitions of protest where the method is used. Where there is a strong 'social' or partnership orientation, in contrast, coalitions tend to be integrative and to take the form of coalitions of influence.

CONCLUSIONS

What lessons can be drawn from this survey of coalition-building for the revitalization of labour movements? We feel that several, albeit rather mixed, conclusions can be drawn. First, while coalition is not a central strategy of revitalization in any of the countries studied, we believe its use is likely to increase. Partly, this is because union movements are being pushed towards coalition. Across the developed world unions have experienced membership decline, and in many cases have lost influence in the labour market and political system. As a result, they are under pressure to develop new tactics and access new resources. In certain respects, coalitions are a symptom of weakness and unions will experience pressure to seek coalition partners if that underlying weakness remains.

Unions are also under pressure to broaden their policy agenda and engage with the questions of environmentalism, identity politics, work–life balance, globalization, and international labour standards. Dealing with all of these questions points towards coalition with other institutions that can offer unions legitimacy, expertise, and other resources. As unions are drawn onto the terrain of other social movements, necessarily, the issue of coalition will emerge. Moreover, union identities are changing and there is greater readiness to accept diversity of interests and an agenda founded on inclusive rather than exclusive definitions of solidarity (Selmi and McUsic 2002). A significant change in union government in recent years has been the development of identity politics and specialist structures for the representation of women, minority, immigrant, gay and lesbian, and other groups among the workforce (Ledwith and Colgan 2002). Developing coalitions with non-labour organizations is perhaps the logical external corollary of this internal change.

Finally, developments beyond the labour movement are likely to pull unions towards coalition. Coalition partners are likely to remain in ready supply, at least in certain fields. The issues of globalization and the regulation of labour standards, gender equality and work–life balance, internationalism, environmentalism, and anti-fascism, with their associated campaigning, advocacy and membership groups will loom large in progressive politics for the foreseeable future. Opportunities for coalition-building also seem set to grow as a result of the double-shift in the structures of government, downwards to regional and city level and upwards to the international level. At these sites, conventional party politics and the link between unions and traditional leftwing parties are less apparent. New forms of union action, founded on coalition, may prove to be more effective above and below the nation state (Ludlam and Taylor 2003).

Second, in terms of the link between coalitions and union revitalization, it can be noted that coalition has frequently represented an innovation in union strategy in the sense of a novel departure in tactics and a broadening of objectives. This is particularly true of the United States but applies in the other countries as well. If for this reason alone, coalition-building is a welcome development. Beyond this point, however, it is difficult to specify the contribution coalitions can make to union revitalization. Partly, this is because of the secondary status of coalition as a union method that is used in conjunction with other primary methods, such as political action or organizing. Partly, too it arises from the multiform nature of coalition-building. Union-backed coalitions are not all the same, but reflect different national contexts and union identities. It follows that the effectiveness of particular forms of coalition will depend on factors that are contingent to union movements and to their environments. In the United States, it has been noted that the most effective coalitions are those that rely upon bridge-builders, involve rank and file mobilization, and leadership support and endure, evolving through iterative action (Brecher and Costello 1990; Hurd, Milkman, and Turner 2003). Our information from the other four cases is just too sketchy to pronounce with certainty whether these same conditions under-pin success elsewhere.

Our final conclusion returns once again to this theme of national differences. Advocates of social movement unionism tend to offer it as a universal solution to labour's ills, appropriate to the general context of globalization or the triumph of neo-liberal political economy. The survey of developments in Britain, Germany, Italy, Spain, and the United States suggest a need for caution before accepting this judge-ment. Coalition-building by unions takes different forms in different countries and reflects enduring variation in union identity and institutional context. It is unlikely that these national patterns will disappear.

References

Adeney, M. and Lloyd, J. (1986). *The Miners' Strike*. London: Routledge and Kegan Paul.

Baccaro, L., Carrieri, M., and Damiano, C. (2003). 'The Resurgence of the Italian Confederal Unions: Will It Last?'. *European Journal of Industrial Relations*, 9/1: 43–59.

Beccalli, B. and Meardi, G. (2002). 'From Unintended to Undecided Feminism? Italian Labour's Changing and Singular Ambiguities', in F. Colgan and S. Ledwith (eds.), *Gender, Diversity and Trade Unions: International Perspectives*. London: Routledge, 113–31.

Behrens, M., Fichter, M., and Frege, C. M. (2003). 'Unions in Germany: Regaining the Initiative?'. *European Journal of Industrial Relations*, 9/1: 25–42.

Bonacich, E. (2000). 'Intense Challenges, Tentative Possibilities: Organizing Immigrant Garment Workers in Los Angeles', in R. Milkman (ed.), *Organizing Immigrants: The Challenge for Unions in Contemporary California*. Ithaca, NY: ILR Press, 130–49.

Brecher, J. and Costello, T. (1990). *Building Bridges: The Emerging Grassroots Coalition between Labor and Community*. New York: Monthly Review Press.

Cobble, D. S. and Michal, M. B. (2002). 'On the Edge of Equality? Working Women and the US Labour Movement', in F. Colgan and S. Ledwith (eds.), *Gender, Diversity and Trade Unions: International Perspectives*. London: Routledge, 232–56.

Crouch, C. (1986). 'Conservative Industrial Relations policy: Towards Labour Exclusion?', in O. Jacobi (ed.), *Economic Crisis, Trade Unions and the State*. London: Croom Helm, 131–53.

—— (1999). *Social Change in Western Europe*. Oxford: Oxford University Press.

Edwards, C. and Heery, E. (1989). *Management Control and Union Power: A Study of Labour Relations in Coal-Mining*. Oxford: Clarendon Press.

Figart, D. M., Mutari, E., and Power, M. (2002). *Living Wages, Equal Wages: Gender and Labor Market Policies in the United States*. London and New York: Routledge.

Flanders, A. (1970). *Management and Unions: The Theory and Reform of Industrial Relations*. London: Faber.

Foster, D. and Scott, J. (1998). 'Conceptualising Union Responses to Contracting Out Municipal Services, 1979–1997'. *Industrial Relations Journal*, 29/2: 137–50.

Frundt, H. J. (2002). 'Four Models of Cross-Border Maquila Organizing', in B. Nissen (ed.), *Unions in a Globalized Environment: Changing Organizational Boundaries and Social Roles*. Armonk, NY: M. E. Sharpe, 45–75.

Hamann, K. (2003). 'European Integration and Civil Society in Spain'. *South European Society and Politics*, 8, 1: 47–68.

Hamann, K. and Martínez Lucio, M. (2003). 'Strategies of Union Revitalization in Spain: Negotiating Change and Fragmentation'. *European Journal of Industrial Relations*, 9/1: 61–78.

Hawken, P. (2000). 'On the Streets of Seattle'. *The Amicus Journal*, Spring: 29–51.

Heery, E. (1998*a*). 'Campaigning for Part-Time Workers'. *Work, Employment and Society*, 12/2: 351–66.

——(1998*b*). 'The Relaunch of the Trades Union Congress'. *British Journal of Industrial Relations*, 36/3: 339–60.

——(2003). 'Trade Unions and Industrial Relations', in P. Ackers and A. Wilkinson (eds.), *Understanding Work and Employment: Industrial Relations in Transition*. Oxford: Oxford University Press, 278–304.

——Simms, M., Delbridge, R., Salmon, J., and Simpson, D. (2000). 'The TUC's Organising Academy: An Assessment'. *Industrial Relations Journal*, 31/5: 400–15.

Hurd, R. W., Milkman, R., and Turner, L. (2003). 'Reviving the American Labour Movement: Institutions and Mobilization'. *European Journal of Industrial Relations*, 9/1: 99–117.

Hyman, R. (2001). *Understanding European Trade Unionism: Between Market, Class and Society*. London: Sage.

Johnston, P. (2001). 'Organize for What? The Resurgence of Labor as a Citizenship Movement', in L. Turner, H. C. Katz and R. W. Hurd (eds.), *Rekindling the Movement: Labor's Quest for Relevance in the 21st Century*. Ithaca, NY: Cornell University Press, 27–58.

——(2002). 'Citizenship Movement Unionism: For the Defense of Local Communities in the Global Age', in B. Nissen (ed.), *Unions in a Globalized Environment: Changing Borders, Organizational Boundaries, and Social Roles*. Armonk, NY: M. E. Sharpe, 236–63.

Juravich, T. and Bronfenbrenner, K. (1999). *Ravenswood: The Steelworkers' Victory and the Renewal of American Labor*. Ithaca, NY: ILR Press.

Kädtler, J. and Hertle, H.-H. (1997). *Sozialpartnerschaft und Industriepolitik*. Opladen: Westdeutscher Verlag.

Koch-Baumgarten, S. (2002). 'Changing Gender Relations in German unions', in F. Colgan and S. Ledwith (eds.), *Gender, Diversity and Trade Unions: International Perspectives*. London: Routledge, 132–53.

Kriesi, H., Koopmans, R., Duyvendak, J. W., and Giugni, M. (1995). *New Social Movements in Western Europe: A Comparative Analysis*. London: UCL Press.

Kriesky, J. (2001). 'Structural Change in the AFL-CIO: A Regional Study of Union Cities' Impact', in L. Turner, H. C. Katz and R. W. Hurd (eds.), *Rekindling the Movement: Labor's Quest for Relevance in the 21st Century*. Ithaca, NY: ILR Press, 129–54.

Krüger, S. (2000). *Arbeit und Umwelt verbinden. Zur Problematik der Interaktion zwischen Gewerkschaften und NGOs*. Berlin: WZB Papers P00-521.

Kusnet, D. (1998). 'The "America Needs a Raise" Campaign: The New Labor Movement and the Politics of Living Standards', in J.-A. Mort (ed.), *Not Your Father's Union Movement*. London: Verso, 167–78.

Ledwith, S. and Colgan, F. (2002). 'Tackling Gender, Diversity and Trade Union Democracy: A Worldwide Project?', in F. Colgan and S. Ledwith (eds.), *Gender, Diversity and Trade Unions: International Perspectives*. London: Routledge, 1–27.

Ludlam, S. and Taylor, S. (2003). 'The Political Representation of the Labour Interest in Britain'. *British Journal of Industrial Relations*, 41/3: 729–49.

Martínez Lucio, M. (1999). 'Union Identity and Strategy in Spain: Negotiating Traditions of Struggle', in M. Upchurch (ed.), *The State and Globalization: Comparative Studies of Labour and Capitalism in National Economies*. London: Mansell, 88–112.

McIlroy, J. (2000). 'The New Politics of Pressure—the Trades Union Congress and New Labour in Government'. *Industrial Relations Journal*, 31/1: 2–16.

Meyer, H.-W. (1992). 'Gesellschaftliche Zukunftsgestaltung und Soziale Bewegung'. *Forschungsjournal Neue Soziale Bewegungen* 3:S8–13.

Milkman, R. (2002). 'New Workers, New Labor and the New Los Angeles', in B. Nissen (ed.), *Unions in a Globalized Environment: Changing Borders, Organizational Boundaries and Social Roles*. Armonk, NY: M. E. Sharpe, 103–29.

——and Wong, K. (2000). 'Organizing the Wicked City: The 1992 Southern California Drywall Strike', in R. Milkman (ed.), *Organizing Immigrants: The Challenge for Unions in Contemporary California*. Ithaca, NY: ILR Press, 169–98.

————(2001). 'Organizing Immigrant Workers: Case Studies from Southern California', in L. Turner, H. C. Katz, and R. W. Hurd (eds.), *Rekindling the Movement: Labor' s Quest for Relevance in the 21st Century*. Ithaca, NY: ILR Press, 99–128.

Moberg, D. (1999). 'Greens and Labour: Two Powerful Movements Gang Up On Polluters'. *Sierra*, January/February: 46–54.

Needleman, R. (1998). 'Building Relationships for the Long Haul: Unions and Community-Based Groups Working Together to Organize Low Wage Workers', in K. Bronfenbrenner, S. Friedman, R. W. Hurd, R. A. Oswald, and R. L. Seeber (eds.), *Organizing to Win: New Research on Union Strategies*. Ithaca, NY: ILR Press, 71–86.

Nissen, B. and Rosen, S. (1999). 'Community-Based Organizing: Transforming Union Organizing Programs from the Bottom-Up', in B. Nissen (ed.), *Which Direction for Organized Labor?*. Detroit, MI: Wayne State University Press, 59–74.

Ogden, S. (1991). 'The Trade Union Campaign Against Water Privatization'. *Industrial Relations Journal*, 22/1: 20–34.

Osterman, P., Kochan, T. A., Locke, R. M., and Piore, M. J. (2001). *Working in America: A Blueprint for the New Labor Market*. Cambridge, MA: MIT Press.

Peters, R. and Merrill, T. (1998). 'Clergy and Religious Persons' Role in Organizing at O'Hare Airport and St. Joseph Medical Center', in K. Bronfenbrenner, S. Friedman, R. W. Hurd, R. A. Oswald, and R. L. Seeber (eds.), *Organizing to Win: New Research on Union Strategies*. Ithaca, NY: ILR Press, 164–77.

Robinson, I. (2002). 'Does Neoliberal Restructuring Promote Social Movement Unionism? US Developments in Comparative Perspective', in B. Nissen (ed.), *Unions in a Globalized Environment: Changing Borders, Organizational Boundaries, and Social Roles*. Armonk, NY: M. E. Sharpe, 189–235.

Rose, F. (2000). *Coalitions Across the Class Divide: Lessons from the Labor, Peace and Environmental Movements*. Ithaca, NY: Cornell University Press.

Russo, J. and Corbin, B. R. (1999). 'Work, Organized Labor and the Catholic Church: Boundaries and Opportunities for Community/Labor Coalitions', in B. Nissen (ed.), *Which Direction for Organized Labor?*. Detroit, MI: Wayne State University Press, 95–112.

Selmi, M. and McUsic, M. S. (2002). 'Difference and Solidarity: Unions in a Postmodern Age', in J. Conaghan, R. M. Fischl, and K. Klare (eds.), *Labour Law in an Era of Globalization*. Oxford: Oxford University Press, 429–46.

Sherman, R. and Voss, K. (2000). 'Organize or Die: Labor's New Tactics and Immigrant Workers', in R. Milkman (ed.), *Organizing Immigrants: The Challenge for Unions in Contemporary California*. Ithaca, NY: ILR Press, 81–108.

Terry, M. (2000). 'UNISON and the Quality of Public Service Provision', in M. Terry (ed.), *Redefining Public Sector Unionism: UNISON and the Future of Trade Unions*. London: Routledge, 214–30.

Turner, L. and Hurd, R. W. (2001). 'Building Social Movement Unionism: The Transformation of the American Labor Movement', in L. Turner, H. C. Katz, and R. W. Hurd (eds.), *Rekindling the Movement: Labor's Quest for Relevance in the 21st Century*. Ithaca, NY: Cornell University Press, 9–26.

Voss, K. and Sherman, R. (2000). 'Breaking the Iron Law of Oligarchy: Union Revitalization in the American Labor Movement'. *American Journal of Sociology*, 106/2: 303–49.

———— (2003). 'You Just Can't Do It Automatically: The Transition to Social Movement Unionism in the United States', in P. Fairbrother and C. B. Yates (eds.), *Unions in Renewal: A Comparative Study*. London: Continuum, 51–77.

Waddington, J. (2003). 'Heightening Tensions Between Trade Unions and the Labour Government'. *British Journal of Industrial Relations*, 41/2: 335–58.

Waterman, P. (1998). *Globalization, Social Movements and the New Institutionalisms*. London: Mansell.

Webb, S. and Webb, B. (1902). *Industrial Democracy*. London: Longmans, Green.

Wells, M. J. (2000). 'Immigration and Unionization in the San Francisco Hotel Industry', in R. Milkman (ed.), *Organizing Immigrants: The Challenges for Unions in Contemporary Capitalism*. Ithaca, NY: ILR Press, 109–29.

Wheeler, H. N. (2002). *The Future of the American Labor Movement*. Cambridge: Cambridge University Press.

Wieshügel (1996). 'Sozialokologische Wende Als Teil Gewerksschaftlicher Reformstrategie'. *GMH*, 3: 150–8.

Wills, J. (2002). *Union Futures*. London: The Fabian Society.

Winterton, J. and Winterton, R. (1989). *Coal, Crisis and Conflict*. Manchester: Manchester University Press.

9

International Trade Union Revitalization: The Role of National Union Approaches

NATHAN LILLIE AND MIGUEL MARTÍNEZ LUCIO

INTRODUCTION

The last two decades have seen a significant increase in the international activity and role of organized labour. Yet, despite a growing awareness of the increasing importance of international linkages and interdependencies in the global economy the global labour movement remains segmented along national, sectoral, and corporate lines. This steers international union strategies towards the defence of the interests of narrowly defined groups of workers, and away from building a viable counterweight to the power of global capital. This chapter explores some of the challenges labour unions face to develop consistent and viable international strategies.

International union strategy is best understood as a set of transnational relationships of and between union organizations, rather than as the outcome of the revitalization strategy of any particular national labour movement. Comparative industrial relations research has traditionally conceptualized industrial relations as occurring within nationally bounded, self-contained isolated systems. International union strategies, by definition, stretch these implicit boundaries. This does not mean that national industrial relations systems are no longer important as reference points for union strategy. Rather, transnational relationships of subnational actors have become so intertwined that it is difficult to understand the strategies of actors within one country without reference to events and actors in other countries. The chapter argues and concludes that labour internationalism is not merely national labour movements extending their strategies into some vague and pre-constituted 'international' arena, but rather involves the extension (for better or for worse) of specific practices, institutions, and patterns of national influence into international contexts, regardless of the internationalist rhetoric of many trade unions.

Unions have often been portrayed as the victims of globalization, stuck in their national frameworks, losing power, and unable to react when faced with dynamic global firms, trade, migration, and all the other international issues labour is now confronted with.[1] This characterization is blunt, but it is also largely correct. Unions by and large, it is argued, have in the past not consistently developed effective strategies and structures for international cooperation. As a result, most international coordination has been official, institutional, and diplomatic rather than substantive in nature during much of the post-war period. As a result of the globalization of production, unions have, however, increasingly been thrown into transnational contact with one another. Transnational extensions of union influence and interactions between unions occur unintentionally through the influences of firms and market forces, as well as resulting from deliberate union strategies. This transnational extension works through a variety of organizational dimensions, for example, corporate and sectoral linkages, and not just the formal and institutional relations between unions within national systems.

Transnational networking is becoming a more systematic and regularized activity for at least some unions in all the countries in this study. It cannot be assumed a priori, however, that specific transnational union interactions will be cooperative. In many cases, transnational union interactions are competitive rather than solidaristic (Tuckman and Whittall 2002), and can result in unions seeking to undermine each other, for example, due to the struggle to maintain levels and clusters of national employment. The interesting questions from the perspective of labour movement revitalization, then, are as follows. First, how do national industrial relations institutions and strategies mediate the development of internationalism? Second, what new challenges are emerging in the realm of international renewal strategies and labour coordination? Third, what preconditions, structures, and strategies generate international worker and union solidarity?

One of the difficulties in discussing international trade union activity is the difference in conception of the role of unions both within and between national union cultures, which results in a great diversity of forms of international labour activity, all of which are potential focal points for academic study. We focus, however, on a subset of international union activities, and look at transnational efforts to organize mutual support in times of crisis and during critical incidents. Obviously, this does not cover the entire gamut of transnational inter-union relationships by any means. However, such events do provide an opportunity to observe those relationships tested when they come under strain.

DIMENSIONS OF LABOUR INTERNATIONALISM

The new labour internationalism is occurring across six dimensions. First, there is increasing union collaboration within multi- and transnational corporations. Networking and coordination among workplace trade unionists in companies such as General Motors has now become commonplace (Martínez Lucio and Weston 1995). The impact of management change, the need for information exchange, and the development of Internet technology have facilitated such developments. Union renewal here is premised on a new dialogue at the micro level but across national boundaries. Second, we have seen since the economic crisis of the 1970s the emergence of new supranational bodies such as the European Trade Union Confederation (ETUC) which bring together the main unions within Europe. This institution has been at the epicentre of the European Union's industrial relations policies. On the micro level, these policies have configured union renewal and revitalization through the development of consultation within European based transnational corporations (through European Works Councils). On the other hand, the drive to European integration has attempted to provide a new symmetry and strength within the various national systems of social rights within the European Union's member states.

Third, there has been a steady shift, for some too steady (Hodkinson 2002), in the cold war mentality and Anglo-American domination of the International Confederation of Free Trade Unions (O'Brien 2000). New forms of global social engagement and distributive politics have emerged prompted by the need to sensitize global regulatory bodies to growing inequities both within and between societies. Fourth, there has been a more formal and systematic approach to joint working within various international sectors. For example, unions in finance and postal services are forging joint agreements and bilateral connections, such as those between the British banking union UNIFI and the German ver.di. International trade secretariats, such as the International Metalworkers' Federation (IMF), and International Transport Workers Federation (ITF), act as information nodes and coordinators of conflict within key sectors. Central to this dimension of renewal and revitalization is the notion that greater formal collaboration and information exchanges may allow workers in different countries to pre-empt restructuring and avoid competition brought about by management whipsawing for example. Fifth, the international labour scene is replete with examples of mutual learning and sharing based on the first four dimensions outlined here. Recruitment strategies, new forms of labour–management collaboration, and new approaches to labour education, are the subject of a multitude of joint international union seminars, secondments, and information exchanges. The 'organizing model', for example, is a form of unionism which prioritizes aggressively seeking to organize new workplaces and expand union membership, through the recruitment of activists and deployment of specialized union staff. Lessons in organizing strategy have been the subject of much joint discussion and information sharing in the United Kingdom, Australia, and the United States. Within the European Union some developments, such as pan-European union initiatives to promote lifelong learning, are assisted by supranational state financial support and policy involvement. Sixth, there is a new discourse of union internationalism grounded in a 'new' radical and, in parts Marxist, critique of global capitalism, but which seeks to embrace non-class based emancipatory struggles as well, such as feminism, environmentalism, and indigenous people's rights. This discourse favours a less traditional, hierarchical, and bureaucratic approach to labour internationalism (Waterman and Wills 2001).

Research on labour internationalism has seen a variety of academic approaches, reflecting the diversity of union activities in transnational arenas. However, despite the growth in new transnational cooperative union projects and structures, union leaders, and academics have not really confronted the way in which union renewal and responses are constructed at the national level, and, in particular, how the interplay of these national constructions affects transnational union cooperation. This chapter will focus on critical incidents in three international sectors to show how the projects of internationalism outlined above are shaped by national structures and contexts of industrial relations and union organization, as well as by competing processes of union renewal.

We have selected three cases that illustrate the leverage opportunities and tensions between unions created by the interaction of transnational productive structures and national industrial relations institutions in the United States, Germany, Spain, and the United Kingdom. The first case, the 2002 collective bargaining on the US West-Coast docks shows international solidarity in the context of well-developed horizontal inter-union relations, low levels of competition between production sites, and strong opportunities for effective solidarity. The second case is the BMW–Rover dispute over plant closures in the late 1990s. In this case differential access to management based in national legislation and industrial relations practices created opportunities for the German union to defend employment at their German production locations at the expense of UK workers. As a result, the closures did not result in any extensive solidarity from the German union. The last case, in the airline industry, demonstrates the ongoing influence of nationally fragmented and vertical structures. These continue to influence and interfere with what otherwise might be very strong opportunities for effective transnational cooperation. All of these cases show how national industrial relations systems interrelate with transnational structures to influence transnational relations between labour unions in both negative and positive ways. National industrial relations systems serve to position unions within transnational inter-union relationships by affording different access to power resources, by influencing discourses and understandings, and by allowing management to exploit these national divisions within the new structures and hierarchies of the global economy.

International Competition and Transnational Union Networks

Inter-union relations are often competitive over jobs and investment, but there is a strong normative presumption within the labour movement that this should not be the case. David Walsh, in looking at union cooperation between crafts in the airline industry, notes that despite occasional competition, unions tend to cooperate with one another because they are part of the same broad social movement, share structurally common interests, and a common set of norms. Unions build networks and develop norms for mutual support so that assistance will be available when needed, even when it is not possible to reciprocate (Walsh 1994: 13). Although inter-union conflicts often erupt where crucial economic interests are at stake, norms of solidarity are strong enough that unions will go to a good deal of effort to resolve, or at least conceal, their differences and present management with a united front.

Although strong networks seem to be a precondition for the expression of concrete solidarity (as one would logically expect, since requests of solidarity would need to be communicated somehow), increased inter-union information exchange between production locations does not automatically remove inter-union competitive dynamics. Historically, international ties between unions have not usually been strong enough to mobilize solidarity, let alone resolve, fundamental interest conflicts (Northup and Rowan 1979). Management strategies, positions within production networks, and the extent of long-term relationships are important in determining whether transnational inter-union relations will be solidaristic or competitive. Sisson and Marginson (2002) show that management can deliberately and strategically interfere with inter-union solidarity. Management is better able to coordinate its bargaining agenda transnationally than unions are, and often uses this ability to pressure local worker representatives. For example, through benchmarking, concessions gained in one country can translate into management demands for concessions elsewhere (Sisson and Marginson 2002). Unions are not helpless to react, but often find themselves with a very difficult collective action dilemma to overcome (Cooke 2002). This is in part because, as Martínez Lucio and Weston (1995) argue, many participants in trade union networks find it difficult to monitor and condition the outcomes of collaborative actions and mutual exchanges of information between unions from different sites of a transnational corporation. Additionally, rapidly shifting transnational structures of ownership and production can interfere with the development of international solidarity, and aid management in its attempts to play unions off against one another. Ramsay (1997) notes that one of the major problems unions encounter when asking for international solidarity is that by the time the need for such solidarity is evident, it is too late to develop the long-term relationships solidarity implies. If union relations are regularly disrupted by changes in corporate and productive structures, stable relationships cannot develop. Lack of stable and systematic relations often leads transnational efforts to emphasize relatively ineffective symbolic shows of solidarity, while concealing the much less solidaristic competitive interest politics underneath. In contrast, systematic, stable, non-hierarchical inter-union relationships can allow unions to overcome competitive interest politics to a degree, facilitating transnational solidarity and the development of new forms of international labour activity.

A TAXONOMY OF NATIONAL STRATEGIES?

Labour internationalism does not occur in some abstract global space, but is rather the interaction between unions who exist within different national spaces. The form of labour internationalism depends on the strength and character of national unions in their national institutions. The nature of union influence within these institutions affects union perceptions and strategic options in their international relations, as will be discussed below. In this respect, national economic regulation on a very basic and implicit level can shape the structures and strategies of national unions. Hence, this section will outline how different national union models and approaches *carry* the regulatory characteristics of their respective national economic and social systems.

Despite the transnationalization of production, the nation state still plays an important role in economic regulation (Panitch 1981). This is, in part, due to the nature of national regulatory systems. Capitalist states pursue a variety of strategies with regards to the deployment and use of labour (Boyer 1988). For example, some states such as Germany continue to underpin employer strategies by enhancing the role of unions and state investment in training—thus supporting a more functional form of labour flexibility based on 'multi-skilling'. Alternately, the state can seek to limit the influence of labour as a regulator and enhance cost-based strategies based on temporal flexibility and low wages as in the United Kingdom during the 1980s (Regini 2000). These national projects are the outcome of a variety of organizational, economic and cultural factors that contribute to the industrial orders underpinning industrial relations (Lane 1994; Coates 2000; Hamann and Martínez Lucio 2003). And although employers often have a transnational strategic perspective to their employment strategy, unions remain primarily national, regional, or local in orientation. This is clear from the day-to-day operations of trade unions. As a result, even when confronted with transnational issues, trade unionists, in great part, still view international activity and union renewal through the lens of the challenges confronting their national labour movement, and through the frame of their national institutions of employment regulation.

In a globally interconnected world, however, these nationally generated strategies, immediately encounter a very different reality than the national context where they were initially generated. From the union perspective, this may result in structural and strategic adjustments to account for the practicalities of operating in a new environment, such as the development of a global industry level bargaining coordination (Lillie 2004). Alternately, hegemonic unions may attempt to impose patterns of influence from their national framework on other national frameworks through transnational space (Williamson 1994). Frustration with transnational encounters can also result in union withdrawal and denial of the transnational relationships and responsibilities, ultimately leading to competitive transnational inter-union relations, as occurred in the Rover case discussed here. The nature of the union response depends partly on the relative strengths, strategies, and ideologies of the union actors internationally and within their national institutions of industrial relations.

In all the countries in this study, Germany, Italy, Spain, the United Kingdom, and the United States, unions view themselves as being under pressure, but the nature and degree of the threat differs from place to place. Unions from countries thought of as 'low road capitalism', such as the United States and the United Kingdom, possess few political and social power resources compared to the so-called 'high-road' countries such as Germany, although in many industries and firms even the so-called 'low-road' country unions can possess a high level of shop-floor industrial strength and influence within the firm.

International labour strategies may therefore be influenced by the role unions have developed historically within particular national industrial relations institutions. Hyman (2001*a*) identifies three major roles for trade unions as actors, each corresponding to an archetypical ideology. First, unions are economic actors, seeking to improve the welfare of their members through industrial strength and collective bargaining. Second, they are 'social partners', and as such are an essential part of a stable, democratic society. Third, they are vehicles for class struggle, fighting the commodification of labour under capitalism. Virtually all unions are all three of these things, in some combination, although each facet is more or less evident at different times and in different contexts. National trajectories of international coordination vary according to Hyman's categories.

The Liberal Market Economies of the United Kingdom and the United States

In the United Kingdom and the United States international solidarity focuses around collective bargaining and formal company-based mechanisms of regulation, as these are central to unions' role in society. For unions in the United Kingdom and the United States employer avoidance of unions, arising from the low wage, low skill strategy of low-road capitalism, is a major strategic challenge and capital often takes an antagonistic approach to unions and joint regulation. Regulatory traditions and institutions are relatively weak when compared to central and northern Europe, configuring an international strategy focused on bolstering union strength in bargaining and organizing, on establishing minimum labour rights, and on establishing a collaborative (for some, 'progressive') relationship with employers in terms of partnership models of political and regulatory engagement (Martínez Lucio and Stuart 2004). UK and US unions, for example, seek transnational regulatory mechanisms, but view these in minimal and (from their perspectives) 'realistic' terms. For example, they are interested in establishing a basic, 'transferable' framework of rights and employer responsibilities that can be applied to a wide variety of industrial relations systems and national political contexts (this is notable in the Anglo-American influence in organizations such as the International Confederation of Free Trade Unions). Hence, in some cases international union activity is based on a partnership approach and on hostility to militant approaches (Gallin 2002).

The German Model

The German model is based on a social approach where the relation with state entities is seen as central to the construction of solidarity. German unions perceive a threat arising from the impact of deregulation and Anglo-American style liberalization on German tripartism, but they do not view this as arising from global capital per se but rather from a political breakdown in the social pact between German labour and capital. German unions are less concerned with union avoidance than UK and US unions are, because the German structure of worker representation and bargaining regulation does not bring this to the forefront as crucial for maintaining union power (Behrens, Fichter, and Frege 2003). Rather, pressure on the system arises from efforts by employers to outflank national regulation through outward investment and the development of a less union oriented system of workplace relations within small- and medium-sized firms. German unions, therefore, prioritize influence over the proximate regulatory processes of the European Union to reduce employer opportunities for 'social dumping'. German unions have expressed this strategy through attempting to extend aspects of the German industrial relations system to EU regulatory processes. However, this runs the risk of turning into a bureaucratic, elitist project of industrial relations within the European Union (Hyman 2001*b*). As the Rover case study will show, this extension of the Germanic model of stakeholder industrial relations does not always lead to solidaristic international behaviour, especially when German firms are involved, due to the considerable political and organizational resources afforded to German unions within their national institutions.

The Mediterranean Economies

In Spain and Italy unions are caught between a discourse of class oppositionalism and the desire to promote and participate in a more socially active and modernizing state role. In those countries, internal class politics in the form of general strikes, social mobilization, and class discourses within most labour unions is located and constrained within an internationalism based on formal European social integration. However, the challenge facing these national labour movements is not viewed in terms of an antagonistic employer class that needs to be politically regulated as in the United Kingdom and United States, nor is it seen just as a case of enhancing the national body of worker rights so as to mimic a north European model. For Spanish unions the 'threat' results from transnational capital finding other arenas in which to invest, and small- and medium-sized indigenous capital failing to culturally assimilate into the social project of European tripartism. More precisely, the Spanish industrial relations system has some of the features of Germany, but in economic terms it exhibits a great deal of defensive flexibility in terms of a reliance on employment flexibility and wage competitive approaches to capital accumulation (Blyton and Martínez Lucio 1995). In Italy the challenge has been the ongoing decentralization and outsourcing of production within firms, the general informalization of the economy and a greater degree of commercialization in such areas as the public sector at the expense of state regulation. Hence, in Italy and Spain, the European Union consumes the energy of confederations in their attempts to integrate, formalize, and modernize further their economic and political relations by 'attaching' them to a social and more progressive view of Europeanization, and the building of a supranational state.

Within these two countries the main unions are attempting to envelop capital within a coordinated system of social and employment responsibilities underpinned by Europeanization. Spanish union strategies are caught in a dilemma. They cannot just nationally enhance the body of employment regulation at the expense of high levels of inward investment that are driven by cost-benefits, so they must strategically locate themselves within the new networks, institutional linkages and bodies that constitute the European Union. The vision of transnational coordination here is not based solely on social 'upgrading' but of creating synergies between social and economic interests and acquiring knowledge assets through European learning and policy networks that allow Spanish employers to become dependent on Spanish labour.

The cost of such projects, for example, is that in Spain international linkages do not always reflect the supposed mobilization-based character of its national activity. For example, relations with unions in Latin America have been less resilient than first expected due to the Europeanization of Spain's political left and the new economic role and interests of Spanish capital in the southern Americas (our case study below of the airline industry will outline tensions in the relations between the Spanish and Argentinean unions within the international airline union networks).

However, the more coordinated economies contain their own fissures, which can generate internal demands for differently structured approaches to international union action. In Germany, for example, the relation between region and nation, on the one hand, and the sector and firm, on the other, leads to a variety of spaces for open and less bureaucratic moments of internationalism. For example, works councils may provide structures for workers seeking to deal with firm level transnational issues, even when these efforts are ignored or opposed by unions, thus creating political demands and developments for alternative approaches.[2] The political dimension of national industrial relations systems can also undermine the mediating role of national frames of regulation.[3] The following three cases focus on critical incidents in three international sectors. They will serve to show how national interests, organizational capacities, and union approaches to regulation can impact both positively and negatively on the process of union revitalization and internationalization.

TRANSNATIONAL STRATEGIES FOR MUTUAL SUPPORT ON THE DOCKS

Dock unions have a long history of internationalism and mutual support arising from the militant ideology of many dock unionists, and from industrial conditions and productive structures that tend to favour cooperative transnational union relations. In response to the transnationalization of maritime employers, many dock unions have established enduring transnational links at multiple levels, from national staff to local representatives, sometimes involving rank and file workers as well. The case of the dispute surrounding the 2002 contract negotiations between the International Longshore and Warehouse Union (ILWU), representing around 10,500 on the US West Coast, and the Pacific Maritime Association (PMA) representing port employers, shows how the transnational strategies of transnational coalitions of labour and capital actors interact within global productive structures and national industrial relations institutions to shape conflict outcomes.

Management's desire to shift the balance of power on the US West-Coast docks reflected the transnationalization of structures of ownership and production in the industry. Before the 1990s, most cargo handling facilities were owned and operated by local companies or government bodies. Since the 1990s there has been a trend to global consolidation. Sometimes this has been through vertical linkages, for example, the transformation of the giant liner companies, such as Maersk-Sealand and P&O Nedlloyd, into vertically integrated logistics companies, in part through the acquisition of port facilities. Alternatively, cargo handling firms such as the Seattle-based Stevedoring Services of America (SSA) and the Singaporean PSA have expanded globally but horizontally, remaining specialized in the operation of port facilities, but transferring their capital and methods (including anti-union tactics in the case of SSA) transnationally (Woodbridge 1999: 99–101). The changing structure of the industry has negative and positive implications for port labour. Increased concentration in a few giant transnational liner companies and stevedoring firms makes it easier for maritime capital to act collectively. Maritime capital is now more ready to get behind port employers who take on dock unions. In past times, port unions could rely on divisions between the interests of relatively smaller and fragmented shipping lines, shippers, stevedoring companies, and governments to put pressure on ports to come to a quick settlement, whatever the cost. This era appears to be coming to an end. Ports have taken on unions with mixed success following a similar pattern around the world. Examples include Santos, Brazil, (Crichton 1995: 95–97; Stares 2000:11) Anonymous 2001), New Zealand (Green 1996) and the Bangladeshi port of Chittagong (Anonymous 1997; Reyes 2001) among others. Very often, the same firms are behind the drive to reduce the power of port unions. For example, in Chittagong and in New Zealand, SSA was a key actor. SSA is also widely thought to be the most influential and hard-nosed actor within the PMA (*Pacific Business Journal,* 18 September 2002). On the other hand, transnationalization makes maritime firms vulnerable to transnational pressure tactics from unions able to muster global support.

Management's willingness to initiate the 2002 contract dispute, however, depended heavily on the constellation of political opportunities in the United States, such as the willingness of the Bush Administration to work hand in glove with the employers. From the outset of negotiations the employers sought to intimidate the ILWU leadership, relying heavily on their political relationship with the Bush Administration. For example, they had the US government's Homeland Security Director Tom Ridge personally telephone ILWU president Joe Spinosa, to threaten him with government action under the new Homeland Security anti-terrorist legislation if the ILWU chose to strike.[4] In past negotiations, after the expiry of the collective agreement, the ILWU engaged in short, localized slow downs, to pressure the PMA in ongoing negotiations.[5] This time, aware that the Bush administration and the PMA were looking for an excuse to lock the union out and militarize the docks, ILWU members continued working under the terms of the old contract. For the PMA even this situation was less than ideal, as the ILWU with no contract *could* legally take industrial action at any time.

The PMA decided to lock the ILWU out for 10 days despite the lack of an excuse, counting on the media incorrectly reporting the dispute as a strike (which in many cases it did). The public impression that the dockworkers were striking gave the Bush administration sufficient political excuse to order an 80-day 'cooling-off' period, during which all industrial action was forbidden. PMA then manufactured 'slow downs' by not ordering enough labour from the union to clear up the backlog from the lockout (the ILWU uses a hiring hall system). Their hope was to establish a pattern of non-compliance with the 'cooling-off' period on the part of the ILWU, which would have justified further anti-union actions. It seemed likely that direct action by the ILWU against PMA members would give the government an excuse to intervene, and perhaps result in militarization of the docks. In order to outflank the employers and pressure them where they were vulnerable, the ILWU turned to dock unions in other countries for help.

In developing a transnational strategy, the ILWU did not start from scratch, but rather drew on a well-developed global network of mutual support. Many unions around the world owed the ILWU debts of gratitude for past solidarity. For example, in 1995 ILWU members refused to work a ship, the Neptune Jade, in support of locked out dockworkers in Liverpool in the United Kingdom (Lavalette and Kennedy 1996). In 1998, the ILWU backed the Maritime Union of Australia in its conflict with Patrick Stevedores, refusing to handle cargo loaded by scab labour (Trinca and Davies 2000). Active participation in International Transport Workers' Federation activities such as the Flag of Convenience campaign to organize seafarers helped the ILWU develop international contacts among mainstream dock unions. Participation in the syndicalist International Dockworkers' Council (IDC) actions gave the ILWU credibility with left wing unionists worldwide (Lillie 2003).

Most of the companies comprising the PMA are foreign-owned, or have substantial foreign interests. The globalization of stevedoring, shipping lines, and logistics makes these companies vulnerable to union action in many locations outside the United States (Turnbull 2000). Furthermore, due to the Flag of Convenience campaign, many major maritime companies have ongoing relationships with the ITF. In an unusual step, ITF general secretary David Cockroft sat in on part of the bargaining, to demonstrate global backing for the US longshore workers. The IDC also announced its support. The ITF asked its affiliates to pressure representatives of shipping lines in their own countries, and many did so. ITF and IDC affiliates in many countries (such as Japan, New Zealand, Australia, Spain, and Denmark, among others) made specific threats that they would not handle cargo from the US loaded by scab labour.[6]

The backing of foreign unions helped define and limit the terms of the conflict, playing a role in preventing escalation by making the option of deploying replacement workers more costly. Replacement workers were not used and the docks were not militarized despite PMA allegations that the ILWU was violating the terms of the Taft-Hartley back-to-work order. As time passed and it became clear that the ILWU would not provide an opening to justify escalation, fissures developed within the PMA. Although the hard-line management of some US-based companies such as SSA continued to push to escalate the conflict, other PMA members softened. On 23 November 2002 the ILWU and PMA signed a 6-year contract. Neither the PMA nor the ILWU was entirely satisfied with the contract,[7] but clearly the PMA had lost an opportunity in failing to break the ILWU.

Strong transnational networks allowed the ILWU to mobilize support from dock unions worldwide to help thwart the attempt by the PMA to break the ILWU. The US West-Coast dock dispute played out a pattern of conflict similar to that on the docks in many other countries. In this pattern, transnational maritime shipping and stevedoring companies mobilize a willing national government to support efforts to reduce or eliminate port union power. As in other countries, intervention by the international dockers' movement directly pressuring these global corporations played an important role in strengthening the unions' hand.

However, despite the transnational aspects, the primary dispute in the United States played out a classic American industrial relations story of hard-nosed employers backed by conservative politicians and an apathetic public taking on an industrially strong but politically isolated union. Typical of the strategies of US unions, the ILWU leadership called in its international solidarity 'markers' to bolster its bargaining position (although the case is unusual in that the ILWU had quite a few markers to call in). Conditions in the United States clearly provided the context in which each actor shaped its strategies. However, the PMA's goals reflected the global strategies of its constituents, and the majority of PMA consisted of transnational companies. The ILWU relied on leverage from international union organizations and foreign unions, which prevented employers from escalating the conflict by introducing replacement workers. The strength and usefulness of the ILWU's transnational networks depended on strong possibilities for mutual support, coupled with very limited transnational inter-union competition, which were conditioned by structures of production in the port industry.

The port transportation sector is known for its strong occupational culture, its common histories of resistance, and the legacy of its international union coordination (McConville 2000; Turnbull 2000). These are not as apparent in other sectors. Tensions remain in terms of the manner in which competitive relations are used by management and even unions; the way in which globalization is in fact structured around competitive and segmented interests; differences in national industrial relations institutions; and the continuing role of national interests, identities and industrial relations discourses. These are tensions that have been overridden to an extent in the West-Coast dispute.

DILEMMAS AND NATIONALISM IN THE CAR INDUSTRY

The case of motor manufacturing shows some of the tensions between national union approaches to industrial relations and the development of transnational links and strategies. In the case of motor manufacturing, international networks have emerged to deal with the exchange of information and workplace related issues, sometimes driven by transnational management strategies of change (Martínez Lucio and Weston 1995; Weston and Martínez Lucio 1997). These networks are quite common in motor manufacturing. They focus on sharing corporate information, but also discuss issues of organizational change and the development of management workplace strategies such as the introduction of teamworking. These networks are known to take an interest in coordinating responses to closures or disinvestments, but they are mainly driven by an interest in changes in workplace regimes and the desire to coordinate and share union responses.

However, their stability is sometimes undermined by competitive relations within and between production plants arising from a company's ability to transfer production. In addition, different national systems of industrial relations provide national constituencies of trade unionists with very different bargaining and information resources. This allows certain constituents of workers within a network to have greater access to information. For example, in General Motors Europe, union leadership within GM's German operations had greater access to information about the location of a new investment in engine production (Martínez Lucio and Weston 1994).

The BMW–Rover case shows how highly positive developments in union coordination may be suddenly undermined by management and union action. The BMW takeover of Rover in the early 1990s was a major opportunity for the British and German labour movements to develop new forms of collaboration and mutual support. This was reflected in the development of the European Works Council (EWC), the consultative forum developed in companies with a presence in at least two European states. There was much trepidation in the early days of the EWC due to the very different national institutions of employee involvement. Initially, German managers had no intention of changing the weaker tradition of worker involvement in Britain (Whittall 2000). The lack of complementary worker rights made networking and collaboration difficult for trade unionists as the German unions had a greater degree of access to corporate information through their national works councils and system of codetermination. Whittall's research shows how this initial problem was steadily overcome. In 1999 internal management changes and rumours of restructuring of BMW's British plants led to a spate of information exchanges and assurances of support between British and German trade unionists in the company. The EWC played a role absent in many cross-border networks by ensuring constant dialogue and reciprocity in a context where productivity coalitions with managers had the potential to undermine long term inter-union networking (Whittall 2000).

However, these relationships failed to generate secure and effective inter-union cooperation when in 2000 BMW decided to offload Rover without any consultation with its British trade unions. The decision was explicitly supported by the German Works Council, and implicitly supported by IG Metall.[8] The lack of worker consultation, the repeated accusations that the UK government had been informed by BMW prior to the decision, and the marginalization of the EWC in the initial decision, resulted in public demonstrations and political activity led by the British unions. Sir Ken Jackson, general secretary of the Amalgamated Engineering and Electrical Union (AEEU), called for a boycott of BMW cars and German goods in general, highlighting the strong nationalist underpinnings of the UK side of the actions. Among the regalia of demonstrations, the flurries of British flag waving, and the desire to seek British owners of Rover, stood the reality of weak and ineffective consultative rights in British industrial relations and the need for ongoing international linkages in such difficult moments. Nationalist sentiment seemed an outcome of the lack of regulatory and political resources of organized labour in the United Kingdom. For their part, the German unions were caught between the imperatives of defending relations with UK unions and maintaining strong relations with their own management. The consensual nature of German industrial relations cooperation has been forged by various historical factors, but the defence of German industry and a strong national manufacturing base is an important one.

The BMW group works council approval of the divestiture highlights the differences between the political and institutional resources of British and German trade unions. These asymmetries in national union power, and the different views of stakeholder interest in each country (Sikka 2000), influence the effectiveness and experiences of trade unionists as they engage with each other, especially in sectors where competition between production units is possible. The case of BMW–Rover shows how quickly fortunes can change and transnational networking can be eroded. It also shows how discourses of national industrial relations can be as important an influence as the differences between national industrial relations institutions. This was clear from the fact that the outcomes of this episode were presented by each union as a 'victory' for both national sets of unions but not as an international union victory for a joint constituency.

The German union saw the outcome as a reaffirmation of their ability to influence management, reflecting the historic gains of German workers in political control and working life issues. The BMW–Rover case also shows the German trade union movement's lack of strategic and consistent interest in extending the German system of industrial relations within defined corporate environments internationally. Instead, German unions prefer to extend their system through political and regulatory processes such as the social dimension of the European Union. The lack of interest in cooperation in specific companies on issues related to bargaining and investment can be seen in other cases as well. For example, in the mobile telephone sector, Deutsch Telecom has kept its T-Mobile operation in the UK non-union; union avoidance has been facilitated by low strategic interest among the German labour movement in networking and joint organizing.

British unions saw their experience as a classic lesson in mobilizing and defending jobs in the United Kingdom. This was very much a reflection of the significance of trade union strategies that has internalized a view of employment based on the centrality of both inward investment and cost effectiveness. The AEEU, which was at the heart of these political discourses (Bassett 1986), has framed the cause as one of defending British jobs and industry, and of adapting to management needs by building productivity alliances, but not on demanding stronger consultative arrangements. The election of a new left wing general secretary in 2002 may shift the political profile of the AEEU and challenge this discourse. However, it remains an implicit feature of UK unions, reflecting a compromise with capital on investment questions in the context of the weak influence of industrial relations institutions on UK corporate governance. During the BMW–Rover affair, nationalist rhetoric and a problematic attitude to Germany weaved into this industrial relations discourse. This was not just a reflection of nationalist personalities such as the then General Secretary of the AEEU Sir Ken Jackson (whose views were evident from his writings on the issue of 'bogus' asylum seekers in the right wing press).[9] More fundamentally, it shows that national systems of industrial relations crystallize in political projects and strategies that configure, shape, and sometimes undermine, transnational union solidarity.

HIERARCHY AND POLITICS WITHIN THE AIRLINE INDUSTRY

New competitive clusters resulting from transnational sectoral capital configurations can also erode attempts at building transnational union solidarity. The airline industry is a case in point. This sector has witnessed a major process of restructuring due to cost pressures and national processes of deregulation (Blyton et al. 1998), especially after the rapid downturn in business in the post-9/11 period (Turnbull and Harvey 2003). Increasingly airlines have restructured and 'globalized' by constructing transnational strategic alliances.[10] These involve sharing of routes and strategic ground-based resources in airports, the interchange of staff, and a common marketing presence. The industry is clustering around key players, such as the Oneworld alliance, which brings together British Airways, American Airlines, Iberia, and others. There have even been forays into each other's ownerships structures: in the case of Iberia, the Spanish government allowed British Airways to buy a significant percentage of shares. Unions have become interested in linking with the worker representatives of strategic allies through a variety of networks, in order to exchange information regarding working practices and new forms of employee management. The Civil Aviation section of the ITF has been a key actor in facilitating these networks and organizing meetings. These networks have given rise to charters and to foundation principles regarding collective action and operational issues. Oneworld and the Star Alliance (which includes Lufthansa, Scandinavian Airlines, United, and others) union networks established codes of conduct regarding the behaviour of their employers and the development of corporate social responsibility. They have begun to establish information networks, which allow for discussion of issues such as the sharing of staff within the corporate alliance and the development of dualistic labour staffing.

Despite explicit attempts by the ITF to follow a union cooperation model borrowed from the successful example of the maritime shipping Flag of Convenience campaign, in airlines many ITF affiliates have resisted the development of effective transnational networks.[11] In many respects the airline union networks that have developed are less action-based and have remained focused primarily on information exchange.

One could argue that airline union networks are in great part linked to the destiny and stability of the corporate alliances themselves. This type of strategic alliance presents a challenge to trade unionists, because such alliances are more fluid than transnational corporations. In addition the ITF cannot really prevent the development of union hierarchies drawn from the dominating partners within the alliance, reproducing the same sort of tensions witnessed in BMW–Rover. Within these networks, dominant players are privy to superior information and resources to influence union and political agendas.

The growth of global alliances presents a challenge both to the ITF and international trade union relations. Whilst such alliances may unintentionally encourage those unions within participating companies to exchange information and frame 'solidarity' principles (as seen with Oneworld) there are alternative challenges also. The relationship and power struggles between the trade union networks of different alliances may lead to new fault lines in the international relations of the ITF. Stronger interest groupings may develop to challenge the internal authority of the ITF, which had previously been based on co-ordinating less organised clusters of national unions. Within these interest groups there may be dominant players, such as the German trade unions, whose resources and institutional role may be much more extensive than those of other member unions. Within Oneworld the dominance of BA and AA labour unions is seen to configure the nature of the internal discussions, according to trade unionists from less central airlines that we interviewed. The upshot is that rather than globalisation being a zero-sum process whereby power is taken or not from the national/local unions, in practice the process will be more complex due to the new sectoral and competing bodies that may emerge at the global level itself, and the way these are internally structured around new hierarchies. (Blyton et al. 2000: 28)

These tensions do not just exist between the dominant and peripheral players of the networks. The restructuring of Aerolinas Argentinas in the late 1990s by their Spanish owners Iberia airlines (who continued to have a major stake held by the Spanish government) led to serious tensions between the relevant unions. Discussions began to reflect the national discourses of their respective employers and governments. The Argentineans mobilized at ITF annual conferences against the Spanish government, who they saw as undermining Argentina's infrastructure and made reference to imperial legacies and national identity. The Spanish airline unions affiliated to the ITF argued that they had themselves borne the costs of such restructuring because of the considerable investments being used by Iberia to sustain Aerolinas Argentinas and avoid closure. Instead of acting as a spur to greater networking and coordination, the cross-ownership issue had created a new politics of ownership that involved the unions in greater cross-national disputes with their colleagues in other countries.

Competitive relations between alliances, and within them through new ownership structures, bring new international fault lines into the labour movement as international action and coordination reflects the politics and economics of the corporate alliances. Dialogue between the respective representatives of various labour networks can be limited or undermined by this clustering of interests around virtual corporations and alliances. And there is a further influence that can underpin labour strength and yet which is not based on international trade union coordination, and that is the pull of national regulatory institutions. Many trade unionists in civil aviation reference the continued effectiveness of traditional forms of union activity as evidenced in a global survey of national airlines (Blyton et al. 2000). Even in a 'deregulated' product market, global airlines still depend on the regulatory support of national governments and global carriers still have a national base.

Not surprisingly, civil aviation unions continue to favour national regulatory policies such as union recognition and collective bargaining, national minimum terms and conditions of employment, statutory worker representation on airline boards and state financial support for national airlines. (Blyton et al. 2000: 17)

In this respect, the process of transnational networking will continue to develop for some time through the prism of national regulatory institutions and the resources they afford trade unionists. And the variation in the form and content of these institutions will, in turn, influence the manner in which internationalism is politically understood, mediated, and negotiated.

CONCLUSIONS

The development of a new international dimension of union activity is real and has both formal and informal characteristics. International union action is sometimes strategic and intentional, but sometimes unions are forced into international contact through shifting production structures, management strategies, or through the international nature of the problem they are dealing with. Any strategy for union revitalization must account for this growing international dimension if it is not to be continually undermined by transnational inter-union competition within firms and sectors. The ability to sustain their role by redefining union structures, interests, and power bases along transnational lines is a fundamental challenge for union revitalization in the coming years.

The first case shows that in some sectors unions are developing strategies and structures for mobilizing solidarity. However, these appear dependent on favourable circumstances. In the docks, these included a lack of competition between production sites, strong inter-union networks, and good opportunities for effective solidarity action. However, the second and third cases highlight some of the challenges facing international labour. They show how traditional national interests and the defence of employment can interrupt the formation of joint union collaboration. The balance between constructing mutual worker interests across national boundaries and sustaining legitimacy within them is unstable. Unions continue to mobilize very different resources from their respective national environments. In terms of revitalization strategies, such as partnership with employers or membership organizing drives, these may actually accentuate the international tensions between unions where there is no higher, transnational forum for collaborating with or influencing employers or for establishing coordinated approaches to defending workers. In airlines there are many points of inter-union collaboration existing within quite sophisticated structures for transnational relations. These create new vehicles for learning and mutual support, but also define new cleavages and hierarchies: there is no zero-sum relation between the national and international as each of these dimensions has its own potential for collaboration and for competition.

Tensions remain between trade unions internationally in terms of five main factors. First, employers and even unions use competitive relations on occasions to keep national groups of trade unionists at odds with each other (Martínez Lucio and Weston 1994). Second, globalization is structured around competitive and segmented interests—there is, as yet, no new international arena that allows for the national and the sectional to be easily overridden or redefined. New global union networking is in turn structured around many of these idiosyncratic features of globalization as an uneven and fractured reality. New economic and corporate hierarchies and fault lines emerge, creating new points of tensions between trade unionists. Fault lines such as those seen in the airlines industry contrast with the older nationally based tensions seen in the BMW example.

Third, there are still differences in national industrial relations institutions and the political and material resources unions can access within them. These tend to be used by trade unionists in their transnational union relations in ways that maintain an imbalance in decision-making influence. Employers and managers tend to exploit these differences during moments of organizational change (Martínez Lucio and Weston 1994). On the positive side however, as the docks case shows, unions can exploit national differences in opportunities for leverage to put pressure on transnational employers, if they are able and willing to coordinate their strategy transnationally. Fourth, national interests and identity continue to be mobilized by trade unionists in a number of ways to legitimate particular campaigns. For example, national identity can be used to create a discourse for legitimating narrowly focused union actions and interests. The case of BMW–Rover demonstrates how this can interfere with the development of broadly based solidarity. Finally, trade union action appears focused around productivist issues and immediate questions of employment—be they of a quantitative or qualitative nature—yet all three cases raise issues of ownership and transparency. The centre of economic and corporate decision-making is often unclear and shifting and the BMW and airlines cases clearly show how the related questions of ownership and control have been unable to bond trade unionists together. Up until now the most effective cases of international coordination tend to arise from mutually supportive conflict strategies which have employment protection or improved bargaining leverage as an objective, or the exchange of information regarding organizational change. What are not so common are international strategies for coping with the way new patterns of capital ownership impinge on economic and social processes.

On the other hand, as the docks case shows, international solidarity does not always require restructuring the labour movement along transnational lines. In some cases, sectoral traditions are not affected by, or can override, transnational competition, and transnational solidarity can be organized on the basis of class, sectoral, or occupational identities. Development of an effective global labour movement may not therefore be as difficult as the previous paragraph would suggest.

On the basis of these points we can argue that the revitalization debate is sometimes fixated with content, that is, what unions do, how they do it, and in relation to whom. Yet the debate fails to look at the form of union responses on an international scale in terms of the way new hierarchies and relations of power develop. In addition much of the current globalization and labour internationalism debate appears to view the national dimension of industrial relations merely as a block on internationalism without understanding how different national traditions *frame* distinct approaches to international action and the interrelations between national constituents of unions (Waterman and Wills 2001; Eder 2002).

The question we must then ask is whether some national institutions and strategies facilitate international relations more than others? There are no clear answers just yet. One might presume, for example, that the German model should be replicated internationally to provide a level playing field for union actors. Yet, the German model is the outcome of specific struggles and compromises which afford German unions considerable regulatory resources compared to unions in other countries—as the BMW case shows. One would not wish to see the Anglo-American model as preferable due to the extent of weaker union roles and greater dependency on management cooperation. On the other hand, it may allow for a more pliable and flexible form of unionism to emerge based on looser networks and shop-floor structures. This model, which is perhaps less dependant than German unionism on an integrated social, political, and legal framework may be better suited to a transnational environment where the only consistent point of reference is the corporate structure and the work-place. Different national institutions and strategies of industrial relations, as well as cultures, may compete in the shaping of the new *internationalism*. Hence, Haworth and Hughes (2002: 76) argue that an international regime of industrial relations is only likely if there is an emergent symmetry between national frameworks, which allows for national union action and roles to be coordinated (Stevis 2002: 150). Yet, as we point out, symmetries will be politically constructed and contested: they will not be a technical exercise in regulatory 'adjustment'. International collaboration at various levels reflects the struggle between different ways of regulating capital and labour and so international labour movement revitalization is likely to be a long and difficult process during which unions and workers will remain at a severe power dis-advantage *vis-à-vis* global capital.

Notes

1. See Tilly (1995), for example.
2. For example, in 1999, workers at an Alcatel fibre-optics factory in Berlin launched a factory occupation and campaign with transnational elements in an effort to stop their factory being closed. IG Metall gave only reluctant support to the dispute, and did not mobilize support at the European level, leaving the workers to make those contacts themselves (Lillie 1999).
3. In the case of Italy and Spain differences emerge in terms of the political fissures within and between unions driven by the political competition and relations between union con-federations (Baccaro, Carrieri, and Damiano 2003; Hamann and Martínez Lucio 2003).
4. 'Ports of Loss'. *LA Times*, 18 October 2002.
5. This tactic is similar to the 'warning strikes' common during collective negotiations in Germany.
6. 'Labour Solidarity Backs West Coast Dockers'. *The Guardian*, 10 July 2002.
7. 'A Storm Still Brews Beneath the Surface'. *Lloyd's List*, 11 March 2003.
8. 'Rover Hätte BMW Gefährdet'. *Die Welt*, 20 March 2000.
9. In 1994 the then General Secretary of the AEEU, Gavin Laird, explained to German academics and trade unionists at a meeting in Berlin that while all unions invoked the lan-guage of solidarity when they met at such meetings, their main objective when they were back home was to prioritize sustaining jobs within their country.
10. The section draws on research by Paul Blyton, Miguel Martínez Lucio, Peter Turnbull, and John McGurk on the airlines industry in Europe financed by the Leverhulme Foundation.
11. Interview with Shane Enright, Chair, ITF Civil Aviation Section, June 2001.

References

Anonymous (2001). 'Santos Hails New Era as Unions Cede Control'. *Lloyd's List*, 4 May.
Anonymous (1997). 'Port Strike in Chittagong Continues'. *Lloyd's List*, 18 March, p. 3.
Baccaro, L., Carrieri, M., and Damiano, C. (2003). 'The Resurgence of Italian Confederal Unions: Will it Last?'. *European Journal of Industrial Relations*, 9/1: 43–59.
Bassett, P. (1986). *Strike Free: New Industrial Relations in Britain*. London: Macmillan.

Behrens, M., Fichter, M., and Frege, C. M. (2003). 'Unions in Germany: Regaining the Initiative?'. *European Journal of Industrial Relations*, 9/1: 25–42.

Blyton, P. and Martínez Lucio, M. (1995). 'Industrial Relations and the Management of Flexibility: A Comparison of Britain and Spain'. *International Journal of Human Resource Management*, 6: 271–92.

—————— McGurk, J., and Turnbull, P. (1998). *Globalisation and Employment Relations in the Airline Industry*. London: International Transport Workers Federation.

—————————— (2000). 'Globalisation and Trade Union Strategy: Evidence from the International Civil Aviation Industry', Cardiff University Working Paper: Cardiff; Reprinted in R. Munck (ed.), *Labour and Globalisation*. Liverpool: Liverpool University Press, 2004, 227–44.

Boyer, R. (1988). *The Search for Flexibility*. Oxford: Clarendon Press.

Coates, D. (2000). *Models of Capitalism*. Oxford: Polity Press.

Crichton, J. (1995). 'S-O-Santos'. *Containerisation International*, June, 93–7.

Cooke, W. (2002). '*The Avoidance of Marginalization of Union Representation Through Foreign Direct Investment: Implications for Transnational Inter-Union Co-operation*'. Paper Presented at the Canadian Industrial Relations Association conference, 25–28 June, Toronto, Canada.

Eder, M. (2002). 'The Constraints on Labour Internationalism: Contradictions and Prospects', in J. Harrod and R. O'Brien (eds.), *Global Unions? Theory and Strategies of Organized Labour in the Global Political Economy*. London: Routledge, 167–84.

Gallin, D. (2002). 'Labour as a Global Social Force', in J. Harrod and R. O'Brien (eds.), *Global Unions? Theory and Strategies of Organized Labour in the Global Political Economy*. London: Routledge, 235–50.

Green, D. (1996). '*Port Reform in New Zealand*', H. R. Nichols Society XVII Conference 1996: Tenth Anniversary of the Society Conference, 17 May, Brighton, Australia.

Hamann, K. and Martínez Lucio, M. (2003). 'Spanish Unions: Dynamics of Revitalization'. *European Journal of Industrial Relations*, 9/1: 61–78.

Haworth, N. and Hughes, S. (2002). 'Internationalisation, Industrial Relations Theory and International Relations', in J. Harrod and R. O'Brien (eds.), *Global Unions? Theory and Strategies of Organized Labour in the Global Political Economy*. London: Routledge, 64–79.

Hodkinson, S. (2002). '*Plus ça change, plus c'est la meme chose*'. *Understanding Globalisation and the New Labour Internationalism: A Case Study of the ICFTU's Core Labour Standards Campaign*', Presented to an International Seminar at the Institut de Recherches Economiques et Sociales, Paris, September 2002.

Hyman, R. (2001a). *Understanding European Trade Unionism*. London: Sage.

——(2001b). 'European Integration and Industrial Relations: A Case of Variable Geometry?', in P. Waterman and J. Wills (eds.), *Place, Space and the New Labour Internationalisms*. Oxford: Blackwell, 164–79.

Lane, C. (1994). *Industry and Labour in Europe*. Aldershot: Edward Elgar.

Lavalette, M. and Kennedy, J. (1996). *Solidarity on the Waterfront: The Liverpool Lockout of 1995/96*. Merseyside, UK: Liver Press.

Lillie, N. (1999). 'Five-week Site Occupation at Alcatel in Berlin'. *EIRO-Online Features*, European Foundation for the Improvement of Living and Working Conditions, December.

——(2003). *A Global Union for Global Workers: The International Transport Workers Federation and the Representation of Seafarers on Flag of Convenience Shipping*. Ithaca, NY: Cornell University, PhD Dissertation.

——(2004). 'Global Collective Bargaining on Flag of Convenience Shipping'. *British Journal of Industrial Relations*, 42/1: 47–67.

McConville, C. (2000). 'The Australian Waterfront Dispute 1998'. *Politics and Society*, 28/3: 393–412.

Martínez Lucio, M. and Weston, S. (1995). 'Trade Unions and Networking in the Context of Change: Evaluating the Outcomes of Decentralisation in Industrial Relations'. *Economic and Industrial Democracy*, 16/2: 233–51.

——and Stuart, M. (2004). 'Swimming Against the Tide: Social Partnership, Mutual Gains and the Revival of "Tired" HRM'. *International Journal of Human Resource Management*, 15/2: 410–24.

——and Weston, S. (1994). 'New Management Practices in a Multinational Corporation: The Restructuring of Worker Representation and Rights?'. *Industrial Relations Journal*, 25/2: 110–21.

Northup, H. and Richard, R. (1979). *Multi-National Collective Bargaining Attempts*. Philadelphia, PA: University of Pennsylvania, The Wharton School, Industrial Relations Research Unit.

O'Brien, R. (2002). 'The Varied Paths to Minimum Global Labour Standards', in J. Harrod and R. O'Brien (eds.), *Global Unions? Theory and Strategies of Organized Labour in the Global Political Economy*. London: Routledge, 221–34.

Panitch, L. (1981). 'Trade Unions and the Capitalist State'. *New Left Review*, 125: 21–44.

Ramsay, H. (1997). 'Solidarity at Last? International Trade Unionism Approaching the Millennium'. *Economic and Industrial Democracy*, 18: 503–37.

Regini, M. (2000). 'The Dilemmas of Labour Market Regulation', in G. Esping-Andersen and M. Regini (eds.), *Why Deregulate Labour Markets?* Oxford: Oxford University Press, 11–29.

Reyes, B. (2001). 'Chittagong Box Terminal Plan Stalled'. *Lloyd's List*, July 10, p. 3.

Sikka, P. (2000). 'Shareholder Capitalism: What Happened to the Stakeholder Society?'. *The Tribune*, 15 December.

Sisson, K. and Marginson, P. (2002). 'Co-ordinated Bargaining: A Process for Our Times?'. *British Journal of Industrial Relations*, 40/2: 197–220.

Stares, J. (2000). 'Special Report–Latin America: Unions Continue to Wield Power in Santos'. *Lloyd's List*, 25 August, p. 11.

Stevis, D. (2002). 'Unions, Capitals and States: Competing (Inter)nationalisms in North American and European Integration', in J. Harrod and R. O'Brien (eds.), *Global Unions? Theory and Strategies of Organized Labour in the Global Political Economy*. London: Routledge, 130–50.

Tilly, C. (1995). 'Globalization Threatens Labor's Rights'. *International and Working Class History*, 47: 1–23.

Trinca, H. and Davies, A. (2000). *Waterfront: The Battle That Changed Australia*. Milsons Point, Australia: Random House.

Tuckman, A. and Whittall, M. (2002). 'Affirmation, Games and Insecurity: Cultivating Consent Within a New Workplace Regime'. *Capital and Class*, 76: 65–94.

Turnbull, P. (2000). 'Contesting Globalisation on the Waterfront'. *Politics and Society*, 28/3: 367–91.

——and Harvey, G. (2003). *Contesting the Crisis*. London: International Transport Workers Federation.

Walsh, D. (1994). *On Different Planes: An Organizational Analysis of Cooperation and Conflict among Airline Unions*. Ithaca, NY: ILR Press.

Waterman, P. and Wills, J. (eds.) (2001). *Place, Space and the New Labour Internationalisms*. Oxford: Blackwell.

Weston, S. and Martínez Lucio, M. (1997). 'Trade Unions, Management and European Works Councils: Opening Pandora's Box?'. *International Journal of Human Resource Management*, 8/6: 764–79.

Whittall, M. (2000). 'The BMW European Works Council: A Cause for European Industrial Relations Optimism'. *European Journal of Industrial Relations*, 6/1: 61–83.

Williamson, H. (1994). *Coping With the Miracle: Japan's Unions Explore New International Relations*. Hong Kong: Asia Monitor Resource Center.

Woodbridge, C. (1999). 'Top Ports and Terminals: Global Players'. *Containerisation International*, March, 97–101.

10

Conclusions: Varieties of Unionism

JOHN KELLY AND CAROLA FREGE

INTRODUCTION

We began our research emphasizing that union revitalization is desirable and important. Despite structural shifts in the economy and in politics at both the international and national levels, unions retain important functions for capitalist economies as well as for political democracy. The ongoing crisis unions are facing all over the industrialized world is, therefore, of major concern. Union decline threatens not only the collective regulation of employment relations (safeguarding better wages, working conditions, and job security), but also affects, if more indirectly, the quality of the broader civil society and political life by weakening one of its largest and most significant civil actors. In fact, unions may even be more necessary than ever before in playing a pivotal role in the growing resistance against corporate-led globalization (cf. Turner, Chapter 1, this volume).

For some observers, the globalization of production, trade, and investment is the driving force behind union decline. Competitive pressures have significantly reduced employment levels in heavily unionized Western manufacturing industries and in some parts of the service sector during the past 20 years. The growing mobility of capital has greatly enhanced its bargaining power, weakening the scope for unions to extract concessions and demonstrate their effectiveness to workers. These same pressures have been reinforced by national states, anxious to retain national production sites and to attract foreign direct investment, and in the case of European countries, eager to comply with the disinflationary regime of monetary union. The logic of this form of globalization thesis is to predict a degree of convergence in the fate of union movements across the advanced capitalist world. Since these movements everywhere are subject to similar economic and political pressures, albeit to somewhat varying degrees, the associated phenomenon of union decline should be common, if not universal.

One major finding is that on the evidence assembled in this volume from the United Kingdom, the United States, Germany, Italy, and Spain, as well as from other sources, this version of the convergence thesis is simply unconvincing. There is sufficient variation both in union strategies and in revitalization outcomes to indicate that there are powerful forces for divergence as well as convergence, a point on which we elaborate shortly. Thus, on the one hand, and consistent with the logic of comparative analysis of labour relations, there is no single strategy that works well for all union movements, irrespective of national context; the same strategy is likely to produce different results in different countries. On the other hand, evidence for variation in revitalization outcomes emerges most clearly when we adopt a multi-dimensional conceptualization of revitalization, moving beyond union membership and density to embrace economic and political power as well as the institutional dimension of union reform. In the first part of this conclusion we discuss how our empirical evidence of cross-country variations in union strategies and revitalization outcomes contributes to the 'varieties of capitalism' debate.

Our second conclusion is about the significance of historical context in evaluating the extent of revitalization. When the evidence for union revitalization is examined in relation to historical precedents, a rather different picture emerges. Compared to the great upsurges of trade unionism in the 1890s, the 1930s through to the late 1940s and the late 1960s into the mid-1970s, the current scale of revitalization is remarkably modest. We speculate on possible reasons for this fact.

VARIETIES OF UNIONISM AND VARIETIES OF CAPITALISM

Theoretical Approach

Interest in the diversity of modern capitalist economies and their industrial relations institutions became widespread from the late 1960s and has focused on two altern-ative trajectories, convergence and divergence, each offering a distinctive view on the interplay between markets, institutions and actors. In recent years the convergence theory originated by Kerr et al. (1960), has been revived and reworked into what is now frequently referred to as globalization theory, although there are several different accounts of the mechanisms that are supposed to produce similar economic struc-tures and outcomes (see Weiss 2003). Technology, the internationalization of markets and market competition, and the erosion of collective institutions by opportunism have all been identified as possible forces for convergence across countries (Traxler, Blaschke, and Kittel 2001: 287). The alternative scenario is a continuing divergence of capitalist economies. The 'new institutionalists' (e.g. Dore 1986; Hollingsworth and Boyer 1997; Hall and Soskice 2001; Weiss 2003) argue that markets and technologies are far from fully determining the structures and performance of capitalist economies and that national economic institutions can make a significant difference. The very idea of variation and choice implies that, to some extent at least, purposeful collective action—in one word politics—can make a difference even and precisely for the nature of advanced capitalism (Crouch and Streeck 1997: 1). Thus, taken one step further, it can be argued that the strategies pursued by the major actors—employers, unions, and political parties—can also make a difference to economic and industrial relations outcomes. While strategies are influenced by institutions, they are not fully determined by them (cf. Crouch and Streeck 1997: 1). In recent years an increasing number of studies—of state economic policies and welfare programmes, for example—have found less evidence of globalization-driven convergence and rather more of 'path dependent' divergence (Boix 1998; Hall and Soskice 2001; Traxler, Blaschke, and Kittel 2001; Swank 2002). These studies have also highlighted the importance of actors' strategies within the different political economies.

In particular, the highly influential work of Hall and Soskice (2001) has forcefully argued that the political economy is a terrain of multiple actors, such as individuals, firms, producer groups or governments, each of whom seeks to advance his interests in a rational way in strategic interaction with others (Scharpf 1997). At the heart of the approach is the capitalist firm, because of its powerful position in market economies. Hall and Soskice (2001: 7) refer to five spheres in which firms must develop relationships to resolve coordination problems in the economy: industrial relations, vocational training and education, corporate governance, inter-firm relations, and relations with their employees. Institutions in each of these spheres form interlocking, national configurations, thereby giving rise to three major 'varieties' of capitalism, namely the liberal market (in our sample: the United Kingdom and the United States), coordinated (Germany), and Mediterranean economies (Italy and Spain). Our five countries were thus chosen to provide instances of each of the three varieties of capitalism.

Although trade unions traditionally play a role in all but one of these spheres (inter-firm relations), more or less significant in some countries than in others, they are hardly acknowledged in Hall and Soskice's approach or recognized as independent, relevant actors (cf. also Howell 2003). As they wrote themselves, 'this is a firm-centred political economy that regards companies as the crucial actors in a capitalist economy.' (Hall and Soskice 2001: 6). We embrace this actor-centred view of the political economy, but see it as perfectly legitimate to concentrate on unions and union movements as key actors in shaping their own destinies.

Discussing unions as independent actors in an era of prolonged union decline is, of course, challenging. We are aware that unions faced tremendous structural constraints in the last two decades, much more than firms, and it is undeniable that such constraints, therefore, determine to a large extent unions' strategies. This becomes particularly evident in a cross-country comparison which illuminates the importance of the national context in the analysis of union strategies and outcomes. Our analysis revealed how unions as actors as well as the external factors shaping unions' strategies (such as the industrial relations institutions, state, and employers actions) are embedded in nationally specific historical and political contexts. Our findings therefore contribute to the growing literature on the role of national institutions by highlighting the national embeddedness of union strategies and national variation in union revitalization.

Comparing Union Strategies

We conceptualized six strategies of union revitalization—organizing, restructuring, social partnership/collective bargaining, political action, coalition-building, and international solidarity. Overall, political action, restructuring, and social partnership were the most frequently used strategies across all five countries. Organizing was very prominent in the United Kingdom and the United States but not in Italy, Spain, or Germany. Coalition-building and international solidarity action were far less common in all five countries.

Moreover, the forms taken by particular strategies differed widely and were often country specific. For example, union political action in the United Kingdom and the United States mainly took the form of electoral activities, especially voter mobilization, the use of party links to influence party and government policy, and lobbying. German unions, by contrast, have attempted to engage government in corporatist arrangements in addition to lobbying. Political action by the Italian and Spanish confederations has in recent years primarily taken the form of negotiations with governments to produce social pacts, in conjunction with general strikes and demonstrations against government policies. Social partnership arrangements also differ strongly across countries. In the United Kingdom and the United States, social partnership agreements are a recent phenomenon and occur almost exclusively at company level. In Italy and Spain, social partnership is most developed at national level although there is an increasing number of partnership agreements at regional and company levels. Finally in Germany, social partnership is a multilevel phenomenon operating primarily at sectoral level (through collective agreements between unions and employer associations) and at company level (between works councils and management). Union organizing, which is currently one of the most prominent union revitalization strategies in the English-speaking world, is a highly formalized and specialized set of activities in the United Kingdom and the United States. In Italy and Spain, by contrast, organizing methods were rather diffuse and bureaucratic, and Germany was somewhere in between theses two groups of countries: there were some innovative activities but the main body of organizing work was being undertaken by works councils. With regard to coalitions, we found an increasing number of mostly local, short-term, project-oriented coalitions in the rich, civil society of the United States, and a limited, but growing, use of coalitions in the United Kingdom, especially around campaigns against the restructuring of public services. German unions have been involved for many years in coalitions in pursuit of shared objectives, for example, on the environment, but most of these coalitions have not been geared towards union revitalization. The Italian and Spanish union movements have made least use of coalition-building, perhaps because their union movements are broadly based groupings which already act in pursuit of a wide-ranging political and social agenda.

Finally, there was less country variation with regard to restructuring strategies and international activities. Variation was due to external and internal union pressures which were found in many countries. For example, declining union density fosters the likelihood of mergers and the growing number and power of multinational companies increases the likelihood of international solidarity.

If we return to the theoretical framework mapped out in Chapter 3 and analyse the sources of these continuing divergences in strategy it becomes clear that many of them are likely to persist because they are deeply rooted in long-standing national institutions, state and employer strategies and union identities. The bias towards union organizing in the United Kingdom and the United States reflects the decentralized structure of collective bargaining and the absence of either state or employer support for extension clauses, so that unions mostly bargain for workers who are union members. Union density and bargaining coverage are very closely correlated, unlike the situation throughout most of Europe where density and coverage are only loosely coupled. The incentive to organize is consequently far more powerful in these two countries (and in the other liberal market economies such as Australia, Canada, and New Zealand) than in the coordinated economies of central and northern Europe. Likewise, the existence of social pacts in Italy and Spain (as distinct from the United Kingdom and the United States), reflects a set of enduring features of those economies and their political systems. Both countries have highly centralized and politically partisan union confederations possessed with the authority to negotiate on behalf of their affiliates with central government. In both countries there are long-standing traditions of extensive state intervention in industrial relations, especially so in Spain. Union political action has both reflected and reinforced this pattern of state intervention. Union identities in turn, in particular the legacies of rank and file mobilizations, have perpetuated the general strike as an item in the union confederations' 'repertoire of contention' in their dealings with governments.

Comparing Union Revitalization Outcomes

Further evidence of divergence appears when we shift our focus from comparing strategies of revitalization to comparing individual countries and the outcomes for their national union movements. In studying revitalization outcomes we emphasized the importance of moving beyond a single and simple measure such as union density, probably the most common indicator of union strength in the literature produced within the liberal market economies (see Behrens, Hamann, and Hurd, Chapter 2, this volume). In the same way that union strategies reflect the specificities of national institutional environments, we argue that evaluation of strategic outcomes needs to be equally sensitive to national context. We proposed that union revitalization could be examined along four dimensions: membership (itself comprising membership level, membership composition, and density), economic (or bargaining) power, political power, and institutional vitality. In the United Kingdom, organizing and partnership relations with employers have dominated the actions of individual unions over the past 10 years or so. The Trades Union Congress (TUC) has encouraged both initiatives through internal restructuring—the creation of the Organizing Academy in 1997 and the Partnership Institute in 2001 respectively—but otherwise it has concentrated on seeking political influence over government. In terms of outcomes, the British union movement has enjoyed a modest degree of success. Membership began to increase from 1998, although it declined again after 2001 and the gender composition has continued its steady improvement: over 40 per cent of UK trade unionists are now women. On the economic dimension, bargaining coverage is still low and closely tied to union density, while partnership agreements with employers are 'isolated experiments', few in number and limited in scope and impact. Politically, the union movement secured significant legislative reforms in the early years of the first Labour government but since then has exercised little influence over the main directions of government economic policy. Institutionally, there have been many innovations in structure, and continuing merger activity, but to date the direct impact on revitalization has been modest.

The experience of the union movement in the other liberal market economy, the United States, could hardly be more different. Despite an impressive array of activities, including coalition-building and international campaigns as well as organizing, part-nership, and political action, American unions have continued to decline on all dimensions of revitalization. Membership and density continued their long down-ward trend through the 1990s, and despite the growth spurts in 1998 and 1999, the 2002 figure dropped below 16 million, a level last recorded in 1952. On the economic dimension, individual unions sought out partnership agreements with employers to try and bolster their bargaining power at company level, but as in the United Kingdom, these initiatives were for the most part isolated experiments. Unions fared little better on the political dimension, because despite unprecedented levels of expen-diture and electoral campaigning, and some successes at state and city level, the Democrats lost control in the 1990s of both Houses of Congress as well as the Presidency. The American Federation of Labor-Congress of Industrial Organizations (AFL-CIO) has restructured itself to free up more resources to support organizing and political campaigning but relative to its Spanish or Italian counterparts, it is a weak federation with a limited budget and little authority over its affiliated unions, few of whom have emulated the AFL's efforts at restructuring.

The *German* trade union movement was once considered by many commentators as a model of power, organization, and effectiveness. When membership and density were declining in many countries throughout the 1980s, German union density stood firm at around 35 per cent. And as unions elsewhere came under mounting pressure from neo-liberal governments (of both left and right variants), the prolonged period of centre-right rule in Germany left the unions and the industrial relations system largely intact. The immediate impact of the 1990 Unification was a dramatic rise in union membership but this was followed almost immediately by a steep decline which has continued ever since. On the economic dimension, the dual structure of works councils and industry-wide bargaining is still in place, but there is evidence of recent erosion in coverage and of employer discontent (Behrens, Fichter, and Frege 2003; Thelen and Wijnbergen 2003). Politically the union movement appeared to have achieved a major breakthrough in 1998 when the Social Democratic Party (SPD) elec-toral victory ended 16 years of conservative rule. The 2001 reforms to the Works Constitution Act were intended to spread works council coverage into smaller firms and symbolized the influence of the German Trade Unions' Federation (DGB) over its political ally. But since then the DGB, like its British counterpart, has faced a govern-ment reform programme it profoundly dislikes but which to date it has proved unable to influence or resist. Institutionally, the major change has been the reduction through merger in the number of DGB affiliates, but it is doubtful whether this will help to safeguard or stabilize the enduring political role of the union movement.

By contrast, the union movements in Italy and Spain have fared significantly better than their counterparts elsewhere. The *Italian* confederations loosened their ties to political parties in the early 1990s and since then have participated in a series of social pacts on a wide range of issues. Both their inclusion in state policy-making and their willingness to use the general strike have consolidated their political power. Institutionally, talks to create a unified confederation broke up in the late 1990s and from time to time inter-confederal unity has been fractured by dissent. Nonetheless, since the early 1990s an unusual degree of unity has been achieved between the confederations, sufficient to enable their effective participation in social pacts. In terms of the economic dimension of revitalization, the earliest pacts also consolidated the bargaining role and authority of the major confederations, in agreement with employers. Finally so far as membership is concerned, Italian unions recorded growth among employed workers from 1998 for the first time in many years.

The *Spanish* story is similar in many respects, with a politically divided union movement making extensive use of political influence over government, backed by the occasional general strike and facilitated by inter-confederal unity. Spanish unions have participated in a series of social pacts since 1996 and exercised some influence over government, most notably in 2002 when strike action forced the government to withdraw its controversial reforms to the unemployment benefit system. Although union density is substantially lower in Spain than in Italy, density began to increase from the early 1990s and has now stabilized at almost 20 per cent. Economically, Spanish bargaining coverage remains high at around 80 per cent of the labour force. However, the Spanish movement perhaps faces a more serious challenge than its Italian counterpart because of the fragility of the collective bargaining structures that are increasingly replacing the state labour regulations carried over from the Franco era. Although the increased role for collective agreements has created the opportunity for unions to consolidate their economic power through collective bargaining, it also poses a threat to unionism because of the inadequacy of employer organization and its opposition to joint regulation, especially in the very significant small firm sector of the economy.

In summary, there is evidence of divergence in the degree of revitalization associated with different union strategies. Amongst the five countries in this study, the Spanish union movement has, perhaps, performed best of all; Italian and British trade unionism have stabilized themselves, albeit in different ways; while the American and German union movements both face serious problems, though they are different in origin and in kind. This picture of variation, drawn from just five countries, is consistent with evidence from elsewhere: the fairly stable and high membership density, political influence, and bargaining coverage of Scandinavian trade unionism contrasts with the sharp decline in these indicators in the 1990s in Australia and New Zealand, for example. Interestingly, although perhaps not surprisingly, the more traditional strategies—political action, organizing, restructuring, and social partnerships—were both more widely used and achieved relatively better results than coalition-building and international activities. Particular forms of political action, notably social pacts accompanied by periodic general strikes, seem to have shown the best results, judged at least by their association with union political power, and to a lesser degree with membership, in Italy and especially in Spain.

Union Strategies, Union Revitalization, and Varieties of Capitalism

How do these findings of variation in union strategy and union revitalization outcomes, link to the broader literature on the varieties of capitalism? The logic of the varieties approach appears at first glance to map closely onto our findings. As outlined above, organizing comprises a significant component of union strategies in the decentralized industrial relations systems of the liberal market economies of the United Kingdom and the United States, but hardly features at all in Italy and Spain, and is rare in Germany. Social pacts, on the other hand, have occupied a central place in the Mediterranean economies of Italy and Spain where the state looms large as a major actor in the system of industrial relations, but are absent from the liberal market economies. Thus, the varieties approach does throw light on broad, cross-national differences in union strategy and seems to account for the major differences between countries.

If we turn our attention from union revitalization *strategies* to union *outcomes*, then the varieties approach is also potentially illuminating. American unionism remains vulnerable to employer hostility within a liberal market economy while by contrast the centralized union confederations in Italy and Spain have been able to engage their interventionist states in social pacts, both exercising and reinforcing their own political power. The decline of German unionism might seem problematic for the varieties account, insofar as the dual structure of works councils and industry-wide bargaining has normally been analysed as an integral component of the 'coordinated economy'. In defence of the varieties approach it could be argued that Germany is unique among Europe's coordinated economies because of the enormous costs of Unification and their impact on German unemployment and economic performance since 1990. Three pieces of evidence could be cited in support. First, if we compare unemployment levels in 1991 and 2001 across the eight main European Coordinated Market Economies (CMEs) (Austria, Belgium, Germany, Netherlands, and the four Scandinavian countries) we find that it fell throughout the decade in five of them but was substantially higher in 2001 only in Finland and Germany (OECD 2002: 303). Second, union density either rose or was stable in six of the CMEs between 1990 and 1998 and fell only in Austria (by eight percentage points) and Germany (by ten points) (Calmfors et al. 2001: 13). Third, disaggregated analysis of union membership figures for 1991–5 shows that 75 per cent of the 2.4 million fall in membership occurred in the eastern Länder (the former GDR) (Jacobi, Keller, and Müller-Jentsch 1998: 201). In short, the 'external' shock of unification could be seen as the prime cause of German trade union decline. On the other hand, Streeck (1997), Thelen and Wijnbergen (2003), and others have argued that in addition to the strains of Unification, the German model may also be internally exhausted for reasons that include growing institutional rigidities in the labour market, deficient product innovation, and divisions among employers exacerbated by increasing international competition in the high quality/high wage sectors of the German economy.

The varieties approach would appear to have more difficulty with regard to the liberal market economies where the British union movement has begun to recover membership and political influence, albeit to a limited extent, but the US movement manifestly has not. Now some variation between countries within the same 'variety of capitalism' is only to be expected. For example, it is clear that while the average CME unemployment level 1961–98 is lower than the Liberal Market Economy (LME) average, there are some CMEs whose recent unemployment record is worse than the LME average, viz., Belgium, Denmark, and Finland (Hall and Soskice 2001: 20). Nevertheless, the differences between the United Kingdom and the United States, modest though they may be, do raise interesting theoretical questions. Within the firm-centred approach of Hall and Soskice (2001) it is not immediately apparent why there should be such differences, given that both sets of employers operate in labour markets that are lightly regulated compared to those in the CMEs and where employees enjoy relatively weak protection. It is true there is evidence that US employers are unusually hostile to trade union presence and in recent years have invested significantly more money into campaigns of union busting and union avoidance than their British counterparts (Kleiner 2002; Heery and Sims 2003).

But employer hostility is in fact only part of the story about recent differences between the United States and the United Kingdom. Another equally critical component is the interaction between union and state strategy and its impact on employers. In both the United Kingdom and the United States, union organizing campaigns seek to obtain a majority vote among a designated group of workers in order to secure bargaining rights. The structure and content of organizing campaigns are similar in the two countries, not surprisingly as UK organizers learned much from their US counterparts. Both union movements used political action in the early 1990s to try and secure changes in the legal regime governing union recognition. But whereas British unions succeeded in altering the UK legal regime, significantly raising the costs to employers of resisting unionization where workers demanded it, US union pressure failed to achieve its intended aims. Survey evidence suggests that a majority of British employers adapted to the new legal regime, occasionally putting up some resistance to union organizing, but agreeing to recognition where a majority of workers was in favour. US employers saw no such need to amend their behaviour and have continued to fight union organizing. The differential outcomes for the two union movements are indeed, therefore, a reflection of differences in employer behaviour. But an equally important part of the story, and one that a firm-centred approach might well leave out of account, is the interaction between union political action, government responsiveness to union pressure, and legal changes that alter the costs and benefits of both organizing and employer counter-mobilization. In other words it is the combination of union strategies, their interaction with the state and the institutional environments of employers that help explain the differential organizing outcomes between the United Kingdom and the United States.

We are, thus, led to a complex judgement on the relationship between the varieties of capitalism and union revitalization. On the one hand there is substantial evidence of continuing divergence among national union movements located in the different varieties of capitalism. This is apparent not only in the types of strategies deployed by those movements, but also in their degree of success. At the same time, however, it is also clear that while employer strategy and institutional environment are important determinants of union revitalization, other factors also come into play. The strategies used by unions, whether party political action and organizing in the United Kingdom or negotiation with governments in Spain, make a significant difference to one or more of the dimensions of revitalization. These strategies in turn, as we saw in earlier chapters, are influenced in part by union identities, long-standing repositories of values and beliefs about union goals and methods. They are also influenced by the responses of the other industrial relations actors: a government which responds positively to a general strike by offering concessions to the union movement thereby reinforces the value of such action and raises the probability of its use in the future. None of this is to say that the varieties approach is inappropriate in studying union behaviour. The point rather is that the firm-centred approach offers an incomplete account of union revitalization, and therefore needs to be supplemented with more attention to the strategies of unions themselves and to their interactions with other actors, and in particular the state.

EVALUATING UNION REVITALIZATION IN HISTORICAL PERSPECTIVE

The question of union strategy effectiveness is complex and we have referred already to the intrinsic difficulties in measuring and correlating union actions and union revitalization (cf. Chapters 2 and 3). National union movements have faced varying degrees of crisis during the past 20 years and these have taken different forms in different countries. As is well known, union density decline, for example, does not mean the same thing in all countries and in the realm of strategies, union political action takes different forms in different electoral and party systems. Nonetheless, our research findings strongly suggest that union strategies make a difference to one or more dimensions of revitalization. In the case of the United Kingdom, for example, union membership began to increase from 1998 and the fall in union density which began in 1979, seemed to have been halted. By contrast US membership and density have continued to decline up to the present day. In a cross-country comparison, confined to the recent past, these differences appear substantial and significant, and from the standpoint of union leaders there is a world of difference between a movement in decline and one that is no longer declining, even if it is not yet back into substantial growth.

However, if we place our findings into a longer historical context, then some of the differences between countries that we have highlighted in this discussion take on a new appearance and we obtain a very different impression of the current scale of union recovery. Consider, for example, the national patterns of trade union membership in the United Kingdom and the United States during the inter-war years. Membership of both union movements peaked in 1920–1 and then began to fall steeply, reaching a low point in 1933. But as both economies began to pull out of the long recession of the early 1930s and unemployment began to fall (from 1933), union membership began to recover quickly. In the United Kingdom, aggregate membership increased by 2 million in the 6 years 1933–9, a rise in density of nine percentage points. In the United States the recovery was even more dramatic, a rise of 3.5 million members in 6 years, giving an increase in density of an astonishing seventeen points in the space of just 6 years (Bain and Price 1980: 37, 88). The US upsurge was closely associated with the strike wave of 1934–7, and a similar connection between union membership and union strike activity was apparent in other countries including the United Kingdom, either in the late 1930s—France 1936, for example, or in the late 1940s—Italy, for example (Kelly 1998: 89–94). Moreover, as left governments came to power in a number of European countries shortly after the end of the Second World War, union movements often acquired increased political power as well as growing membership and many played key roles in the construction of welfare states and the design of post-fascist systems of labour relations.

By comparison, the recent very limited and tentative signs of revitalization in a few countries are of a quite different order of magnitude. In none of our five countries has union membership or density begun to climb dramatically, for example. Not only that, but viewed from an historical perspective, it is the similarities across countries that stand out rather than the differences. There is no contemporary union movement in the advanced capitalist world that has made a dramatic recovery, on the scale of Belgium, France, the United Kingdom, or the United States in the late 1940s and decisively raised its membership, as well as its economic and political power (Kochan, Katz, and McKersie 1986; Ebbinghaus and Visser 2000); nor is there evidence of a resurgent unionism, as in the earlier period, forcing its concerns onto the agenda of employers and the state, whether it be ambitious wage claims, welfare programmes, or labour market measures to maintain full employment. Indeed, the union movements of Europe and North America are still engaged in fighting defensive battles against welfare and labour market reforms and are still submitting modest wage demands that are only fractionally higher than the rate of inflation (EIRO 2003). Even more surprisingly, this union moderation has occurred against a backcloth of modest economic growth. If some union movements have managed to halt the decline that began from around 1980 onwards, to date it would be hard to identify any that are making substantial and dramatic advances along one or more of our dimensions of revitalization.

We should, of course, be careful to note the differences, as well as the similarities, in the economic and political contexts between the middle of the previous century and the present. In the United Kingdom, for example, post-war reconstruction boosted employment in engineering and in central and local government, areas of the economy that were already quite heavily unionized (Bain and Price 1980: 50, 76). Consequently, union growth could occur more readily in job territories where there was a strong union presence.

Why this should be the case, why union recovery has been timid or non-existent, is a question that raises major theoretical issues for our understanding of labour movements. Long wave theorists for instance have argued that a new phase of capital accumulation should entail a new period of trade union revival, as it has normally done in the past (cf. Franzosi 1995; Kelly 1998; Silver 2003). To date, however, it is hard to discern the germs of a dramatic union upsurge. In order to conceptualize the overall weakness of union revitalization, Lukes' well-known framework of power

(1975) may be utilized. Lukes distinguishes three dimensions of power: the first dimension focuses on the behaviour of actors (unions, employers, etc.) in the making of decisions on issues where there is an observable conflict of interest. Where a final outcome could be identified and was closer to the initial position of one of the actors, then this actor was deemed to be the more powerful. A second, deeper, level of power is expressed through control of the agenda, that is power operates through regulating the issues that are available for debate. The third dimension entails the most powerful actor shaping the dominant discourse by influencing the ideology, in particular the beliefs and perceived interests, of the other actors. In other words, the more powerful actor within a system occupies a hegemonic position, in a Gramscian sense, controlling the ways in which issues and problems are defined and thought about (Simon 1991).

Viewed from this perspective, many union movements today merely engage in 'surface conflicts' with employers and the state over the terms of neo-liberal reforms of labour markets and welfare states. Although there are exceptions, unions' major successes these days often consist in slowing down or modifying neo-liberal reforms. The price paid for corporatist inclusion through social pacts has been the acceptance of anti-union reform agendas. In other words, that governments continue to talk to unions is sometimes seen as a major success independent of the outcomes of these negotiations. In the worst case, corporatism risks being degraded to the preservation of discussion rather than the pursuit of joint policy-making.

Thus, in Lukesian terms neither the agenda of reforms, nor the neo-liberal frameworks within which many of them are presented by state policy-makers, have been effectively challenged by union movements. Unions are forced to respond to the demands of neo-liberalism and globalizing capital rather than creating their own agendas, as they have managed to do at various stages in their history. For example, after the 1930s Depression, union movements in a number of advanced capitalist countries came to pursue ambitious programmes of progressive reforms that placed capital and its political allies on the defensive, from the completion of universal suffrage through the construction of welfare states to labour market policies geared to full employment (Sassoon 1996: 137–66).

But why have union movements failed in recent years to challenge the hegemonic ideas of neo-liberalism? The reasons are complex and vary from one country to another, notwithstanding the fact that neo-liberalism itself takes different forms in different countries and has been reworked over the past 20 years (Held et al. 1999: 2–21). One possibility is that, the role and influence of trade unionism may be in the throes of decline as global capitalism enters a new phase of development. There are several different conceptualizations of the transition that may now be in progress and the new form of society and economy that may be emerging: Post-Fordism, Post-industrialism, the second modernity or the 'risk society' are perhaps the most common formulations (Sennett 1998; Beck 2000). Beck (2000: 18), for example, characterizes the 'second modernity' in terms of ecological crises, the decline of traditional paid employment, job insecurity, individualization, globalization, and gender revolution. Despite a number of significant differences among these formulations of transition, we can discern a common set of propositions about the restructuring of work and employment and its negative impact on trade unions. The dimensions of restructuring most frequently discussed are the expansion of the skilled and professional labour force, the growth of contingent labour contracts, and the increased variation in patterns of working time and working lives. For all these reasons, trade unions are thought to be proving both less attractive to potential members and less able to regulate an increasingly complex and diverse set of labour market conditions (for a review see Heery 2003). However, there is evidence from the United Kingdom and the United States that despite these labour force and labour market trends, a substantial minority of non-union employees would join a union, if one were available at their workplace (Freeman and Rogers 1999: 69). A related argument is that in the 'second modernity' class conflict as the major division in society is challenged by the rise of individualism and identity politics. One consequence is that union movements face an increasing challenge from new progressive social movements to their long-standing, near-monopoly position as the major social movement in society since the late nineteenth century. However, potential conflicts between trade unions and 'new social movements' should not be exaggerated. Unions in the United Kingdom, the United States, and Germany, for example, have been able to build coalitions with a diverse range of 'new' social movements (Frege, Heery, and Turner, Chapter 8, this volume).

A rather different approach to the question of union weakness and the limits of revitalization, starts from trends in politics rather than the economy and the labour market. One reason for the weakening position of union movements may be that ideologically, they face similar problems to their left political counterparts, following the collapse of the communist states in 1989 and the end of the cold war, understood as a form of anti-communist politics. As is well known, the political Left in Europe and elsewhere has so far failed to construct a distinct identity for itself since 1989 and to respond to the new problems of the globalizing capitalist world. In particular, almost every major European social democratic party has undergone a significant ideological shift during the past 20 years, absorbing many of the tenets of neo-liberal economic policy, especially on the subjects of labour market and welfare reform (Sassoon 1996; Glyn 2001). To this set of developments should be added the collapse of Europe's communist parties after 1989 and the decline, disintegration, or social democratization of those parties in subsequent years. One consequence of these profound political and ideological changes has been to deprive union movements of both ideological positions and resources that could be deployed in order to challenge neo-liberal hegemony. In the absence of such a challenge unions are forced to participate in negotiations and debates with governments and employers on highly unfavourable terrain. Their continued inclusion in policy-making by employers and states may help ensure their survival, but participation on a broadly neo-liberal agenda may simultaneously constrain their effectiveness as agents of reform and thereby seriously hinder significant revitalization.

On the other hand, unions are becoming more independent from their political party allies and this development could be contradictory, constituting both a threat to union movements but also an opportunity (see Hamann and Kelly, Chapter 6, this volume). In order to revitalize themselves, unions as democratic actors need to strengthen their involvement in broader ideological debates about contemporary global capitalism. This, in turn, may allow them to engage more freely in a new discourse on labour and work, framing developments in the labour market in their own language, and challenging the hegemony of neo-liberal ideas and values with alternative visions for the achievement of social justice and greater democracy.

References

Bain, G. S. and Price, R. (1980). *Profiles of Union Growth: A Comparative Statistical Portrait of Eight Countries.* Oxford: Blackwell.

Beck, U. (2000). *The Brave New World of Work.* London: Polity Press.

Behrens, M., Fichter, M., and Frege, C. M. (2003). 'Unions in Germany: Regaining the Initiative?'. *European Journal of Industrial Relations,* 9/1: 25–42.

Boix, C. (1998). *Political Parties, Growth and Equality: Conservative and Social Democratic Economic Strategies in the World Economy.* New York: Cambridge University Press.

Calmfors, L., Booth, A., Burda, M., Checchi, D., Naylor, R., and Visser, J. (2001). 'The Future of Collective Bargaining in Europe', in T. Boeri, A. Brugiavini, and L. Calmfors (eds.), *The Role of Unions in the Twenty-First Century.* Oxford: Oxford University Press, 1–155.

Crouch, C. and Streeck, W. (1997). 'Introduction: The Future of Capitalist Diversity', in C. Crouch and W. Streeck (eds.), *Political Economy of Modern Capitalism: Mapping Convergence and Diversity.* London: Sage, 1–18.

Dore, R. (1986). *Flexible Rigidities.* Stanford, CA: University of California Press.

Ebbinghaus, B. and Visser, J. (eds.) (2000). *Trade Unions in Western Europe Since 1945.* London: Macmillan.

EIRO (2003). 'Pay Developments—2002'. 11 March. www.eiro.eurofound.ie.

Franzosi, R. (1995). *The Puzzle of Strikes: Class and State Strategies in Postwar Italy.* Cambridge: Cambridge University Press.

Freeman, R. B. and Rogers, J. (1999). *What Workers Want.* Ithaca, NY: ILR Press.

Glyn, A. (2001). 'Aspirations, Constraints, and Outcomes', in A. Glyn (ed.), *Social Democracy in Neo-Liberal Times: The Left and Economic Policy Since 1980.* Oxford: Oxford University Press, 1–20.

Hall, P. A. and Soskice, D. (2001). 'An Introduction to Varieties of Capitalism', in P. A Hall and D. Soskice (eds.), *Varieties of Capitalism: The Institutional Foundations of Comparative Advantage.* New York: Oxford University Press, 1–68.

Heery, E. (2003). 'Trade Unions and Industrial Relations', in P. Ackers and A. Wilkinson (eds.), *Understanding Work and Employment: Industrial Relations in Transition.* Oxford: Oxford University Press.

——and Simms, M. (2003). *Bargain Or Bust? Employer Responses to Union Organising.* London: Trades Union Congress.

Held, D., McGrew, A., Goldblatt, D., and Perraton, J. (1999). *Global Transformations: Politics, Economics and Culture.* Cambridge: Polity Press.

Hollingsworth, J. R. and Boyer, R. (eds.) (1997). *Contemporary Capitalism: The Embeddedness of Institutions.* Cambridge: Cambridge University Press.

Howell, C. (2003). 'Varieties of Capitalism: And Then There Was One?'. *Comparative Politics,* 36/1: 103–24.

Jacobi, O., Keller, B., and Muller-Jentsch, W. (1998). 'Germany: Facing New Challenges', in A. Ferner and R. Hyman (eds.), *Changing Industrial Relations in Europe*. Oxford: Blackwell, 190–238.

Kelly, J. (1998). *Rethinking Industrial Relations: Mobilization, Collectivism and Long Waves*. London: Routledge.

Kerr, C., Dunlop, J. T., Harbison, F. H., and Myers, C. A. (1960). *Industrialism and Industrial Man: The Problems of Labor and Management in Economic Growth*. Cambridge: Harvard University Press.

Kleiner, M. M. (2002). 'Intensity of Management Resistance: Understanding the Decline of Unionization in the Private Sector', in J. T. Bennett and B. E. Kaufman (eds.), *The Future of Private Sector Unionism in the United States*. Armonk, NY: M. E. Sharpe, 292–316.

Kochan, T. A., Katz, H. C., and McKersie, R. B. (1986). *The Transformation of American Industrial Relations*. New York: Basic Books.

Lukes, S. (1975). *Power: A Radical View*. London: Macmillan.

OECD (2002). *Employment Outlook 2002*. Paris: OECD.

Sassoon, D. (1996). *One Hundred Years of Socialism: The West European Left in the Twentieth Century*. London: I. B. Tauris.

Scharpf, F. (1997). *Games Real Actors Play: Actor-Centered Institutionalism in Policy Research*. Boulder, CO: Westview Press.

Sennett, R. (1998). *The Corrosion of Character*. New York: Norton.

Silver, B. (2003). *Forces of Labor: Workers' Movements and Globalization Since 1870*. New York: Cambridge University Press.

Simon, R. (1991). *Gramsci's Political Thought: An Introduction*. London: Lawrence and Wishart.

Streeck, W. (1997). 'German Capitalism: Does it Exist? Can it Survive?'. *New Political Economy*, 2/2: 237–56.

Swank, D. (2002). *Global Capital, Political Institutions, and Policy Change in Developed Welfare States*. New York: Cambridge University Press.

Thelen, K. and van Wijnbergen, C. (2003). 'The Paradox of Globalization: Labor Relations in Germany and Beyond'. *Comparative Political Studies*, 36/8: 859–80.

Traxler, F., Blaschke, S., and Kittel, B. (eds.) (2001). *National Labour Relations in Internationalized Markets*. Oxford: Oxford University Press.

Weiss, L. (2003). 'Introduction: Bringing Domestic Institutions Back In', in L. Weiss (ed.), *States in the Global Economy: Bringing Domestic Institutions Back In*. New York: Cambridge University Press, 1–33.

Index